BACKGROUND TO
INDIAN LAW

BACKGROUND TO
INDIAN LAW

by

RT HON. SIR GEORGE CLAUS RANKIN

LL.D. (Edin.)

Sometime Chief Justice of Bengal

CAMBRIDGE

AT THE UNIVERSITY PRESS

1946

CAMBRIDGE
UNIVERSITY PRESS

University Printing House, Cambridge CB2 8BS, United Kingdom

Cambridge University Press is part of the University of Cambridge.

It furthers the University's mission by disseminating knowledge in the pursuit of education, learning and research at the highest international levels of excellence.

www.cambridge.org
Information on this title: www.cambridge.org/9781316603710

First published 1946
First paperback edition 2016

A catalogue record for this publication is available from the British Library

ISBN 978-1-316-60371-0 Paperback

CONTENTS

PART I: CIVIL LAW

PART II: CRIMINAL LAW

PREFACE

I HAVE been impressed at times with the peculiarity of the fate of very learned and able friends of mine who, as the reward of exceptional knowledge and skill in the business matters of England and Scotland, are suddenly required to turn a large part of their attention to Indian appeals. What, at first, do they think of them or make of them? What is their approach? So too with learned counsel taken in to lead in a case about a waqf or a debutter. Not many people in this country have any settled notion of what we are doing in India administering law to Indians, nor have means of readily acquiring a well-founded notion of how we come to be doing so or of the principles which we apply. Certain I am that when I went in 1918 to India to engage upon the task, I had the smallest amount of information and no real explanation of many facts of great historical importance. It has occurred to me that a book could be written of some interest and even, if but rarely, of some little help to English lawyers and others forced or induced to embark upon this very special law. This accounts for my having written the present book, and I hope that it will not be without its uses. These, however, will be indirect, occasional and fragmentary, as the book is not really a manual of Indian law. I trust it does not detract from its usefulness that I have desired to press upon the English lawyer the really great work for India of Lord Romilly, Maine and Stephen. That the Indian codes are worthy of a better and more elaborate introduction than this will be obvious, and someone better able than I am will assuredly write it. The chapters on 'Civil Law before the Codes' and on the 'Indian Penal Code' were written originally as part of the series of chapters which is now published, but they have already appeared in the *Law Quarterly Review* of October 1942, and January 1944, respectively. This accounts in the latter case for a certain amount of repetition. It should be explained that the references to Parliamentary Papers are throughout to the House of Commons series.

G. C. R.

EDINBURGH
12 *June* 1945

PART I: CIVIL LAW

CHAPTER I

CIVIL LAW BEFORE THE CODES

LAW IN THE 'FACTORIES'

THE first provision for the exercise of judicial powers by the East India Company was made by a charter of Charles II in 1661, and its responsibility for the administration of law in India was confined until 1765 to the 'factories' of the Company and their branches. That different authorities functioned as courts of law in Madras, Bombay and Calcutta after 1661[1] is only to be expected from the different times and circumstances in which the Company's authority at each of these places took its origin. It had come to exercise authority in Madras under grants from Indian rulers (1639); in Bombay as representing the King of England (1668) who had accepted the island of Bombay as part of his Portuguese bride's dowry; in Calcutta as a zemindar to whom the villages of Satanuti Govindpur and Calcutta had been granted (1698). But by charter of George I of 1726 there was introduced into all three Presidency towns a Mayor's Court, not a court of the Company as it had been in Madras but a court of the King of England, though exercising its authority in a land to which the King of England had no claim to sovereignty. That the law intended to be applied by these courts was the law of England is clear enough from the terms of the charter though this is not expressly stated; and it has long been accepted doctrine that this charter introduced into the Presidency towns the law of England—both common and statute law —as it stood in 1726. Thus arose, not for the first time but in an acute form, the problem whether the civil law of England was to be applied to Indians. After the capture of Madras by the French in 1746 and its restoration in 1749 a new charter for all the Presidency towns was granted by George II in 1753; and in this it was expressly provided that the Mayors' Courts were not to try actions between Indians, such actions being left to be determined among themselves unless both parties by consent

---

1 Cf. Sir Charles Fawcett, *First Century of British Justice in India* (1934).

submitted the same for determination by the Mayors' Courts. This provision is said by Morley (*Digest*, i, clxix) to be the first reservation of their own laws and customs to Indians, though he considers that it was never made effective in Bombay.

LAW IN THE PROVINCIAL COURTS OF THE LOWER PROVINCES, 1772

The principle of this provision—the word 'reservation' is not in all respects exact—was taken as a basis when in 1772 Warren Hastings came to set up civil courts for Bengal, Bihar and Orissa, pursuant to the Company's determination to 'stand forth as *dewan*' under the grant obtained by Clive in 1765 from the puppet Mogul emperor at Delhi. The 'Plan' of 1772 provided, in terms of which the substance regulates to this day the greater part of British India, that in certain matters Hindus and Mahomedans were to be governed by their own laws—namely, in 'suits regarding inheritance, marriage and caste and other religious usages and institutions'. This is the twenty-seventh article of what is called Regulation II of 1772, though the word 'Regulation' was to take on a more technical meaning after 1773 and 1781 when Acts of Parliament had conferred certain powers of legislation. It provided no specific directions for any suits other than those expressly mentioned; and when in 1781 Sir Elijah Impey added the word 'succession' to the word 'inheritance', and declared that where no specific directions were given the judges should act 'according to justice, equity and good conscience', the scheme was complete so far as regards the 'rule of decision' which the new courts were required to apply to the matters which might come before them. Hastings seems to have appreciated, as Cornwallis did after him, that this did not amount to 'a good system of laws', and that greatly to be desired was 'a well digested code of laws compiled agreeably to the laws and tenets of the Mahometans and Gentoos'. He realized that from the inhabitants of Bengal in his day 'a perfect system of jurisprudence was not to be expected'. With the other members of the 'committee of circuit' of 1772 he claimed that the plan was 'adapted to the manners and understandings of the people and exigencies of the country, adhering as closely as possible to their ancient usages and institutions'.

The scheme of civil justice which was thus brought into force had two main features; first, that it did not apply English law

to the Indian provinces; secondly, that Hindu law and Mahomedan law were treated equally. As early as 1772, Alexander
Dow, a lieutenant-colonel in the Company's service, in his
Enquiry into the State of Bengal, had maintained that 'to leave the
natives to their own laws would be to consign them to anarchy
and confusion', since they were divided into two religious bodies
almost equal in point of numbers and 'averse beyond measure
to one another' (p. cxliii):

'It is therefore absolutely necessary for the peace and prosperity
of the country that the laws of England in so far as they do not
oppose prejudice and usages which cannot be relinquished by the
natives should prevail. The measure besides its equity is calculated
to preserve that influence which conquerors must possess to retain
their power.'

This view was not accepted by Hastings who, as a new Governor,
was in 1772 carrying out the decision of the Company 'to stand
forth as *dewan*'. What could the law of England have to do with
the exercise of the *diwani*? In due course, no doubt, Hastings
was to show how little he would let the Company's power be
trammelled by the notion that it was a mere vice-gerent of an
emperor at Delhi. But he could hardly begin in the spirit of
the gallant Dow:

'The sword is our tenure and not the firman of an unfortunate
prince who could not give what was not his own. The thin veil of
the commission for the Dewanny is removed....It is an absolute
conquest and it is so considered by the world' (p. cxvi).

Before ten years had passed Hastings was to have some
experience of the impact of the law of England upon the Lower
Provinces, and before the beginning of the nineteenth century
it was the accepted view of Indian administrators that the
law of England was not suitable to Bengal. Harington in his
Analysis (1805)[1] carefully defends this conclusion—stressing the
differences in the genius of the peoples and the fact that property
had been acquired by Hindus and Muslims under settled and
indeed written laws of their own.

To place the Hindu and the Mahomedan laws upon the same
footing, notwithstanding centuries of Muslim rule, was another
act of enlightened policy. There had, of course, been times of
massacre and persecution, but it does not appear that Hindus
under the Mogul empire had of late been refused the enjoy-

---

1 *Analysis of the Laws and Regulations*, by John Herbert Harington, p. 11.

ment of their own family and religious laws and usages. Still, as another lieutenant-colonel in the Company's service was to point out (*Observations on the Law, Constitution and Present Government of India*, by Lieutenant-Colonel Galloway, 1st ed. 1825, 2nd ed. 1832) the law of the Mogul empire upon this subject was to be found in the *Fatawa Alamgiri*, a collection of decisions made in the reign of Aurungzebe which had ended in 1707— only fifty-eight years before the grant of the *diwani*. In the course of centuries practice might have become more tolerant than theory, but in theory the position of the Hindus was at best that of *zimmis*—infidels who inhabited a country which had fallen to a Moslem conqueror but who had been left in comparative freedom on terms of a land tax and a poll tax. Thus, Galloway maintained, the *Fatawa Alamgiri* allowed the progeny of a Hindu marriage to inherit, but as to the parties themselves the marriage was illegal if it was illegal by Moslem law. We need not take Galloway as a final authority on the Mahomedan law as to marriage and inheritance among *zimmis* (cf. *Dictionary of Islam*, by Hughes, 1885, art. 'Zimmi', and authorities there cited) but he was right in that under the Moguls Mahomedan law was the law of the land as Hindu law was not. He followed James Mill and others in thinking very meanly of Hindu law and complained that its 'ashes had been raked up'. This brings home to us that the decision to treat the two laws as 'co-existing and co-equal', to borrow Macaulay's phrase, was far-sighted policy—not matter of course.

And if it does not, we may refer to the protest by the Naib Diwan forwarded in May 1772 by the Council of Revenue at Murshidabad to the President and Council at Calcutta. It is to be found in the seventh Report of the Committee of Secrecy on the state of the East India Company dated 6 May 1773, and was referred to in the Lex Loci report of 1840. There the Naib Diwan strongly remonstrates against allowing a Brahmin to be called in to the decision of any matters of inheritance or other dispute of Gentoos, saying that since the establishment of the Mahomedan dominion in Hindostan the Brahmins had never been admitted to any such jurisdiction; that to order a magistrate of the faith to decide in conjunction with a Brahmin would be repugnant to the rules of the faith, and an innovation peculiarly improper in a country under the dominion of a Mussulman Emperor. That where the matter in dispute can be decided by a reference to Brahmins, no interruption had ever been given to that mode of decision; but that where they (*sc.* Gentoos) think fit to resort to the established judicatures of the country, they must submit to a decision according to the rules and principles of that law by which alone these Courts were authorized to judge. That there would be the greatest absurdity in such an association of judicature, because the Brahmin would determine according to the precepts and usages of his caste and the magistrates must decide according to those of the Mahomedan law: in many instances the rules of the Gentoo and Mussulman law, even with respect to inheritance and succession, differ materially from each other.

But a negative if noticeable feature of the scheme was its limited character. No law at all was prescribed save for special topics—inheritance, marriage, caste, religious institutions. The entire scheme was conditioned by the fact that the persons available for appointment as judges knew no law. It was intended that the ordinary run of disputes about contracts and debts should be dealt with by referring them to arbitrators of the parties' own choice, while for cases to which the Mahomedan and Hindu law applied the judge was given the assistance of 'law officers' to declare the rule of law applicable to the case. These officials represented an adaptation of the Mahomedan system which provided a *mufti* to expound the law for the benefit of the *kazi* who administered it; but the similarity was more apparent than real, since in many cases the *kazi* was himself a man learned in the Muslim law. The initial workings of this system came before Impey and his colleagues on the Supreme Court in the case known as 'the *Patna Case*'; it was found that the 'law officers' were left to take the evidence and even to pass orders. Though it seems now to be accepted that in no other way could the work have been got through, the practice was illegal and the law officers were cast in heavy damages (*Nuncomar v. Impey* by Fitzjames Stephen, vol. II, ch. 12). But independently of any irregularities in its working the system was far from satisfactory. Its defects were obvious enough. 'This as a judicial system can be approved by no intelligent being', was Galloway's verdict. But on the whole its defects were unavoidable defects. It was right to aim not at completeness but at taking due account of the British administrator's ignorance of the habits and character of the people. Certain advantages were secured by the defects. It was a greater service to postpone the problem of a 'common' law than to adopt any of the solutions then available.

Yet a fourth feature of the scheme of 1772 deserves attention. The laws to be applied to succession, marriage, caste, etc., were described in the Regulation as 'the laws of the Koran with respect to Mahomedans and those of the Shastras with respect to Gentoos'. Though these phrases had been changed when the rule was restated in section 15 of Regulation IV of 1793, which spoke of 'Mahomedan laws' and 'Hindoo laws', these laws were conceived of as religious laws ascertainable by study of the sacred books. Neither Hastings, nor in all probability anyone else, appreciated that, while both were religious laws, the religions were very different, and the part played in each by law and by usage was not the same. Thus certain chapters (*suras*) of the Koran may be said to contain the fundamentals of Mahomedan law on basic subjects, e.g. the second, fourth, fifth and sixty-fifth; but most of its detailed rules and even of its principles cannot be found in the Koran alone. Three other main sources are recognized—tradition (*hadis*), consensus of the learned (*ijma*) and analogical reasoning (*kiyas*). Shia and Sunni law are widely different, but till 1810 or later the former was almost ignored in Bengal.[1] There are at least four schools of law among the Sunnis. There are, moreover, cases where custom has trenched upon the sacred law, e.g. to provide for single-heir succession, or in the case of converts to retain the law of succession which governed them before conversion to Islam, or in the case of agriculturists to conform to the life of village communities. Until so late as 1913 it was in doubt whether the rules of the Mahomedan law as to succession could be altered by custom so far as regards the provinces of Bengal, Bihar, Agra and Assam; though the Madras Civil Courts Act (III of 1873) contained an express provision giving effect to custom. The High Court of Allahabad refused for a long time to recognize usages in derogation of the sacred law until the decision of the Judicial Committee of the Privy Council in *Muhammad Ismail* v. *Lale Sheomukh* (1913) 17 Calcutta Weekly Notes 97.

As regards the Hindu law, to regard it as ascertainable in any given case from 'the Shastras' was to forget that the root of that law is custom; that the Bengal and Benares Schools went upon

[1] See *Mt Hayat-un-Nissa's* case (1890) L.R. 17 I.A. 73.

very different lines of family law; that many races of different origin had become imbued with Hinduism; and that in different places and times Hindu law or usage meant different things. As Elphinstone was to write in 1823:

'The Dhurm Shaster, it is understood, is a collection of ancient treatises, neither clear nor consistent in themselves, and now buried under a heap of more modern commentaries, the whole beyond the knowledge of perhaps the most learned pandits, and every part wholly unknown to the people who live under it. Its place is supplied in many cases by known customs, founded indeed on the Dhurm Shaster, but modified by the convenience of different castes or communities and no longer deriving authority from any written text.'[1]

The standpoint of the Regulàtion of 1772 is well seen in the attitude adopted towards the custom of 'impartibility' or single-heir succession which was abrogated by Regulation XI of 1793. Section I of that Regulation states:

'This custom is repugnant both to Hindu and Muhammadan laws which annexed to primogeniture no exclusive right of succession to landed property and consequently subversive of the rights of those individuals who would be entitled to a share of the estates in question were the established laws of inheritance allowed to operate with regard to them as well as all other estates.'

It should be noted, however, that in 1800, by Regulation X of that year, a local custom of single-heir succession obtaining in the jungle mahals of Midnapore and other entire districts, as distinct from individual zemindaries, was recognized as long established and 'founded on certain circumstances of local convenience which still exist'.

SUPREME COURT AT CALCUTTA, 1773–1781

In the town of Calcutta the Supreme Court had in 1774 super-seded the Mayor's Court, and by 1781 had so applied the powers —wide and ill defined—with which its Act and Charter had endowed it, as to create an impasse. The Governor and Council had in the *Kasijura* case employed the military to prevent execu-tion of the process of the Court by apprehending the sheriff's officers with all their followers. As Lord North put it in the House of Commons the judicial and political powers were in arms against each other. In their petition to Parliament,

1 Minute of 22 July 1823. *Life of Elphinstone*, by Sir T. E. Colebrooke, 1884, vol. II, pp. 111 *et seq.*

Hastings, Francis and Wheeler claimed that they had been 'obliged to yield their protection to the country and people... from the controul of a foreign law and the terrors of a new and usurped dominion'. They objected to 'the attempt to extend to the inhabitants of these provinces the jurisdiction of the Supreme Court of Judicature and the authority of the English law, and of the forms and fictions of that law which are yet more intolerable because less capable of being understood'. Certain Europeans in Calcutta protested in like manner against 'giving to the voluminous and intricate laws of England a boundless retrospective power in the midst of Asia'. These protests were by no means free from exaggeration, and Macaulay in his narrative of these events was to carry their extravagance still further, painting a reign of terror throughout the land.[1] As regards civil law at least, there is no reason to attribute to Impey and his colleagues any intention to depart from the general principles which the Mayor's Court had theretofore applied to the ordinary affairs of life in Calcutta. It is not shown that they were minded to disregard native customs as to marriage or succession. Indeed, in Morton's Reports (p. 1) we find Impey, Chambers, Lemaistre and Hyde in 1776 granting administration to the goods of Hindus with directions that they be administered according to Hindu customs. But it is true that the Act of 1773 was silent as to the law which the Supreme Court should administer and contained nothing effective to restrict its jurisdiction over Indians. After all that Fitzjames Stephen had to say in defence of the Supreme Court, we may agree in the view, which was clearly taken by the Parliament of 1781, that its interference with the courts and authorities established by the Company throughout the Lower Provinces, whether it was or was not within the terms of the Act of 1773, was tolerable neither in method nor in substance. It was pointedly demanded in the Commons debate which resulted in the appointment of the committee over which Burke presided and thus in the Act of 1781: 'What is the object of public expediency in presenting native Indian subjects with English Courts and laws? Is it on the supposition that they have no laws of their own?' 'I think', said one hon. member, 'it has been held as a maxim that it is only to an unpolished people that a legislator can give what laws he pleases.' And Lord North explained on behalf of the

1 Essay on Warren Hastings, *Macaulay's Essays*, 7th ed. 1852, p. 279.

Government that the Regulating Act of 1773 had not been intended 'to extend the British laws in their unintelligible state (for so might they appear to the natives of a country in which they never had been promulgated) throughout that vast continent'.

THE ACT OF 1781

As Parliament's considered judgment upon the applicability of the English law to Indians in Calcutta the Act of 1781 is worth a careful scrutiny, all the more that its provisions were to be extended to the other Presidency towns of Madras (1800) and Bombay (1823) and have governed all three Presidency towns to the present time. It gave civil jurisdiction to the Supreme Court over Indian inhabitants of Calcutta, but directed (section 17) that 'their inheritance and succession to land rent and goods and all matters of contract and dealing between party and party' should be determined in the case of Mahomedans and Hindus by their respective laws and where only one of the parties should be a Mahomedan or Hindu 'by the laws and usages of the defendant'. This provision, in the view of Sir Courtenay Ilbert (*Government of India*, 2nd ed. p. 249), 'constitutes the first express recognition of Warren Hastings' rule in the English statute law'. But two ways of giving expression to the same principle could hardly show more variety. 'Marriage, caste and other religious usages and institutions' are not mentioned in the Act of 1781: 'matters of contract and dealing' were not mentioned in the Regulation of 1772. The Act where one party only is a Hindu or a Mahomedan introduces for the first time the law of the defendant: the Regulation had left such a case to justice, equity and good conscience—that is, to the good sense of the court. And between the two provisions there was an underlying difference—namely, that within Calcutta the residual law, the law to be applied whenever no express direction required some other law to be applied, was the law of England—not *ius naturale* nor the unfettered discretion of any judge. Calcutta in 1726 was neither a ceded nor a conquered territory, nor was it an unoccupied or savage country in which Englishmen had founded a plantation; but the Charter of 1726 and the principles laid down by Lord Mansfield in *Campbell* v. *Hall* (1774) 1 Cowper 204, 208 operated to make all persons within Calcutta amenable *prima facie* to the English law. True, well-known cases (*Mayor of Lyons* v. *E.I. Company* (1836) 1 Moo. P.C. Cases 175; *Advocate General*

v. *Rani Surnomoyee* (1863) 9 M.I.A. 387) were later to place it beyond controversy that the English law administered in Calcutta, whether to Indians or others, was not the whole English law but so much only as was not 'inapplicable to the circumstances of the settlement'; as was, for example, the rule against aliens owning land, the forfeiture of a suicide's property or the mortmain statutory law.

English law had not been treated as having any claim to a say in the Company's Courts where the judges acted in the exercise of the *diwani*. Hence it was possible in the interior of the province under the Regulation of 1772 to apply the Hindu law of contract to a case between Hindus as a matter of good conscience, though contract was not one of the subject-matters mentioned in the Regulation; and the Mahomedan law of gift and of pre-emption came to be extended on this principle to Mahomedans. Outside the Presidency town there was no *lex loci*. But to the Supreme Court it was in theory at least more difficult to extend the native laws beyond the matters indicated in section 17 of the Act of 1781, and these matters were really only two—inheritance and contract. No doubt, in section 18 there were words saving the rights of fathers and masters of families and excepting from the criminal law 'any acts done in consequence of the rule and law of caste respecting the members of the said families only'—provisions prefaced by the words 'in order that regard should be had to the civil and religious usages of the said natives'. There was therefore some ground in the Act itself for giving a benevolent construction to section 17, particularly since the word 'caste', as is generally agreed, was not used in any strict sense which would make it inapplicable to Mahomedans.

Arguments to a like effect but manifestly defective have been drawn[1] from the words 'justice and right' in the clause which appeared first in the Calcutta Charter of 1772 as clause 14 (afterwards clause 26 of the Madras Charter of 1801 and clause 33 of the Bombay Charter of 1823); but the clause has no bearing upon the law to be applied by the court, being directed only to the duty of the court to give judgment on a consideration of the merits of the case notwithstanding the state of the pleadings, the absence of any of the parties and so forth.

---

1 *Re Kahandas Narrandas* (1880) I.L.R. 5 Bom. 154; *Mool Chand* v. *Alwar Chitty*, I.L.R. 39 Mad. 543, 552–3.

W. H. Macnaghten in his *Principles of Hindu Law* (1829) said that questions connected with succession and inheritance were frequently litigated in the established courts while marriage, caste, religious usages were for the most part adjusted by reference to private arbitration (p. vii). The work of the Mayors' Courts, if one may judge from the records of that court in Madras, which have been published in the series *Records of Fort St George*, supports this opinion. The authority of the caste and the Panchayet has always been fundamental with Hindus—'*panchmen Parmeshwar*', God is with the five—and it may be that Parliament was not anxious that this authority should be exercised by barrister judges from England, at least to any greater extent than might prove necessary. One remembers how in the Elphinstone Code (Bombay Regulation II of 1827, section 21) caste questions were excluded from the jurisdiction of the civil courts.

But whatever be the explanation of the fact that the only two 'titles' of the law specifically mentioned in section 17 of 1781 are inheritance and contract, still in the nature of the case the laws as to inheritance and succession draw after them the marriage laws and much else which they presuppose. This is particularly true of the Hindu law where succession by survivorship lies at the heart of the joint family system. Thus Sir Thomas Strange in the preface to his *Elements of Hindu Law* (1825), pointing to this consideration, explains that it 'gives a scope to these elements beyond the exigency of the two specified titles strictly considered' notwithstanding that as he has said 'it is to these two subjects chiefly that the following attempt at arrangement and elucidation is intended to be confined'. Looking back upon the history of over a century and a half, we may say with confidence that the family laws and religious usages of Hindus and Mahomedans have been on the whole as fully respected by courts of law within Calcutta as elsewhere.

Again the Company's Courts by the discretion given to them in 1772 were entitled, even though not obliged, to give to persons who were neither Hindus nor Mahomedans the benefit of any laws ascertained to be their own laws. Hastings may safely be supposed to have known what he was doing when he made no express provision for Englishmen, Jews, Armenians, Parsees, etc. It was not until after 1833 that the interior of India was open to settlement by Europeans save on the most restricted scale, and Hastings knew well that his new courts would not be manned by persons with any legal training. As time went on endeavours to ascertain and apply, in the exercise of the court's discretion, the laws of succession which Englishmen and others would acknowledge as appropriate to their individual cases, put a great strain upon the country courts and was a cause of much uncertainty in the law. The Supreme Court at Calcutta, on the other hand, seems never to have extended to persons other than Hindus and Mahomedans the provisions of section 17 of the Act of 1781 by analogy and without further statutory warrant: though one may doubt, with Sir Erskine Perry, whether Parliament intended any special treatment for Hindus and Mahomedans.

'I think it quite clear that the clause in question was framed solely on political views.... It was believed erroneously that the population of India might be classified under the two great heads of Muhammadan and Gentoo.... It may be questioned whether one individual in the Legislature—with the exception perhaps of Mr Burke—was aware of the sectarian differences which distinguished Shéa from Sunniy; and not even that great man, we may be assured, was at all conscious that there were millions of inhabitants in India such as Sikhs, Jains, Pársis, Hebrews and others who had nothing or next to nothing in common with Brahminical worship.' (*Hirabai* v. *Sonabai* (1847) Perry's Oriental Cases 110.)

In the Government of India Act the original terms of section 17 of 1781 have now been widened so as to make it applicable to all classes of persons (cf. section 112 of 5 & 6 Geo. 5, c. 61) subject to a 'personal law or custom having the force of law'.

LAW OF THE DEFENDANT

The reference in the Act of 1781 to the law of the defendant is worth attention. It applies where one and one only of the parties is a Mahomedan or Hindu but it is very difficult to give to the language used a sensible or workable meaning. In *Sarkies* v. *Prosonomoyee Dossee* (1881) 6 Cal. 794 Pontifex J. did his best to expound it, suggesting that the words 'inheritance and succession' must be confined to 'questions relating to inheritance and succession by the defendants'; but there is force as well as acid in the remark of West and Bühler that 'it can hardly have been intended that a Gentoo should lose his law of inheritance whenever he entered a Court of law to enforce it' (*Hindu Law*, 4th ed. p. 6). It may be, as these learned authors think, that such a provision would have reasonable application if confined to 'matters of contract and dealing'; though there seems to be little room for this view as a matter of construction there is some authority in its favour.[1] . The 'law of the defendant' appears again in the Bombay Regulation (IV of 1827, section 26) which still prescribes the law to be applied in that province outside the Presidency town. Though the matter is no longer of great practical importance it derives a certain interest from the fact that the 'law of the defendant' had as such a place in the classical days of the 'personal law'—the system which obtained on the continent of Europe[2] between the sixth and the ninth centuries when the provinces of the Roman Empire had been overrun by the 'barbarians'. Parliament in 1781 may not have remembered Archbishop Agobard of Lyons (A.D. 816). 'It often happens', says he, 'that five men each under a different law may be found walking or sitting together'—Frank, Burgundian, Goth, Lombard, Roman and so forth. But of the law of the defendant as introduced into the Supreme Courts it is best to confine oneself to negative statements and to thanking Heaven that it plays little part in the High Courts of to-day.

'It may not be very easy to define what the concluding words of the section mean; but whatever their proper construction may be, it is clear that they do not mean this, that when a Hindu purchases land from a European, in which the vendor has only a limited interest, the Hindu purchaser is to be in any better position as regards his purchase than a European purchaser would be.' (Garth C.J. in *Sarkies'* case, I.L.R. 6 Cal. at p. 806.)

'That does not mean that whenever the defendant in a suit is a European British subject no law but the law of England shall be applied to ascertain the validity of any past transaction which may be brought under consideration in the suit.' (*Azim-un-Nissa Begum v. Dale* (1871) 6 Mad. H.C. 455.)

It stands to reason that in any court the Hindu law of succession or inheritance is applied to cases in which the deceased was a Hindu, whatever the race or religion of the defendant and although there might be many defendants of different races and religions. In like manner the law applied to the succession to a Mahomedan is the Mahomedan law, and so as to other 'personal laws'.

---

1 *Azim-un-Nissa Begum* v. *Dale* (1871) 6 Mad. H.C. 455; *Ali Sahel* (1895) I.L.R. 21 Bom. 85.
2 Savigny, *History of Roman Law in the Middle Ages*; transl. Cathcart (1829), vol. I, p. 99; Gibbon, *Decline and Fall*, ch. xxxviii.

LAW IN THE BOMBAY PROVINCIAL COURTS

The law of the defendant was to appear again as a rule of
decision laid down for the courts in the Bombay Presidency
outside the Presidency town itself. Section 14 of Bombay Regulation IV of 1799, unlike its Madras counterpart (section 16 of
Madras Regulation III of 1802), did not follow the scheme
which Hastings had devised in 1772. It directed in effect that
in every claim to personal or real right and property 'the cause
is to be decided, so far as shall depend on the point of law, by
that of the defendant' in the case of Mussulmans and Hindus;
and 'with respect to Portuguese and Parsee inhabitants, when
they are defendants the Judge is to be guided by a view to equity
in his decisions, making due allowance for their respective
customs as far as he can ascertain the same'. In all cases of
succession to landed property, the judge was to try to ascertain
whether they had been regulated by any general usage of the
district or any particular usage of the family of the defendant
and to consider in his decision the weight due to such evidence.
And in all cases whatsoever he was to see if there were not 'an
unwritten yet ascertained common law (called in Hindostan *ralje-
al-moolk* or "the customary rule of the country") and whether
this be not usually applied to cases like the one before him
whether the claim be by a Hindu or Mussulman'. If there was
such a customary law and it appeared consistent with equity,
it was to be recorded and was 'to operate to the exclusion, so far,
of the written and formal code of the Hindu and Mussulman
law books and treatises as being more essentially and nearly the
rules to which the natives have become habituated'. In these
directions the most noticeable departure from the Bengal scheme
of 1772 lies in the care taken to give effect to usage as distinct
from the requirements of the ancient texts of the religious law.
That the native laws are not reserved for the few subject-matters
mentioned in the Bengal regulation—inheritance, marriage,
etc.—but are applied to all sorts of claims, is another departure.
The repeated reference to the Hindu and Mahomedan laws as
applicable by reason of their being the law of the defendant is
also noticeable. In the preamble to Regulation II of 1808 this
principle is further emphasized as being the reason why, in
Bombay, Hindu criminal law was applied to Hindus.

'Hitherto the Regulations of this Government have been generally
framed as nearly conformable as local circumstances would admit to

those enacted by the Governor General in Council, with, however, this exception (which has equally obtained the Supreme Government's approbation) that whereas the Mahomedan law is alone applicable in Bengal to the decision of criminal trials, the Gentoo natives living under this presidency are allowed the benefit of the laws of their religion in all trials of whatsoever description, wherein they are the defendants or accused parties.'

In the Elphinstone Code of 1827 section 26 of Regulation IV provided for all suits that in the absence of an Act of Parliament or Regulation, the law to be observed should be 'the usage of the country in which the suit arose; if none such appears, the law of the defendant and in the absence of specific law and usage, justice, equity and good conscience alone'. West and Bühler[1] say on this: 'Here the law of the defendant prevails, failing statute law and usage of the country, but such usage there is governing inheritance, partition, adoption, and the whole province of family law amongst the Hindus.' Their exposition of the reference to the law of the defendant is, however, in negative terms: 'The provision in favour of the defendant is not meant to have an operation such as to enable one man to dispose of another's rights.' They refer to the negations of Westropp C.J. in *Lakshmandas Sampchand* v. *Dasrat* (1880) I.L.R. 6 Bom. 168, 183-4, where he approves *Sarkies'* case (*supra*) and says that a previous decision 'is open to doubt in respect of the view then entertained that the validity of a mortgage by a Mahomedan to a Hindu, if the latter be defendant in the suit, should be tested by the Hindu law—a proposition which seems to involve a serious misapprehension and misapplication of Bombay Regulation IV of 1827, section 26. It could not have been intended by the Legislature that the power of a Mahomedan to convey should be measured by the Hindu law.' 'The law of the defendant', as we have seen, is inveterate in Bombay, but it does not seem to mean the law of the defendant.

THE PUNJAB SYSTEM

The Bombay rule as laid down in 1827 has been identified by very competent jurists[2] with the rule laid down long afterwards for the Punjab. Section 5 of the Punjab Laws Act of 1872 introduced custom as the primary rule of decision. It was adopted at the instance of Sir George Campbell, who was not

1 *Hindu Law* (4th ed.), p. 7.
2 Sir Courtenay Ilbert, *Government of India* (2nd ed.), 1907, p. 330; Professor van Vollenhoven of Leyden in *Asiatic Review*, vol. XXIII for 1927.

content with the old Bengal rule which was originally proposed by the Bill—the Mohamedan law in cases where the parties were Mohamedans and the Hindu law in cases where the parties were Hindus. 'Not one out of ten—perhaps not one out of a hundred—persons in the Punjab was governed by the strict provisions of the Hindu and Muhammedan law' (Progs. of Council, 20 March 1872). The prevalence of *deshachar* or local custom confounding distinctions of race and even of religion and keeping people together in village communities is explained by the fact that the Punjab was the corridor through which so many Eastern races entered the peninsula.[1] Fitzjames Stephen as legal member of Council accepted Campbell's amendment to his Bill, being influenced greatly by the fact that for twenty years the customs had been 'most scrupulously registered' in connection with land settlements.

But the Punjab enactment makes no reference to the law of the defendant and it makes custom the primary rule not on all subject-matters but on certain specified topics. The list of topics specified is an expanded version of Warren Hastings' list: succession, special property of females, betrothal, marriage, divorce, dower, adoption, guardianship, minority, bastardy, family relations, wills, legacies, gifts, partitions, any religious usage or institution. There is little real analogy between the prevalence of local custom in the Punjab and the conditions of the Bombay Presidency. In particular, Elphinstone's outlook on such matters cannot be appreciated by reading section 26 of Regulation IV of 1827, but is explained in his celebrated and most interesting minute of 22 July 1823.[2]

THE PRINCIPLE

Returning, however, from this excursion into the Punjab of the seventies, we may now claim to have before us a rough note of

1 'There is no regular history of the Punjab prior to the Muhammadan invasions. But we know that for at least two thousand years before that era, there were mighty movements of the people north and west of the Himalayas into the Punjab and India. Wave after wave of conquest and migration broke through the western passes leading into the Punjab and swept over its broad surface; sometimes spending themselves there, sometimes receding towards their source, sometimes penetrating, though in steadily diminishing volume, into the valley of the Ganges and Central and Southern India, and in their course exterminating or driving back or slowly amalgamating with the aboriginal races' (Sir Michael O'Dwyer in *Journal of the Royal Society of Arts*, 1926, vol. LXXIV, p. 420).

2 *Life of Elphinstone*, by Sir T. E. Colebrooke, 1884, vol. II, pp. 111 *et seq.*; Arthur Steele, *Law and Customs of Hindu Castes*, 1827 (Preface); *Elphinstone*, by J. S. Cotton, 1892, pp. 179 *et seq.*

the sorts or systems of law administered in the different parts of British India in the critical year 1833. The Charter Act of that year forms a watershed in the legal history of India. That the law as it then stood could be damned loudly and long for its lack of completeness, uniformity and certainty was shown by Macaulay's famous speech[1] upon the second reading of the Bill. But its deficiencies were due in great measure to the fact that it had respected Indian usages—not without some exceptions, yet not sporadically but carefully and upon principles deliberately accepted.

In 1788 Sir William Jones in his well-known letter to Lord Cornwallis (19 March 1788) had offered to direct and supervise the compilation of a digest of Hindu and Mahomedan laws 'confined to the law of contract and inheritance (to which the legislature has limited the Supreme Court)'—a task which so far as regards Hindu law was completed, though not until after Jones had died, by the Pandit Jagannatha and is well known in Colebrooke's translation. In his letter Jones gives expression to the view that 'the principle of decision between the native parties in a cause appears perfectly clear but the difficulty lies (as in most other cases) in the application of the principle to practice'. The principle could hardly be more persuasively stated:

'Nothing could be more obviously just than to determine private contests according to those laws which the parties themselves had ever considered as the rules of their conduct and engagements in civil life; nor could anything be wiser than by a legislative Act to assure the Hindu and Mussulman subjects of Great Britain that the private laws, which they severally hold sacred, and violation of which they would have thought the most grievous oppression, should not be suppressed by a new system, of which they could have no knowledge, and which they must have considered as imposed on them by a spirit of rigour and intolerance.'

CONTRAST WITH THE PRESENT DAY

To-day the impression made by the law of British India upon the skilled observer from without is not what these considerations would lead one to expect. As seen by a great authority on the common law of England the position is very different from anything that Jones or Hastings had in mind:

'In Blackstone's day the Common Law was the law of a few million people in England and Ireland, and if the colonies, planta-

1 10 July 1833.

tions and settlements were added, perhaps a quarter of a million more. Now in these islands there may be perhaps forty millions living under English law, but the Common Law has long passed its old boundaries. Under its sway live the teeming millions of the United States, the greatest nation living within a ring fence that the world has ever seen. Then there are Canada, Australia, New Zealand, great now but with unforeseeable potentialities. The enormous sub-continent of India has adopted, except for family and other racial or religious law, the Common Law which there regulates the great mass of dealings between man and man. In each of these great collections of mankind there are judges enunciating the law and schools teaching it, and professors meditating upon it, seeking to criticize and reform it. England cannot have a monopoly or even a primacy in this great and widespread development.' (Lord Wright, *Legal Essays and Addresses*, Preface, p. xiii.)

This picture of to-day contrasts not merely with the first beginnings of 1772 in which the law of England had no place, but also, though of course less strongly, with the outlook of Parliament in 1781; though Parliament was dealing then with a city which had grown up as an English settlement, and had been for over fifty years (since 1726 at least) ruled, if not by English lawyers, at least by English law as laymen understood it and with certain necessary adaptations when applied to Indians. Parliament had not accepted Impey's notions as to the Indian inhabitants of Calcutta, that 'their submission was voluntary and if they disliked the laws, they had only to cross a ditch, and were no longer subject to them'; that while 'the state of an inhabitant in the provinces at large was that of a man inhabiting his own country, subject to its own laws', the state of a Hindu inhabiting Calcutta 'did not differ from that of any other foreigner from whatsoever country he might have migrated and he partook of the protection of the laws and in return owed them obedience'. No doubt he owed the laws obedience, but that was no reason why they should not be so framed as to be suitable to his case; after all the Englishman and not the Indian was the real 'foreigner'.

The contrast between outlook and result may be due to the wisdom of experience, and it profits to notice what the difference is and how the intervening history accounts for it. Without making too much of a summary phrase we may note the distinction taken by Lord Wright between 'family and other racial or religious laws' and those which regulate 'the great mass of dealings between man and man'. The former phrase serves well to point to Warren Hastings' Regulation of 1772: 'inheritance, marriage, caste and other religious usages and institutions'; and the latter phrase can hardly be much different from 'all matters of contract and dealing between party and party' in section 17 of the Act of 1781. Both phrases were used originally to define matters reserved for the native laws. But while we can agree with Sir Courtenay Ilbert (*Government of India*, 2nd ed. p. 336) that 'Warren Hastings' famous rule still indicates the class of subjects with which the Indian legislatures have been chary of interfering and which they have been disposed to leave to the domain of native law and usage', we confront a problem when we note that though contracts between Indians were directed to be governed by Indian laws even in the city of Calcutta, they and much else are governed throughout India to-day by the principles of the common law.

INFLUENCE OF THE LAW OF ENGLAND

It will take us part of the way towards an explanation if we bear in mind two things. The first—a reflection which must often have been made and for which many learned persons might doubtless be cited as authority but which was well expressed by Henry Colebrooke, than whom I know no greater authority upon Indian laws—that

'the rules of decision in the law of contracts are in general dictated by reason and good sense but the rules of succession to property being in their nature arbitrary are in all systems of law merely conventional.' (*Two Treatises on the Hindu Law of Inheritance*, 1810.)

The second may be put in Maine's words:

'Nobody who has inquired into the matter can doubt that before the British Government began to legislate India was, regard being had to its moral and material needs, a country singularly empty of law....The result is that if the legislature does not legislate the courts of justice will have to legislate; for indeed legislation is a process which perpetually goes on through some organ or another wherever there is a civilised government and which cannot be stopped.' (Grant Duff, *Sir Henry Maine*, p. 51.)

Apart from the need for a higher degree of uniformity or certainty there was a need for law in the sense that there were 'vast gaps and interspaces in the substantive law'—subjects on which no rules existed (cf. *ibid.* p. 244).

The influence of the common law in India is due not so much to a 'reception', though that has played no inconsiderable part, as to a process of codification carried out on the grand scale, not merely with a view to putting into form a system of law which already was in force, but to lay down a rule of decision where there seemed to be none, or where different rules were competing for the same ground. Fitzjames Stephen was only one of a number of distinguished lawyers who had a share in this work, but both to Leslie Stephen and to Ilbert he appeared as one who 'hurled together huge blocks of rough-hewn law'—a Cyclopean builder ('Life of Stephen', *L.Q.R.* July 1894, p. 280). The urgency of the work lay partly in the need to prevent Indian courts from filling up gaps in the law by borrowing haphazard from England rules which had grown up in the special context of English history.

The origin of this important movement has been traced to a correspondence which took place in or about 1829 between Sir Charles (afterwards Lord) Metcalfe and the judges of Bengal (cf. Sir Edward Ryan's evidence before a committee of the House of Lords, 15 March 1853).[1] But of course Bentham began it. On the passing of the Charter Act of 1833 one Legislature was established over the whole of British India with authority not over Indians only but over Europeans and others to whom India was being thrown open by the Act. Part of Macaulay's speech upon the second reading was devoted to the uncertainty of the laws administered in India and the need for codification to ensure uniformity and certainty.

'We do not mean that all the people of India should live under the same law; far from it;...we know how desirable that object is but we also know that it is unattainable....Our principle is simply this—uniformity where you can have it; diversity where you must have it—but in all cases certainty....A code is almost the only blessing—perhaps it is the only blessing—which absolute governments are better fitted to confer on a nation than popular governments.'

To Macaulay, India under the system of 1772 laboured not only, like part of Europe after the fall of the Roman Empire, under 'several systems of law widely differing from each other but co-existing and co-equal', but under the further disadvantage that neither the Hindu nor the Mahomedan law was ascertainable even with the aid of *pandits* or *kazis*, so that in practice the decisions of the tribunals were altogether arbitrary. 'Sir Francis Macnaghten tells us', he says, 'that the first lesson

1 *Parl. Papers,* 1831, vol. VI, p. 13; 1852–3, vol. XXXI, p. 237.

to be impressed on a functionary who has to administer Hindu law is that it is vain to think of extracting certainty from the books of the jurists.' And he makes some remarks of his own about the Koran and the Institutes of Manu which can only provoke a smile. He, at least, had no intention of being warned off by Warren Hastings from codifying and even making uniform so far as possible inheritance, marriage, caste and so forth. To him the vague residuary phrase 'justice, equity and good conscience' was not the only source of 'judge-made law' or 'a rude and capricious equity', and the Indian Law Commission which the Act established was not merely to fill in the content of that phrase.

Of the project of 1833, notwithstanding the strenuous labours of the first Commission under Macaulay and his successors, no results had reached the statute book before the Mutiny. 'The Afghan disasters and triumphs', says Fitzjames Stephen, 'the war in Central India, the war with the Sikhs, Lord Dalhousie's annexations, threw law reform into the background and produced a state of mind not very favourable to it.' Judges and others annotated copiously upon all drafts and suggestions. Two false steps were taken by the Commission and had to be retraced —proposals that the Hindu and Mahomedan laws should be codified and that the law of England should be made the *lex loci* throughout British India. But the Mutiny precipitated the codes. The Charter Act of 1853 had established a second Commission to sit in England with English judges as its leading members, and by 1855 a limited scheme for a civil code upon English lines had received its approval. The time taken by the Indian Legislature, once it got to work, to pass the enactments which were so greatly to transform the law of India is surprisingly short, since it may be said to have begun with the passing of the Civil Procedure Code and Limitation Act in 1859 and to have come to an end in 1882 when Sir Whitley Stokes left India. But none of the civil codes have had the same success as the Penal Code which was drafted by Macaulay in 1837, finally revised by Sir Barnes Peacock as Law Member,[1] and passed in 1860: it came into force on 1 January 1862, when the Indian High Courts Act of 1861 superseded the old dichotomy—of King's Courts with the Supreme Court at their head and Company's Courts under the Sudder Diwani and Sudder Nizamat Adalats.

1 1852–9.

CHAPTER II

CODES AS LAW OF THE LAND

I

THE influence and authority of the law of England and the part which it should be allowed to play in British India were the immediate subjects of a report by the Indian Law Commission soon after Macaulay had left India in 1837. This report, dated 31 October 1840, has come to be known as the 'Lex Loci' report. Mr Andrew Amos had succeeded Macaulay in the office of Law Member and as Chairman of the Commission. Messrs Cameron and Millet remained as members but Messrs D. Eliott and H. Borradaile had succeeded Macleod and Anderson[1] as civil servants from Madras and Bombay. The 'plan' of Warren Hastings as regards civil courts was at that time embodied in two provisions of the Cornwallis Code of 1793—section 21 of Regulation III and section 15 of Regulation IV. The latter provided that in suits regarding succession, inheritance, marriage and caste and all religious usages and institutions, the Hindu and Mahomedan laws were to be considered as the general rules by which the judges were to form their decision. This provision applied only to Hindus and Mahomedans and only to suits of the specified types. For other persons and for other types of suit there was no provision save that Impey's direction of 1781 was repeated by section 21 of Regulation III that in cases for which no specific rule may exist the judges were to act according to justice, equity and good conscience. For Madras the same arrangements held good under Madras Regulation III of 1802. In Bombay, under section 26 of Regulation IV of 1827 'custom of the country' and 'law of the defendant' were not *necessarily* restricted to the Hindus and Mahomedans: but the position, for example, of Portuguese and Parsis who had been left to equity by Regulation IV of 1799 was neither clarified nor bettered by the phrases of 1827.

By 1840 the population of mofussil India could no longer be regarded as consisting for practical purposes of Hindus and Mahomedans, and great effects were to be expected from the

---

1 Sir John Macpherson Macleod and Sir George William Anderson. The former served also on the Law Commissions of 1853 and 1861 which sat in England.

Act of 1833 which had thrown India open to Englishmen and other Europeans. European British subjects had by Act XI of 1836 been made amenable in civil cases to the country courts without that right of appeal to the Supreme Court which had been given by the Act of 1813. Act IV of 1837 had enabled them to hold land: indeed, the Privy Council had decided that even aliens were competent to do so in Calcutta.[1] The number of Indian Christians was considerable and was increasing by the efforts of the missionaries; there was the great body of the domiciled community—'East-Indians', 'Eurasians', now called (in the new sense) 'Anglo-Indians'; also Parsis and Armenians whose laws in their country of origin were difficult or impossible to ascertain; and Portuguese in large numbers. Jews also must be accounted as a separate community, especially in Malabar. These were large classes, and, as the Commission most properly insisted, many individuals were cut off by the illegitimacy of themselves or of some ancestor from any legal connection with the country from which they had sprung: many, also, by reason of mixed ancestry or otherwise, were not, in the circumstances prevailing in the East, able to trace and prove their pedigree and establish it as valid according to the appropriate law. For all such no specific system of law had been prescribed to the courts outside the Presidency towns: justice, equity and good conscience was to be their only guide. We might perhaps make some small saving for 'custom of the country' and 'law of the defendant' in Bombay, but it comes to little or nothing. Sir Erskine Perry, who well knew the position in Bombay province, says that Parsis, Jews, Portuguese and Anglo-Indians were persons 'as to whom there is a somewhat discreditable state of doubt as to what the law is'.[2] Within the Presidency towns all that was not covered by section 17 of the Act of 1781— a section which referred only to the Hindu and Mahomedan laws and specifically mentioned only two 'titles' of these laws, namely, succession and contract—was covered by English law as the law of the place administered by the courts of the place. The Law Commission recognized that decisions had established that English law for this purpose was not the whole law of England, but so much only as was applicable to the circumstances of the country; also that it did not include amendments

1 Mayor of Lyons case (1836) 1 Moo. P.C. Cases 175.
2 27 March 1845, *Parl. Papers*, 1847, vol. xliii, p. 656.

made after 1726 by Acts of Parliament not specifically extended
to India, though legislation binding upon the Supreme Courts
had recently become possible in India by the Act of 1833.

Thus, a marked contrast presented itself to anyone who took
a broad view of law in British India—not merely a contrast
between two unrelated sets of courts, the Company's and the
Queen's—but between two systems of law. Both within and
without the Presidency towns provision was made for the enjoyment by Hindus and Mahomedans of their respective laws,
though in some respects it was not in both areas the same provision. But apart from special provision thus made for these
two personal laws, there was within the towns of Calcutta,
Madras and Bombay, a general law applicable *prima facie* to
everything and everyone as the territorial law. That this general
law was the law of England was readily established upon the
terms of the Charter of 1726: that it applied within these towns
not only to Englishmen and other Europeans but to Indians,
save in so far as special provision had been made for Indians,
was no more than an application of the fourth proposition laid
down by Lord Mansfield in *Campbell* v. *Hall*, 1774, 1 Cowper
204, 208: 'Whoever purchases, lives or sues there, puts himself
under the law of the place.' Had the areas in question been
larger the law prevailing in these towns would perhaps have
been called *lex terrae*: the Commission used the phrase *lex loci*
as meaning 'territorial law'. The contrast was that within these
towns a *lex loci* prevailed in the absence of personal or other
special law; outside these towns justice, equity and good conscience were at large.

What then had been happening in the provincial civil courts
to cases to which the Hindu and Mahomedan laws were inapplicable? How had 'equity' been interpreted and 'good conscience' applied? The information of the Commission on this
question of fact was:

> 'The mofussil courts have had to decide some cases, though hitherto
> probably very few, in which they have felt that the equity they are
> to administer must follow some law....The doctrine they have
> adopted is, that there is no *lex loci* in British India, and their practice
> has been to ascertain in the best manner they could, what was the
> law of the country of the parties before them.'

On this doctrine and practice, the Commission comment that
it reproduces the remarkable state of things mentioned by

Agobardus in the ninth century—'five·men each under a different law may be found walking or sitting together'[1]—subject, indeed, to the principle that all European British subjects had English law administered to them—a principle which excluded Scots law. They explain in detail that this 'doctrine of personal law' leaves important classes unprovided with any law; instancing Armenians and Parsis as persons of whose country of origin the laws could not be ascertained or applied, and pointing out that many persons could not be connected with their country of origin by reason of illegitimacy or difficulties of proving pedigree. On the other hand, they note that under this system the English law is already the law administered to a great portion of the new population in the mofussil.

The Commission's account of the working of the Company's courts in cases not governed by Hindu or Mahomedan law would not appear to be unfair or materially inaccurate, since it allowed for the fact that in many of such cases the courts found it possible to do justice on common-sense lines without having to ascertain and follow any particular system of law. Cases of contract would in general be resolved according to the intention or presumed intention of the parties, or on some simple principle manifestly just. Many cases would depend upon local custom or settled rules as to land revenue and tenures. Cases which could not fairly be decided without reference to the particular positive institutions of a developed system of law, would in general be cases of succession: on which topic as between East and West or even between one western country and another, there is little to be regarded as common ground. Sir Herbert Maddock, in a minute of 14 June 1845, disputed the Commission's account of the practice—denying that the mofussil courts tried to administer the substantive law of the country of the party or parties concerned, and maintaining that they endeavoured to decide such cases according to equity and good conscience after admitting evidence as to custom in certain matters.[2]

On the other hand, Mr H. T. Prinsep in his minute of 29 April 1842[3] would not agree that the country courts were allowing a new practice to grow up. He maintained that they only recog-

---

1 Gibbon, *Decline and Fall*, ch. xxxviii.
2 *Parl. Papers*, 1847, vol. xliii, p. 689.
3 *First Report of* 1861 *Commission*, 23 June 1863, App. B, p. 90.

nized and acted upon a law which they found in force—'the law applied to Europeans when they were mere licensed settlers and traders residing under sufferance in the ports and cities of India'; that it was 'a well-known and fully recognized principle in all Eastern countries...that foreigners, denizens, zimmees (*i.e.* submitting enemies) and licensed residents of all kinds... shall bring with them for all domestic transactions their own customs and laws including their own rites of marriage and rules of inheritance'.

The criticisms of Maddock and Prinsep do not really detract from the accuracy of the Commission's statement of the facts, though to attribute to the courts a settled 'doctrine of personal laws' is to go beyond the evidence. The courts considered that there was no *lex loci* and they certainly had regard at times, in succession cases at least, to the law of the parties either as existing custom or as the law of their country of origin. But this they would seem to have done as a good exercise of the very general discretion given to them by the direction to observe justice, equity and good conscience. Indeed, that nothing like a rigid or settled rule had been established may be seen from the cases—they are four only—cited by the Commission from the Sudder Dewanny reports, which are tentative and inconclusive save indeed upon the point that there was no *lex loci* in mofussil India. The 'somewhat discreditable state of doubt' is still more plainly to be seen from the discussion which took place in 1843 in the Supreme Court in the case of *Stephen* v. *Hume*,[1] a case where an Armenian in Dacca had died possessed of land. When the law of England was applied to govern the succession to the property of an Englishman, it is difficult to say dogmatically that it was done on a basis of custom and not upon a notion that the *lex domicilii* or law of the country of origin had a claim to govern the matter. But as Armenian law was not ascertained or perhaps ascertainable from law books, questions of succession in the case of Armenians were according to Sir Edward Ryan 'dealt with by a reference to the customs of the people as they are supposed to have existed in former days and by a reference to their priests who advise upon those customs, but there is no established law'.[2] The Commission's report disclosed that 'no settled rule of law whatever' had resulted: some judges, it would

1 Fulton's *Reports*, p. 224.
2 *Parl. Papers*, 1832–3, vol. XXXI, p. 240.

seem, applied English law to Armenians, some their own notions of equity, and some made vain inquiries of Armenian ecclesiastics. The rule that foreigners should be allowed their personal laws was doubtless recognized by Mahomedan courts: it is no more than Lord Stowell stated in the 'very celebrated and beautiful passage' of his judgment in 'The Indian Chief'.[1] 'By the paramount custom of Asia', wrote Sir Frederick Pollock in 1926, 'every group of men is entitled to its own customs so long as they are not actively offensive to others (exceptions of fanatical despots like Aurangzib excepted).'[2] But this Eastern system (if system be the word) had not been reproduced in its entirety by the British: the Mahomedan and the Hindu laws had been put on a similar and equal footing by Warren Hastings: each was a personal law; but it cannot be said that the courts were required to administer other personal laws on the same footing, except perhaps in Bombay after 1827.

The statements in the Introductory Note prefixed to Appendix B to the report (25 June 1863) of the Law Commission which drafted the Succession Act of 1865, are careful and free from exaggeration:

'A practice has grown up in the Country Courts of administering to every person, not being a Hindu or a Mahomedan, in all cases not specially provided for, the substantive law of the country of such person, or of the country of the ancestors of such person whenever such substantive law is not inconsistent with equity and good conscience.... It is chiefly in matters relating to Inheritance and Succession and to Personal Relations that the Country Courts endeavour to observe and apply the substantive law of the country of the suitor. ...As regards those matters in which the Country Courts have endeavoured to apply the substantive law of the country of origin, much inconvenience has arisen.'

When Sir Henry Maine came as Law Member to put forward the draft in 1863 of the Bill which became the Indian Succession Act[3] without substantial alteration, he clearly showed that no settled doctrine had established itself in the mofussil courts as to the succession to persons who were not Hindus or Mahomedans.

'To Europeans settled in the mofussil the new law will be of far greater importance than to the inhabitants of Calcutta, Madras and

---

1 1800, 3 C. Rob. Adm. Rep. 22 at 29. The phrase is Lord Kingsdown's (*Att.-Gen. v. Rani Surnomoyee* (1863) 9 M.I.A. 387, 425).
2 *Pollock-Holmes Letters*, p. 192, Letter of 15 Nov. 1926.
3 Statement of Objects and Reasons, 3 June 1864; cf. Sen-Gupta's *Indian Succession Act*, Calcutta, 1928, p. clxii.

Bombay. The papers appended by the Commissioners to their report show the extraordinary uncertainty and fluctuation of professional opinion as to the legal status of persons so situated. While many authorities of no mean repute hold that there is no certain law applicable to the European settler; another, and probably the better opinion, is that every European brings to India the law of his country of origin and transmits it to his legitimate descendants. It seems, however, to be admitted by most of those who maintain this doctrine that a Scotchman in India holds immovable property under English Law.'

The remedy proposed by the Indian Law Commission was that an Act should be passed making the substantive law of England the law of the land outside the Presidency towns, applicable to all persons except Hindus and Mahomedans—but omitting from the law of England for this purpose (1) so much as was not applicable to the situation of the people, (2) the general statute law passed after 1726, (3) whatever was inconsistent with local Regulations, (4) the English system of land tenures and of conveyancing, and (5) the English rules as to inheritance of land (so as to make land outside the Presidency towns inheritable and distributable on the same principles as movables). The rule was to be observed that land should descend according to the law of the place where it is situate and movables according to the law of the domicile. The mofussil courts were to administer on these terms the English law as modified by English equity. As regards marriage, divorce and adoption, the English rules of law were not to apply to persons professing any religion other than the Christian religion. There was to be a saving for law or usage immemorially observed by any race or people not known to have been ever seated in any other country than India and generally for any good and lawful custom.

This was the effect of the proposals of 1840 as elaborated by the Commission in the proposed Act drafted by them in 1841 and published in 1845. This draft was also designed to give effect throughout India, on the complaint of Christian converts and missionaries, to the principle already enacted for Bengal (section 9 of Regulation VII of 1832), that renunciation of the Hindu or Mahomedan religion should not entail the loss of rights to property—a principle to which legislative effect was given in 1850 by Act XXI of that year. This Act of 1850 has come to be known as the 'Freedom of Religion Act' or 'Caste

Disabilities Removal Act', but it is sometimes called the 'Lex Loci Act' by a misnomer, since by that time the *lex loci* provisions had been dropped.

II

The arguments employed by the Commission in its report to recommend its proposals are apt to distract attention from the question of their merits as a practicable measure of law reform. Having posed the question: what is the *lex loci* of British India?—they answered first, that neither Hindu nor Mahomedan law could be so regarded and that either there was no *lex loci* or English law must have that character. Strong swimmers against the stream of authority, they opposed the view taken by the Supreme Court at Calcutta that English law was introduced into the Presidency Towns by the Charters, maintaining that no intervention of legislative power was required to introduce the English law.

'If there had been no authority in favour of this last proposition [*sc.* that there was no *lex loci*] we should have had little hesitation in denying it, and in asserting that when any part of British India became a possession of the British Crown, there being in it no *lex loci*, but only two systems of rules for the government of two religious communities, the English law became *ipso jure* the *lex loci* and binding upon all persons who do not belong to either of these two communities. There is certainly no express authority for this doctrine, but if it be admitted that neither the Hindu nor the Mahomedan law can be considered as *lex loci*, then British India must, we think, be considered with regard to all persons not Hindus nor Mahomedans as an uninhabited country colonised by British subjects. And then according to the doctrine said to have been laid down by the Lords of the Privy Council, 2 Peere Williams 75[1] with the reasonable limitations assigned to it by Sir William Blackstone I. 107[2] those British subjects must be held to have carried with them to this country so much of English law as is applicable to their situation. And so much of the English law must be held to be and to have been, ever since the country became subject to the British Crown, the *lex loci* of British India.

'This seems to us a fair application of principles of international law to a combination of circumstances to which they have not been before applied...but we are afraid that there is very grave authority which is not reconcileable with this view.'

1 A case of 1722. It has no name.
2 These limitations were not in Blackstone's first edition (1765), but they appear in the fifth edition published by Blackstone in 1773 and it may be in earlier editions. They were quoted by Sir William Grant M.R. in *Att.-Gen.* v. *Stewart* (1817) 2 Merivale 143.

This line of reasoning—provocative and precarious as abstract and deductive argument in legal matters is apt to be—was regarded as somewhat beside the mark by Mr Amos, the President; who was in general agreement with the proposals of his colleagues, though he was not, as they were, in favour of excluding the English doctrines of tenures and conveyancing or the English rules as to succession to real property. The Commission of 1853 took the same view of the 'retrospective question discussed by the Commissioners in India' and did not think fit to revive it. It cropped up again as regards the Presidency towns in *Advocate General* v. *Rani Surnomoyee* 1863 9 M.I.A. 387, where the Judicial Committee followed the *Mayor of Lyons* case, emphasizing that in 1726 and for long afterwards the King of England had no claim to be regarded in Calcutta as the local sovereign: he had at this time no claim to be considered sovereign in any part of India with the exception of the Island of Bombay.

That the Mahomedan civil law was the law of the land throughout the territories formerly possessed by the Moguls had been maintained by Galloway[1] in his *Observations in the Law etc. of India*, of which the first edition had been published anonymously in 1825 and the second edition under his own name in 1832. In *Stephen* v. *Hume* (Fulton's *Reports*, p. 224), Sir John Peter Grant in a dissenting judgment appeared in 1843 to accept the Mahomedan law as the law of mofussil India and applicable, for example, to Armenians in Dacca. But this view and the view of the Commission giving the character of *lex loci* to the law of England throughout British India at large are unhistorical: being legal theory founded on a wrong appreciation of the facts. If we examine the footing upon which British power came to have effect over Bengal, Bihar and the Upper Provinces, we find that it began as the exercise of the *diwani* in circumstances which could raise no questions comparable to those presented by an uninhabited country being colonized. There were few or no English settlers. The breakdown of the Mahomedan system of civil courts was indeed complete. Englishmen with law officers to assist them were indeed the judges. But they were not English lawyers. The language of the courts was to be Persian. Questions of disputed debt and similar disputes were intended to be settled

---

1 He was an able and distinguished Lieutenant-Colonel in the Company's service with a long experience in Upper India. He became a Major-General (1841), a K.C.B. (1848) and Chairman of the Company (1849).

by arbitration. The Hindu and Mahomedan laws were to be ascertained from *pandits* and *maulavies*. These laws were to be administered as to certain matters; as to other matters, express provision was made which may have been sadly inadequate but which was a determination of the legislative power quite inconsistent with their being governed by the Mahomedan law as such or the law of England as such. The very Regulation which the Commission cited upon the question of religious converts—Bengal Regulation VII of 1832—had provided in section 9 that the provision for justice, equity and good conscience 'shall not be considered as justifying the introduction of the English or any foreign law or the application to such cases of any rules not sanctioned by those principles'. The civil courts had as a matter of good conscience applied the Mahomedan law where that course was considered to be called for, e.g. in matters of preemption and of gift, which were not mentioned in the Regulation as matters to which Mahomedan law was applicable of its own force. The contrast between the civil and the criminal law in this respect is too plain to permit of mistake: the Mahomedan criminal law was the law of the land, the Mahomedan civil law was not. Indeed, whether the mofussil courts in any given case applied the Hindu, the Mahomedan or the English rules as to contract or tort, they did so as a matter of discretion and good sense in the circumstances of the particular case, no one of these laws being prescribed as such or having any general priority. This was exactly what they were directed to do by the clause which Impey introduced in 1781, and which was repeated by the legislatures of all the provinces. The idea that there was a gap or vacuum into which the law of England necessarily rushed —if it were otherwise well warranted by *Calvin's* case,[1] *Campbell* v. *Hall*,[2] and other authorities—is excluded by the facts. Provision had been made to prevent any such force being given to the English law, which was known neither to the courts nor to the people and was not thought to be suited to the country. Apart, therefore, from the fact that it was the deliberate policy of Clive in 1765 to accept for the Company in its own interests the position of *dewan* under the Moguls, the Indian Law Commission of 1840 cannot be regarded as taking due account of the 'combination of circumstances' to which they applied 'principles of international law' derived from English decisions.

1 1609 Rep. 17 *b*.   2 1774 1 Cowper 204.

Nor do they seem to have fully appreciated the consequences arising from the fact that 'justice, equity and good conscience' in the Regulations had no special sense importing, like the word 'equity' in the English courts, that there was law which it 'followed' in the exercise of its 'concurrent' and other jurisdictions, precedent by which it was bound, equitable as distinct from legal interests and estates, and limits beyond which it left parties to their rights at law. They did indeed firmly perceive that the generality of the direction made it inadequate to afford any guidance in certain cases 'where no specific rule exists'— as, for example, in questions of succession. On this subject the report of the Commission is both reasonable and impressive, though their talk of the mofussil courts as courts of conscience and courts of equity gives an English twist to their views.

'The courts of the mofussil have to decide upon all kinds of rights, not only those which are the same in all countries, but those which, depending upon more positive institution, are different in different countries. A man who borrows money and refuses to pay it, acts unconscientiously whether he does so in England or in France. But a man who withholds from his younger brothers a share of his deceased father's land, acts conscientiously in England but unconscientiously in France. In these cases, as one of our old law books expresses it, "the diversity of law maketh the diversity of conscience". Before therefore a court of conscience can decide a question of this latter sort, it must know under what law the parties are living.

'The position of the mofussil courts, therefore, in regard to law, is much more analogous to that of those courts of conscience in England which have now got the name of courts of equity. The mofussil courts in order to decide rightly, must and do adopt that maxim on which the English courts of equity act; viz. that equity follows the law. Surely, therefore, it is of importance that a judge in the mofussil should know what law it is that his equity is to follow.'

Much of this is well said. Not only in matters of succession, but in other matters, some of which affect both Hindus and Mahomedans, to lay down the rule of 'justice, equity and good conscience' was in Stephen's phrase 'to throw the reins on the neck of the judges'.[1] But its vagueness or inadequacy or other demerit did not prevent the prescribed rule of decision being the law of India. As law it held the field in all the Indian provinces by positive enactment: unlike 'equity' in England, it carried no implication that 'law' must be found elsewhere. On this footing

1 *Life of Earl of Mayo* (Hunter), ch. VIII, by Stephen, vol. II, p. 181. *Life of J. F. Stephen*, by Leslie Stephen, p. 288.

no principles of international law applied to cover the same ground by a different provision—to let in the English law or any other law. In no province had the English law been recognized as binding on the country civil courts whether in 1765 or at any later date. If there has been in India a 'reception' of the English law or parts thereof, the 'principles of international law' to which the Commission appealed do not account for it. The suggestion of Alexander Dow[1] that 'the laws of England in so far as they do not oppose prejudice and usages which cannot be relinquished by the natives should prevail' was definitely rejected; though he had claimed that it was based on equity, on the need 'to preserve that influence which conquerors must possess to retain their power', and on its necessity for 'the peace and prosperity of the country'. The Regulations of 1781 and 1793 expressed a different view—that the people could be regarded as Hindus or Mahomedans, that in certain matters these great classes must have their own laws, that in other matters it was a mistake even as regards them to undertake with the resources at the Company's disposal to administer the positive institutions of any developed system of law. The few 'European British subjects' to be found in the country districts were mostly in the service of the Company; it was doubtful how far the Company could bind them by its Regulations; and, after 1774, there was the Supreme Court administering to them the principles of the English law. It is not easy to see what English law could have to do with the *diwani*; but in any case the attitude adopted towards the English law by John Herbert Harington in his *Analysis* (1805) is implicit in the elaborate Code of Cornwallis which was fully approved by his successor, Lord Wellesley.

'The fixed habits, manners and prejudices and the long established customs of the people of India formed under the spirit and administration of an arbitrary government, totally opposite in principle and practice to that of England, would not admit of a more general application of British laws to the inhabitants of the country; who are not only ignorant of the language in which those laws are written, but could not possibly acquire a knowledge of our complex, though excellent, system of municipal law.... The impossibility of introducing English laws as the general standard of judicial decision in these provinces, without violating the fundamental principle of all civil laws that they ought to be "suitable to the genius of the people and to all the circumstances in which they may be placed", has been

1 *Enquiry into the State of Bengal*, 1772, p. cxviii.

ably stated by Mr Verelst....His sentiments are also supported by Sir John Shore (now Lord Teignmouth)..."the grand object of our government in this country should be to conciliate the minds of the natives; by allowing them the free enjoyment of all their prejudices and by securing to them their rights and property". Moreover, when the provinces of Bengal, Bihar and Orissa were virtually conquered by the British arms, as well as when the civil government of them was formally vested in the Company by the dewany grant... the inhabitants, Mahomedans as well as Hindus, were in possession of their respective written laws, under which they had acquired property by descent, purchase, gift and other modes of acquisition; and which from their religious tenets and prejudices, they had been educated and habituated to regard and venerate as sacred.'

These views may have been too general; they may or may not be thought to stand in need of some reservation on particular topics. But after 1781 at least, at whatever date it be supposed that 'the country became subject to the British Crown' Regulations were in force to exclude arguments which would introduce the law of England whether on the ground of conquest, colonisation, the non-Christian character of the country, or the personal character of the native laws. That the introduction of the law of England 'ought to have taken place tacitly according to the analogy of the general principles of international jurisprudence' is a notion which adds nothing to the value of the Report of 1840.

III

If we jettison the Commission's argument that the law of England had, of right, sway and authority over all British India by virtue of the mere fact that it was British, and if we look to their views as to the best practicable reform in 1840, we find in their report a fully reasoned exposition of the need of a *lex loci*. This is only, in other words, what the Charter Act of 1833 by its 53rd section had laid down—that 'it is expedient...that such laws as may be applicable in common to all classes of the inhabitants...should be enacted'. The general proposition was advanced by the Commission that

'in every country there ought to be a law which is *prima facie* applicable to every person in it. The number of classes which, in any particular country, should be exempted from this law must always depend upon the circumstances of that country; but, be these classes few or many, small or large, the necessity of a law for persons whose condition cannot be defined beforehand, or who cannot be brought by evidence within any of the defined classes, is desirable.'

The inquiring mind may hesitate to accept statements about law that ought to be in every country, and it has been said that 'to the Oriental mind a personal law is more familiar and appears more natural than a territorial law'.[1] But the Commission made good its case as regards British India by showing on the facts of 1840 that

'though British India may appear on the one hand to have less need of a *lex loci* than any other country, because the great mass of its population consists of two sects whose law is contained in their religion, yet on the other hand there is probably no country in the world which contains so many people who, if there is no law of the place, have no law whatever.'

Left to their own notions of what was fair, mofussil courts distributing the assets of Armenians or Parsis upon intestacy had in many cases failed to find any body of rules of succession special to the intestate's class; and some judges had proceeded to apply their own notions of a just distribution, others the English law. But where the special law for the case was not in doubt, any law in the world might have to be ascertained and applied by the court, and to decide what law should be held appropriate questions of pedigree might have to be investigated, and in some cases the conflict of different laws might have to be considered. On the other hand, Englishmen and their descendants were likely to be much more numerous in India than any other persons not Hindus or Mahomedans. The law of England was, moreover, the law of the Presidency towns. It was also the law which the British might be expected to administer with more success than any other and which they might most readily impart to Indians.

Assuming that a body of law could be presented as such to British India, the law of England was an obvious choice. The Commission thought that there was nothing in the English substantive law which prevented it from being easily adapted to the condition of all persons in India, not Hindus or Mahomedans—with the possible exception of the Parsis. Taking advantage of the hope that in due course codes of substantive law would be prepared, they recommended that during the considerable interval which must elapse before this was done, the law of the mofussil should be assimilated to that of the Presidency

---

1 Hall, *Foreign Jurisdiction of the British Crown*, 1894, p. 133.

towns, and the English law made applicable to all who were not Hindus or Mahomedans.

The limited character of the proposal should perhaps be emphasized. It was restricted to substantive law; it did not apply to take away their personal laws from Hindus or Mahomedans; and it was safeguarded by a number of reservations as already mentioned—in particular the English law as to realty was not to be followed, and the English law of marriage and divorce was not to be applied to persons who were not Christians. The mofussil courts were to administer English equity as well as English law. Peoples not known to have been ever seated outside of India were to have a special right to their immemorial usages.

Such a proposal was not answered by the general considerations which Harington had brought forward against the application to the Indian people at large of the English law—whether with Harington (1805) we think of it as 'our complex though excellent system of municipal law', or with Lord North (1781) as 'the British laws in their unintelligible state', or with Ilbert[1] speak of

'the unregenerate English law insular, technical, formless, tempered in its application to English circumstances by the quibbles of judges and the obstinacy of juries, capable of being an instrument of the most monstrous injustice when administered in an atmosphere different from that in which it had grown up.'

Nor could the Commission's proposals be dismissed by reviving the protests of Warren Hastings and others against the Supreme Court's interference with the country courts upon principles of English law and practice. In 1829 Sir John Peter Grant had renewed this form of iniquity in Bombay but had been overruled by the Privy Council[2] who would have none of it. The English law of arrest upon mesne process—'one of the worst and most oppressive points of the law of England as it stood down almost to our own times'[3]—would not have been reintroduced by the Commission's proposals, which were limited to the substantive law and did not affect procedure. Indeed, the Commission's notions of the range of 'substantive law' erred not in excess but in defect, since in their view the law of tort and the criminal law were not substantive law.

1 Ilbert, *Government of India*, 2nd ed. 1907, p. 53.
2 1 Knapp's Reports, p. 1.   3 Stephen, *Nuncomar and Impey*, vol. II, p. 145.

'In this Act we intend the term to include only the definition of rights and obligations; and we consider the definitions of civil injuries and the definitions of crimes as parts of adjective law. This we think is clearly the correct import of the expression. The definitions of civil injuries and of crimes are evidently only necessary for preventing infractions of rights and obligations. If we suppose every member of the community to have sufficient motives, independently of legal proceedings, to respect the rights of his neighbour and his own obligations, there would be no use in defining civil injuries or crimes....'

This view may be disputed: the law of tort, it may be thought, defines or tells me the limits of my rights.[1] In any view neither the law of tort nor of crime seems to be adjectival in the same sense as the law of evidence or of procedure. The Commission may be allowed their own language, but their omission of the law of tort is not without significance and has not been without effect. The law of crime was not included in the proposals of 1840 because the Penal Code had been drafted by 1837.

Even when full account is taken of the limits and safeguards stipulated by the Commission, the introduction of the general law of England as applicable in default of special law or custom to everyone and everything would have been a bold experiment. It was to do a great deal at one stroke—so much so indeed, that one could only expect to find out what one had done after one had done it. To apply a fusion of law and equity before the English Judicature Acts had worked out such a system, to apply this to a number of different classes of people, many of Oriental origin and having habits and notions which were foreign to the Common Law—here was indeed a task for the mofussil courts.

Part of its difficulty had not been clearly appreciated by the Commission, who appear to have thought that in 1840 English equity was being administered to British subjects by the mofussil courts. Mr Amos in his separate Minute to the Report, and also Sir Lawrence Peel and Sir H. W. Seton,[2] found it necessary to correct this impression and to insist that the defined principles of the English Chancery Courts were not the same thing as 'good conscience'.

---

1 'Strictly speaking, therefore, there can be no such thing as a distinct law of wrongs. By the law of wrongs we can only mean the law of duties, or some class of duties, considered as exposed to infraction and the special rules for awarding redress or punishment which come into play when infraction has taken place.' Sir F. Pollock, *First Book of Jurisprudence*, 6th ed. 1929, p. 70.
2 Letter to the Governor-General, 25 March 1845.

'In equity or any other system that is governed by precedents and fixed rules, it cannot be said of every claim or defence which a party is permitted to establish that it is a conscientious one; particular injustice must occasionally result from the observance of general rules and the lesser evil is tolerated that the graver one of uncertain law may be avoided.'

We may here note in parenthesis that in fact the fusion of law and equity in the English sense came in 1861 to be the task of the High Courts in their original jurisdiction—some twelve years before the Judicature Acts took effect in England. The Indian High Courts Act of 1861 terminated the procedure whereby law and equity were administered on different sides of the Supreme Court—the 'Plea' side and the 'Equity' side. This procedure had sometimes given cause for scandal—at least in the opinion of the Law Commissioners of 1840 who remarked upon a case[1] where an Equity bill of 1834 was dismissed in 1840 on the ground that there was a remedy at law—that is, on the 'Plea' side of the same court. Certain observations of Peacock C.J. in the *Tagore* case[2]—a case arising from within Calcutta—are directed to the fusion of law and equity in a case governed by the Hindu law. They seem to show that by 1869 it was beginning to be expected of mofussil courts that they should follow and apply English notions of equity in the technical sense, now that the appeal from them lay to the High Court—a court which might be considered to profess skill and competence in that body of doctrine, a claim which the Sudder Court could hardly have made. All the same, justice, equity and good conscience retained their old meaning in the mofussil courts. In 1882 we find Sir Richard Garth insisting:

'But in Calcutta the case is very different...and moreover we are bound by the language of the charter not by the law of equity and good conscience which prevails in the mofussil but by the law of equity and good conscience which was administered by the Supreme Court (see sections 19, 20 and 21 of the Charter of 1865). That law I consider is generally speaking the selfsame law of equity which is administered by our Courts in England.'[3]

The idea that justice, equity and good conscience could be 'interpreted to mean the rules of English law if found applicable

---

1 The name of the case is given in the *Lex Loci* Report as *Gopee Mohun Deo* v. *East India Co.*

2 1869 4 Ben. L.R. (O.J.) at 163–4.

3 *Juggut Mohinee Dossee* v. *Dwarkanath Bysack* (1882) I.L.R. 8 Calcutta 582 at 590. A house had been built in Calcutta on land in which only the estate of a widow had been acquired.

to Indian society and circumstances', though accepted by the Judicial Committee in 1887,[1] had not established itself in the sixties. Sir Richard Couch[2] put it forward in 1865 as an interpretation of a judgment delivered by Lord Kingsdown in 1862.[3] Had this doctrine obtained in the thirties or even in the forties, the Law Commissioners and their many critics must have written in very different terms from those which they employed.

Perhaps the most prescient comment to be found among the opinions elicited from officials by the circulation of the *Lex Loci* Report is that dated 13 April 1843, and sent by Mr J. Davidson as Commissioner of the Agra Division:

'It appears to me then that whatever department of the substantive law of England is to become "the substantive law of the place" for our Indian territories in general, should be introduced gradually by embodiment with all requisite modifications into individual successive Acts of the Indian Government as practical necessity might arise or be foreseen; and in this way the Indian Courts might draw light from English jurisprudence, and a body of law be created, than which a greater legislative boon could hardly be given to the country, both immediately as a safeguard to private rights and indirectly in its influence on the character of our Indian courts of justice.'[4]

Sir John Peter Grant had resigned his judgeship at Bombay rather than become the 'wild elephant between two tame ones' as Lord Ellenborough had intended.[5] Admitted to the Calcutta bar on 13 May 1831, he had been made a judge of the Supreme Court there in 1833. Sir Lawrence Peel was the Chief Justice and Sir H. W. Seton the other puisne. Grant's views were far from unfavourable to the *lex loci* project,[6] but he had a poor opinion of the draftsmanship of the proposed Act, and smothered it with criticism. The joint letter (25 March 1845)[7] of his two colleagues was destined to be much more helpful. They thought that the Act as drafted showed a 'want of precision as to the extent to which the Law of England is to be introduced'.

'The system of English law is so vast and the application of it is attended with so many difficulties, that, to judges not previously

1 *Waghela* v. *Sheikh Masludin* L.R. 14 Indian Appeals 89, 96.
2 *Dada* v. *Babaji* 2 Bom. H.C. Reports 38.
3 *Varden* v. *Luckpathy* 9 Moo. I.A. 307.
4 *Parl. Papers*, 1847, vol. 43, Accounts and Papers 10, pp. 625–6.
5 Greville's *Journals of the Reign of George IV and William IV*, 1874, ed. Henry Reeve, vol. I, p. 271.
6 *Parl. Papers*, 1847, vol. XLIII, p. 664 at 673 (17 April 1845).
7 *Parl. Papers*, 1847, vol. XLIII, p. 635; also *First Report of the* 1861 *Commission*, app. B, p. 89.

trained to its study, the difficulties in this country would be almost insurmountable; since they would have to administer a law with which they were unacquainted, and they would not have the assistance of a bar or other professional agents, or of officers possessing the knowledge in which the judges were deficient. . . .

'It would be a laborious task but it would not be impracticable, to point out the portion of the common law of England intended to be introduced; and the difficulty would be less as to the statute law, from the record of it being collected and accessible. It would be of the greatest aid to those who would have to apply its provisions if the Draft Act were accompanied by some digest or authoritative exposition of the law to be introduced.'

To this criticism they added others, but they offered their aid in framing provisions in accordance with their views as to the specification and explanation of the law to be introduced. Their letter was taken by Mr Cameron, who had in 1843 become Law Member, as approving the Commission's proposals subject to a digest of the *lex loci* being *afterwards* prepared; and as 'opening the fairest prospect of accomplishing that great object, the enactment of a code of English substantive law so far as it is applicable to India (both Presidencies and Mofussil) that has ever yet presented itself' (Minute of 4 April 1845).[1]

Sir Henry Hardinge—a busy General fighting the first Sikh war—was new to the post of Governor-General, having arrived in Calcutta in July 1844. He was nervous lest the *Lex Loci* Act, even if accompanied by a digest of English law suited to Indian conditions, might increase complication, technicality and uncertainty in the mofussil courts, and asked the Chief Justice (15 July 1845) for his views on this aspect of the matter. Sir Lawrence Peel's reply of 2 August greatly influenced the course adopted:[2]

'The Lex Loci Act, if accompanied by a digest of such parts of the English law as it was deemed expedient to introduce into the mofussil, would introduce no difficulties, subtleties or technicalities whatever. It is, in my opinion, indispensable to the success of this experiment that a digest should form a part of it; which might readily be enacted. Sir Harry Seton's and my recommendation of the measure proceeded on this view. . . . A suit in the mofussil under the Lex Loci Act if enacted would, for anything that that law proposes to the contrary, proceed in precisely the same course in which any other suit proceeds. The mere difference would be that instead of taking evidence as to the law of foreigners of all nations from doubtful sources the judges would look to a written digest of the law for a rule

to govern their decisions in the cases to which the Act would extend.
...Of course the personal laws of Hindus and Mahomedans are to
be held inviolate but there is no rational ground for maintaining
personal laws in other cases.... Without going so far in praise of the
English law as some have gone, I can say with truth that I think it
an excellent system of laws, and that it should be of inestimable
benefit to enact for the general mass of people in the same Empire,
save those for whom necessity required peculiar laws to be retained,
one and the same body of laws. This could not be done by a code
enacting a mere body of laws, for it would not do to supersede English
law in an English dependency, closely connected in commercial
relations with the parent state: and a code or a digest embodying
the main principles of the English law differ only in name.'

This letter has a more particular importance in connection
with the policy adopted towards the law of contract:

'I may observe, in addition, that the English law as to contracts,
the most fruitful source of litigation, is so much in harmony with the
Mahomedan and Hindu laws as to contracts that it very rarely
happens in our Courts,[1] which are bound to administer to Hindus
and Mahomedans their respective laws as to contracts, that any
question arises on the law peculiar to those people in actions on
contracts.'

By 1845 it was getting to be plain that the completion of a
digest or code of English law for India would be no rapid
process. It was unkindly remarked that in 1840 when this
prospect was first held out by the Commission that learned body
consisted, apart from the Law Member, of three members and
a secretary: these had by January 1845 become reduced to one
member without a secretary. Indeed, Sir H. Maddock's
minute[2] of 6 September 1845, roundly asserts that 'it was as
much owing to accident as design that the Commission had not
ceased altogether to exist'. The hard and detailed work done
upon draft bills by the Commission was not generally known
and its value could not readily be estimated. The disabilities of
native Christians were separately dealt with in 1850. Lord
Dalhousie having become Governor-General in 1848 had the
second Sikh war (1849) and the second Burmese war (1852) on
his hands and a new Charter Act was due in 1853. Dalhousie
did not think it fitting to administer the Mahomedan criminal
laws as amended by the Regulations to British subjects in the
mofussil.[3] Bethune, Law Member from 1848 to 1851, carried

1 Only the Supreme Courts and minor courts in the Presidency towns were so
bound. 2 *Parl. Papers*, 1847, vol. XLIII, p. 714.
3 *Parl. Papers*, 1852-3, vol. XXXI, p. 238.

out an extensive if misguided revision of Macaulay's Penal Code. Meanwhile he resisted its enactment. Its revision fell to his successor Peacock to complete: a civil code was still further off.

Section 28 of the Charter Act of 1853 recited that the Indian Law Commission had recommended extensive alterations in the law and had set forth in detail the provisions which they had proposed for giving effect to certain of their recommendations. It authorized Her Majesty to appoint 'such and so many persons in England as to Her Majesty might seem fit' to examine and consider these recommendations and proposed enactments and such other matters as might be referred to them. The persons so appointed were required to make their reports 'within three years after the passing of this Act'. The new Commission had among its members Sir John Romilly, Sir Edward Ryan, Messrs Cameron and Macleod who had been on the former Commission, and Mr T. F. Ellis. That Indian legislation should be prepared in England was a course recommended to some extent no doubt by the history of the first Commission, which, in spite of a highly auspicious beginning and of prolonged and strenuous labours, had shrunk to a state of ineffectiveness if not of inanition. The Government of India had not cherished it and its vitality had been more protracted than its influence. Even so, the course adopted in 1853 was rendered possible only by the high doctrine entertained by the home authorities as to their right to require obedience from the legislature functioning in India—doctrine afterwards asserted fully and explicitly in a Minute by John Stuart Mill[1] and by successive Secretaries of State.[2]

The first report of the new Commission furnished a draft Criminal Procedure Code, and its second report dated 13 December 1855 dealt with 'the wants of India in respect of substantive Civil Law'. It agreed with the *Lex Loci* report that outside the courts of the Presidency towns there ought to be a *lex loci*—a substantive civil law for persons who have not special laws of their own which our courts are required to enforce.

'This is a great want which ought to be supplied. It is, however, a want which in our opinion is merged in another want, larger and not less urgent, and can best be supplied by a measure adapted to meet the whole of the actual emergency.'

1 *Parl. Papers*, 1876, vol. LVI, p. 32.
2 *Ibid.* pp. 20–8, 31–2, 486–7, 549–601.

This further want was the need for making the law within and
without the Presidency towns uniform not only as regards the
general law but also as to the terms upon which the special laws,
e.g. of Hindus and Mahomedans, were to be administered. The
proposed union of the Supreme and Sudder Courts, afterwards
effected by the Indian High Courts Act of 1861, made this need
all the more striking, but they little understand English methods
of procedure who suppose that the terms of Warren Hastings'
principle[1] differently stated for the mofussil courts and the
Supreme Court by section 15 of Regulation IV of 1793 and
section 17 of the Act of 1781 would be restated for both in the
same way. These stand to-day in their separate language, though
Civil Courts Acts have superseded Regulations and the Government of India Act has superseded the Act of 1781 which Edmund
Burke and his committee had prepared.

The Commission laid down certain governing principles,
which served well to correct the over-confident Benthamism of
1833 and the incautious theory of 1840, marking out lines on
which law reform might reasonably proceed. The need of codification was not shirked—not even temporarily as by the *Lex Loci*
Report of 1840. It was laid down (1) that a body of substantive
civil law was wanted for British India as a whole; (2) that the
English law should be its basis, but that for this purpose the law
of England should be greatly simplified and in some matters
modified with regard to Indian conditions; (3) that some subject-
matters of civil law should not be included in the code and that
particular classes should sometimes be excepted as regards particular matters from its general provisions; (4) that while any
special laws should be inserted in the code unless cogent objection existed to this course religious laws like the Hindu and
Mahomedan should not be codified by or under a British
legislature; (5) that save for exceptions made by the code it
should be the law of the land applicable to everyone.[2] Sir John

---

1 Cf. Ilbert, *Government of India*, pp. 249, 326.
2 'In the present state of the population of India, it is necessary to allow certain
  great classes of persons to have special laws, recognized and enforced by our
  Courts of Justice with respect to certain kinds of transactions among themselves.
  But we think that it is neither necessary nor expedient that for any persons the
  law should vary according as they reside within or beyond the boundary of the
  Capital....
     'We have arrived at the conclusion that what India wants is a body of sub-
  stantive Civil Law, in preparing which the law of England should be used as
  a basis; but which, once enacted, should itself be the law of India on the subjects

Jervis and Mr Robert Lowe dissented from the other members, and recommended that the law of England should be introduced at once,[1] but the requirements above stated show of themselves why a Code was necessary for British India. No other country's law taken as a whole could be introduced, in Hegel's phrase, 'out of a pistol'; and a digest was not, as Sir Lawrence Peel had thought, the same thing as a code. Only by due provision for exceptions and exemptions was a *lex loci* possible for India. Whether the effect of simplification on English law and equity would be a good working scheme of civil law was in 1855 matter not of empirical knowledge but of faith. The Anglo-Indian Codes were experiments which put it to the test—with different results in different branches of the law.

In their three years of life this Commission could not attempt to complete such an edifice as they projected or even to lay its foundations, but they did a great work when they laid out the scheme. On 14 December 1861 a commission was issued to

it embraced. The framing of such a body of law, though a very arduous undertaking, would be less laborious than to make a digest of the law of England on those subjects, as it would not be necessary to go through the mass of reported decisions in which much of English law is contained. And such a body of law prepared as it ought to be with a constant regard to the condition and institutions of India, and the character, religions, and usages of the population, would we are convinced be of great benefit to that country.

'Being designed to be the law of India on the subjects it embraces, this body of law should govern all classes of persons in India, except in cases excluded from the operation of its rules by express provisions of law. Not only must there, however, be large exceptions in respect of amenability to this body of law, but there are important subjects of Civil Law which we think it would not be advisable that it should embrace. It would be premature to attempt now to define either the exceptions or exclusions.

'We see no reason, however, why, on very many important subjects of Civil Law—we shall only name one, contracts, as an example—such law cannot be prepared and enacted as will no less be applicable to the transactions of Hindoos and Mahomedans, by far the most numerous portions of the population, than to the rest of the inhabitants of India.

'If on any subject embraced in the new body of law it should be deemed necessary that for a particular class of persons or for a particular district or place there should be law different from the general law, and if there shall be no particular and cogent objection to the insertion of such special law into the proposed body of law, such special law, we think, ought to be provided in that way. But it is our opinion that no portion either of the Mahomedan or of the Hindoo law ought to be enacted as such in any form by a British Legislature....'

1 *Parl. Papers*, 1856, vol. xxv, p. 259. Jervis declined to sign the third and fourth reports of the Commission dated 20 May 1856, on the ground that no Code of Procedure for all India was being drafted. By his letter of 22 May 1856 'he formally and it may perhaps be said somewhat petulantly' declined to take any further part. Morley, *Administration of Justice in India*, 1858, p. 169. He died in 1856.

certain persons for the purpose of preparing a body of substantive civil law for India and they were directed to do so on
the principles laid down by the Report of 1855. This set on foot
the work of drafting and may be taken as the end of the discussion on policy and as closing—if not a chapter—at least a
paragraph of British Indian history which may be entitled 'The
Codes are Coming'.

CHAPTER III

INDIAN SUCCESSION ACT

THE 1861 COMMISSION

THE Commission signed by Sir Charles Wood on 2 December 1861 was the acceptance by Government of the policy laid down in the second report of the previous Commissioners dated 13 December 1855; and the new Commissioners were requested to report the result of their labours separately on each branch of the civil law as it was dealt with. From the *Lex Loci* Report of 1840 and the discussions which had ensued, it appeared plain that for persons other than the Hindus and Mahomedans the law most urgently required was a law to regulate the devolution of property on death. This had been the topic which had called forth the attempt on the part of the country courts 'to ascertain in the best manner they could what was the law of the country of the parties before them'. That method indeed was not well established in point of practice or free from doubt in point of principle, and at the best 'if the Indian Mofussil Courts were really obliged to be prepared to combine at any moment the law of any given European country with the local law of any given Indian province, these Courts would have a burden imposed on them heavier than that which presses on any set of tribunals in the world'.[1] The draft which with little change became the Indian Succession Act of 1865 was submitted on 23 June 1863 in a unanimous report signed by Sir John Romilly,[2] Sir William Erle,[3] Sir Edward Ryan, Mr Robert Lowe (Lord Sherbrooke), Mr Justice Willes and Mr J. M. Macleod, the last mentioned having been one of the Indian Law Commissioners of Macaulay's time.

The membership of the Commission changed somewhat as time went on; and a draft law of Contract was submitted on 28 July 1866, of Negotiable Instruments on 24 July 1867, of Evidence on 3 August 1868, and of Transfer of Property on 28 May 1870. On 18 December 1867 an additional report on the draft for a law of Contract was made in view of the Govern-

1 Statement of Objects and Reasons, Act X of 1865.
2 Lord Romilly, 1865; Master of the Rolls, 1851–73.
3 Chief Justice of the Common Pleas.

ment of India's objections against the inclusion of sections dealing with specific performance. This was the Commission's fourth report. Their seventh and last was dated 11 June 1870 and dealt with the revision of the Criminal Procedure Code. In 1870 the Commissioners resigned, complaining that their drafts were not being enacted by the Indian Legislature. The main occasion of this grievance was that Sir Henry Maine, who was Law Member till 1869, when Sir James Fitzjames Stephen succeeded him, had maintained his objections in connection with the Contract Act on the subject of Specific Performance— a subject which was not codified till 1877 when Sir Arthur Hobhouse[1] was Law Member. But by 1870 the Government of India were becoming somewhat nervous at the speed and extent of the projects for a civil code and afraid that the distinguished Commissioners might outrun public opinion in India.

THE GENERAL SCHEME

The draft Succession Act must be adjudged a most valuable and distinguished piece of work, carried out by a body of real experts who devoted their knowledge and abilities to the cause of clearness and simplicity, and took right and bold decisions on major questions of principle. Archaisms were rigidly eschewed.

It was decided that marriage should not of itself have any effect to change the ownership of the property of a party and that succession to immovable property should follow the same rules as applied to movables. Wills were required to be in writing, to be signed and to be attested by two witnesses, though the formalities were made somewhat lighter than in Lord Langdale's Act (Wills Act 1837). A grant of probate or letters of administration was required to constitute representation of the deceased and authorize administration of his property. Apart from funeral and testamentary expenses and certain wages an executor or administrator must pay all such debts as he knows of, including his own, equally and rateably as far as the assets will extend. The perpetuity limit was framed as the lifetime of one or more persons living at the testator's death and the minority of some person who shall be in existence at the expiration of that period and to whom if he attains full age the thing bequeathed is to belong.[2] A bequest to a person not in existence

---

1 Later Lord Hobhouse.
2 As distinct from 'a life or lives in being plus 21 years'.

at the testator's death, subject to a prior bequest, was made void unless it comprised the whole of the remaining interest of the testator in the thing bequeathed. Directions for accumulation were made void, save for one year after the death; and bequests to religious and charitable uses if made by one having a nephew or niece or any nearer relative could only be made by a will executed not less than a year before his death and deposited within six months of execution with a registrar.

Thus a simplified system based on principles taken from the law of England was provided as the general law governing all who were not expressly exempted from it. Europeans, Eurasians, Jews, Armenians and Indian Christians were subject to this general law. Hindus and Mahomedans and Buddhists were excluded from the Act, and the Governor-General in Council was given power to exclude any Indian races or tribes not falling within these classes. Thus, while to the ordinary practitioner in the British Indian courts the Act governed a comparatively small minority of cases, the Act was nevertheless the general law of the land, *prima facie* applicable to the devolution on death of any land in British India and of all movables belonging to anyone dying domiciled in British India.

The merits of this particular piece of codification lie not merely in the clearness of its expressions in matters of detail. It was a well-drawn Act, and the qualified praise of Whitley Stokes in 1887 hardly does it justice:

'It has now been in force for more than twenty years and has worked smoothly though its arrangement is not very scientific, though some of its provisions might be more clearly and accurately expressed, though its illustrations are lacking in local colour, and though it provides hardly any of the common forms necessary to give effect to its provisions as to probate and administration.' (*Anglo-Indian Codes*, vol. 1, p. 321.)

GAIN IN SIMPLICITY

Its chief merit is that it began a systematic attempt to frame a Code of Civil Law on an English basis by showing in this, the first chapter to be attempted, the maximum gain in simplicity. Of the distinction between realty and personalty Maine had stated in the 'Objects and Reasons' that 'it has been calculated that but for its existence, the largest part of the law contained in the English Equity Reports might at once be dispensed with'.

And he said when he introduced the bill into the Council (25 November 1864):

> 'It was quite certain that when you had once enacted that marriage should not *per se* confer any rights on husband and wife, and that the law of succession to land should be the same as the law of succession to personalty, you at one stroke introduced an amount of simplicity into English law which was almost incredible.'[1]

But the Commissioners had done more. They had carefully stripped away a number of other complications. Some of these arose out of attempts by the courts in England to inquire whether the will did in the end represent what the testator desired to happen at his death; as, for example, the presumption that a legacy to a creditor was given in satisfaction of the debt, or that a legacy to a child was in satisfaction of the right to a portion. So, too, the rule that by the advance of a portion the father adeems a legacy to his child. These 'presumptions' are said to be rules of the Roman or civil law which obtained a lodgment in English law, but being disapproved of by courts of equity are allowed to be repelled by evidence which would have been admissible in the law from which they derive.[2] The plain meaning of the words of an *unrevoked* will was to be taken as the testator's intention in such cases, and in other cases also; e.g. a condition subsequent if valid need not be accompanied by a gift over.

CONSTRUCTION RULES FORMULATED

Principles adopted by the courts for the interpretation of wills were formulated in precise terms with the aid, it is said, of the late Mr Francis Vaughan Hawkins's book on the *Construction of Wills*, the first edition of which was published in 1863.[3]

MARRIAGE

The rule laid down in section 4 that no person shall by marriage acquire any interest in the property of the person whom he or she marries nor become incapable of doing any act in respect of his or her own property which he or she could have done if unmarried, was challenged in Council by such eminent and

1 Grant Duff, *Memoir of Sir H. Maine*, p. 198.
2 Hawkins's *Construction of Wills*, 2nd ed. pp. ix, 15.
3 Died 1908. 'A most accurate writer and pre-eminent authority upon that branch of the law with which his name will always be specially associated by the title of that model text-book "Hawkins on the Construction of Wills"' (Joyce J. in In re *Hewing Murray* v. *Hewing* (1908) 2 Ch. 493, 495).

respectable persons as Mr William Muir[1] and Mr Justice Seton-Karr.[2] Maine with both skill and humour allayed the doubt 'Whether on moral grounds the complete proprietary independence of husband and wife was justifiable', and emphasized that the English law on the subject involved the English law of dower and the English equitable doctrines about the wife's right to a settlement and other matters. The question need not be reargued at this time of day. It is plain that the Commissioners were right in thinking that the introduction of the English property law of husband and wife would not be acceptable to any of the classes for whom these rules of succession were intended. Where the intestate leaves no kindred his widow takes the whole estate and the husband who survives his wife is given the same rights in her property as she would have had in his property had she survived him.

IMMOVABLES

The rule which treated realty and personalty alike seems to have been generally accepted without opposition. Many of the peoples to whom the Act would apply knew of no fundamental distinction on this ground. The Supreme Court's charter of 1774 had made lands and houses subject to execution for the simple contract debts of the owner, and it had long been the custom in Calcutta for executors to sell immovables at their own hand in the course of administering the estate, although this latter practice was not expressly authorized by the charter. In the great case of *Freeman* v. *Fairlie*[3] which in 1828 had settled after long controversy that Calcutta land was freehold of inheritance and not personal estate, these features of the law were much discussed both by the Master in Chancery[4] in his very able report and by Lord Lyndhurst L.C. at the end of his judgment. Neither was satisfied with the argument of Chief Justice East in which he referred this right exercised by executors wholly to the charter:

'I think', said the Lord Chancellor, 'that it is not improbable that it crept in at a very early period, when the law was not much attended

---

1 Sir William Muir became Lieutenant-Governor of the United Provinces and Principal of Edinburgh University.
2 Walter Scott Seton-Karr, Judge High Court Calcutta, 1862–8; Foreign Secretary, 1868, under Lords Lawrence and Mayo.   3 1828 2 Moo. I.A. 305, 309, 348.
4 James Stephen, grandfather of Sir J. Fitzjames Stephen. He had had experience of Colonial Law, had practised at 'the Cockpit' before the Privy Council, and has much of the credit for the doctrine of 'continuous voyage' in our Prize Courts.

to in that country; it got established by use; it was continued as being found convenient; and perhaps it has no legal origin; it now has, however, the sanction and authority of an Act of Parliament.'

The opinion that there was no need to maintain for the benefit of Englishmen in India different orders of succession for movables and immovables was reinforced in the view of the Commissioners by the consideration that 'the English who possess immovable property in India, generally look upon it merely as a temporary investment, not intending to establish their families there permanently'.

APPRECIATION IN INDIA

It is, indeed, clear that to begin with the Commissioners can have had no complaint of the reception accorded in India to their work. It received from Sir Henry Maine, the Law Member, all the admiration which he had previously reserved for the French codes. He told the Council 'even in England this body of rules has never been put into so intelligible and accessible a shape as it is placed by this law', that when they had examined it 'the strongest impression left on their mind will be respect for the Commissioners who prepared it'; and that the labours of the Commission 'are probably destined to exercise hardly less influence on the countless communities obeying English Law than the French codes have exercised, and still exercise, over the greater part of the continent of Europe'.

CLASSES EXCLUDED

The task of the Commission, however, had been a limited one from the Indian standpoint. The exclusion of Hindus, Mahomedans, and Buddhists was not confined to the order of succession upon intestacy but was complete. It had long been settled that for the purpose of construing enactments giving to Indians the benefit of their religious laws the widest meaning would be given to the terms 'Hindu' and 'Mahomedan'. Only in that way could the 17th section of the Act of 1781 be given its proper scope as regards the jurisdiction of the Supreme Courts, or the Regulations (e.g. Bengal Regulation IV of 1793 section 15) applied in the districts. No standard of orthodoxy would be laid down by the courts: on the contrary, different schools or sects were considered to be entitled to their own variety of the Hindu or Moslem law. Sikhs and Jains were treated as Hindus, and the subsect of the Shias, like the different schools among the Sunnis, as Mahomedans; but they were not made to conform in point of law to any single model.[1] The best exposition of the attitude of the courts and of the legislature is doubtless that given by Sir Arthur Wilson delivering the judgment of the Judicial Committee in the case of a Sikh who was held in 1903 to be a Hindu within the meaning of section 331 of the Succession Act and section 2 of the Probate and Administration Act of 1881.[2] The same view had been taken of the Jains in earlier cases, and for the purpose of giving them their own law this was clearly right; though it may be doubted whether the ordinary Hindu law should in the absence of proof of special custom be regarded as applicable to Jains as the·courts have hitherto held. Historically and otherwise Jainism seems to have some claims to be regarded as more than a variant of the Hindu religion, but to define Hinduism is an almost impossible task.

The exclusion of Buddhists was not perhaps free from misconception, since while some Buddhists, e.g. certain hill tribes, were not at a stage which made the terms of the Succession Act suitable to their case, and Burmese Buddhists had a religious law of their own, it does not appear that Buddhists in general and as such follow any particular law. Thus, when Chinamen in large numbers came to settle in Burma it was found that, though Buddhists, Burmese Buddhist law meant nothing to them; and that in China they might have been governed by any one of a number of laws, none of which had any particular reference to the Buddhist religion.[3] This is only one more illustration of the fact, alluded to by Sir Arthur Wilson in the Sikh case, that the legislature and the courts have only come to know gradually the varieties of the religious beliefs which obtain among the people. The Commissioners had not thought that the Parsis had made out a case for a special law of their own, but an Act of the same year gave them their own law as to intestate succession (Act XXI of 1865).

HINDU WILLS ACT, 1870

From the very beginning Maine intimated in Council a hope that the provisions relating to testamentary disposition might be

---

1 *Hirabai* v. *Sonabai* (1847) Perry Oriental Cases 110. *Rajah Deedar Hossein's* case (1841) 2 M.I.A. 441.
2 *Ram Bhagwan Kuar* v. *Jogendra Chandra Bose* (1903) L.R. 30 I.A. 249.
3 Cf. *Tan Ma Shive Zin's* case (1939) A.C. 527. Grant Duff *Memoir*, p. 199.

extended to all the races of India who have the power of making wills. In 1870, while the *Tagore* case was pending in appeal before the Judicial Committee and Mr Justice Willes's historic judgment had not yet clarified the principles which bound Hindu testators in making testamentary dispositions, a very short Act, called the Hindu Wills Act, was passed to bring certain Hindu wills within the main sections of the Succession Act. The Act as originally introduced into the Legislative Council was only intended to apply within the Presidency towns, but its local limits were enlarged to include the whole of Bengal as the power of making wills was found to be much employed throughout that province by reason of the great extent of the power of disposition which was asserted and enjoyed by the father under the Dayabhaga even when he had sons. As passed it applied to the wills of Hindus made in the territories subject to the Lieutenant-Governor of Bengal or in one of the Presidency towns and to all which affected the title to any immovables situate within these areas. This Act was expressly stated to apply to the wills of Hindus, Jains, Sikhs, and Buddhists. It introduced for them the requirements of 1865 as to writing, signature, and attestation; the necessity of a grant of probate, or letters of administration; most of the rules of construction and many of those which applied to legacies and bequests. The words 'son and child' were made to include persons adopted; the meaning of 'grandchild' and 'daughter-in-law' was similarly extended. It was provided that marriage should not revoke any such will or codicil. The Act authorized no one to create in property any interest which he could not have created theretofore.

PROBATE AND ADMINISTRATION ACT, 1881

Even so, the statute book had left untouched the wills of Mahomedans and wills made by Hindus outside the province of Bengal (as it then was) or the towns of Madras and Bombay, unless indeed the latter affected immovables in a Presidency town or in Bengal. Neither Hindu nor Mahomedan law required a will to be in writing, but Mahomedan law allowed only one-third of the nett estate to be disposed of by will, and Sunni law had an objection to a legacy being given to an heir. As mere documents of title or conveyances Hindu and Mahomedan wills were put forward in the ordinary course of civil suits, but the law provided no effective method of conferring on anyone a complete and conclusive title as representative of the deceased. The grants obtained in the Supreme Courts were held to be evidence of such authority, conclusive only between the parties before the court. In any case, there was no arrangement whereby the ordinary Indian will was required to be deposited with an official for safe custody. The Probate and Administration Act of 1881 gave facilities for obtaining probate or letters of administration where such grants were desired in respect of the estates of persons not governed by the Succession Act. It was a purely permissive measure. Such grants were to make the grantee the deceased's legal representative for all purposes and to vest in him all property of the deceased though not, of course, property which had passed by survivorship on his death. But the grants were not made indispensable. It was left to the option of the parties to ask for them. When a grant had been made, the power of disposing of the deceased's property was not at first granted to the executor or administrator in the absolute terms of section 269 of the former Act, but was given subject to the consent of the court, unless the court had dispensed with this restriction. It was widened in 1889 in the case of an executor. Many of the sections which in the Succession Act governed the right to obtain a grant of probate or of letters were repeated by the Act of 1881.

THE PRESENT CODE

In 1925 a consolidating measure called the Indian Succession Act 1925 was passed and its comprehensive statement of the law superseded the Indian Succession Act of 1865, the Hindu Wills Act of 1870, the Probate and Administration Act of 1881, the Succession Certificate Act of 1889 and certain other Acts. It has since been amended on important points.[1] As regards the future —we are not at the moment interested in the many savings for wills duly made and acts duly done under the previous law— the main scheme and the exceptions now permitted to the operation of the simplified English system of 1865 are in the case of the chief classes of the population as follows: As regards all wills, the Act vests in the executor a representative title and permits of application for probate or letters; and as regards all intestacies it permits of applications for letters of administration.

1 Acts XXXVII and XL of 1926, XVIII of 1927, and XVIII and XXI of 1929.

Where such grants are made the grantee or grantees are the only representatives of the deceased. Apart from these facultative provisions, succession to Mahomedans is left to be governed by the Mahomedan law. Hindus (using the term to include Buddhists, Sikhs and Jains) when they are intestate are not within any requirement that letters of administration should be taken out; and the Act leaves intestate succession to Hindus to the Hindu law. As regards their wills, since 1927 these must be made, if unprivileged, with the formalities of writing signature and two witnesses which were first laid down for Europeans and others in 1865. But a grant of probate is not necessary to establish title as executor or legatee except in the case of wills made in, or affecting immovables within, the territories subject to the Lieutenant-Governor of Bengal in 1870 or a Presidency town. Letters of administration are not required in the case of Indian Christians who die intestate but probate is necessary for their wills. Parsis have a special law of intestacy prescribed by the Act (sections 50–6). Where a grant of probate or letters of administration is not necessary, a debt due to the deceased cannot be recovered by suit unless a Succession Certificate is taken out, having the debt specified therein.[1]

HINDU WILLS SINCE 1927

A long list of sections which appear in Part VI—the part of the Act which deals with Testamentary Succession—are by Schedule III made applicable *inter alia* to all Hindu wills and codicils made after 1 January 1927. This was effected by Act XVIII of 1929. A few of the sections of Part VI are omitted as inapplicable to Hindu wills. Savings are made to ensure that a Hindu can only dispose by will of property which is his to dispose of; that he cannot create any interest unknown to the Hindu law; that adoption should have effect; that marriage should not revoke a will. But much of the detailed work of the Commission of 1861 now stands good for all Hindu wills made since 1927 as well as for those which formerly came within the Hindu Wills Act 1870—the chapters on Construction of Wills, on Void Bequests, the Vesting of Legacies, Specific and Demonstrative Legacies, Ademption of Legacies, Election and so forth.

---

1 An *ad valorem* tax is charged by the Court Fees Act on grants and on Succession Certificates: to be free of the necessity to obtain a grant is a valuable right.

PERPETUITY

We must here take special notice of the rules enacted in 1865 to provide against 'remoteness'—the perpetuity section and the preceding section which made void a gift made subject to a prior bequest to a person not in existence at the testator's death, unless it comprises the whole remaining interest of the testator in the thing bequeathed (sections 100 and 101). These sections did not of course apply to Hindus originally, as Hindus were excepted from the Act of 1865, but as the *Tagore* case laid down, a bequest to a person not in existence at the testator's death was invalid by Hindu law. When the Hindu Wills Act of 1870 applied to certain wills the provisions of the Act of 1865 the two sections above-mentioned (100 and 101) were included, although section 100 assumes a power of disposition (or a capacity to take) greater than the Hindu law allows. Indeed, Fitzjames Stephen's first speech in Council was on 21 January 1870 upon this Act, and its main purpose was to give reasons for applying section 101 to Hindu wills. He explained how 'in England both wills and perpetuities are comparatively ancient; and the safeguards provided by the judges and by the legislature against the abuse of the one by the introduction of the other are to the last degree intricate and technical'. But Hindu wills were of recent origin and Hindu law had not developed the necessary doctrines to safeguard them.

'If we do not legislate the courts of justice will; and inasmuch as they will have to legislate *ex post facto* on each particular case as it arises, and no further than that case will warrant, it is probable that if the matter is left to them, we shall get at an immense expense to litigants, and after the lapse of generations a system as complicated as that of the English Real Property Law. We must, therefore, lay down some rules. What are they to be? Our answer is the 101st section of the Succession Act. Apply those three lines to Hindu wills and you settle the question. If we do not do that we must make perpetuities legal by express words, and I think no one would propose so monstrous a system.'

Stephen did not claim to understand why the Act of 1865 had limited accumulations to one year as in England these were allowed for twenty-one years, and for a number of purposes might be legitimately employed for the longer period. He was speaking when the rule that no unborn person could take a gift by will had been laid down in the High Court but before it had been accepted as good Hindu law by the Privy Council. When in 1929 the Act of 1925 was amended, the corresponding sections (113 and 114) were among those applied to Hindu wills made after 1 January 1927, the Hindu law rule which invalidates any gift to an unborn person having been abrogated in 1916 as to future wills.

THE GENERAL LAW AMENDED, 1927

In 1925 there had also been retained as applicable to Hindu wills the section (102 in 1865, 115 in 1925) which incorporated the principle laid down in *Leake* v. *Robinson* 1817 2 Mer. 363 that a gift to a class of persons is wholly void if any members may have to be ascertained beyond the limits of the perpetuity rule. This rule had long been held by the Calcutta High Court and the Judicial Committee to be a rule inapplicable to Hindu wills, being an English rule of construction. The Hindu rule against gifts to an unborn person had never been so applied in Hindu law as to affect the right of other members of the class. In a case governed by the Hindu Wills Act of 1870 which came in 1925 before the Judicial Committee (*Soundara Rajan* v. *Natarjan* 1925 L.R. 52 I.A. 310), a gift to grandchildren had to be held bad as regards the whole of the class because it was invalid as to children of the daughter who were born after the death. So too in 1925 the section had been retained (104 of 1865, 117 of 1925) which forbade accumulations beyond a year after the testator's death though this section was not applied to Hindus. These matters were all ironed out in 1929. The law for the future was laid down for all alike, Hindus and others (not being Mahomedans or persons specially exempted from the Act by order of the Government). The rules against remoteness were to be the two rules which in 1865 had been taken with modifications from the English law. Accumulations were to be allowed for 18 years after the death and for longer, if directed for the purpose of paying debts, providing portions for issue, or preserving property; this section (117) was added to those which by Schedule III were applied to Hindu wills. The rule of 1865 taken from *Leake* v. *Robinson* was reversed for all alike, it being provided that in the case of gifts to a class the bequest is void as regards those members only who are hit by the rule against remoteness, not as regards the whole class.

RECENT AMENDMENTS OF THE SCHEME OF 1865

We may also notice two recent amendments of the law as it affects persons who are neither Hindus nor Mahomedans. They bring up to date the English law which the Commission simplified and stated in the sixties. The consent of the husband is not now necessary before probate or letters of administration can be taken out by a married woman. Where an intestate has left a widow but no lineal descendants, the widow is now given a first charge on the nett estate for Rs. 5000 in addition to her other rights. The same applies *mutatis mutandis* to a widower on the death of his wife intestate.[1]

1 Cf. Intestate Estates Act 1890, 53–54 Vic. c. 29.

CHAPTER IV

CODES AND LEGISLATIVE INDEPENDENCE

I

AIMS OF THE ACT OF 1833

THE Charter Act of 1833 had allowed the territorial possessions of the East India Company to remain under its government for a further period of twenty years, but when that time had elapsed little or nothing had been effected by the legislative power which it had established with authority over all persons within these territories. The Law Commissioners had at times been consulted on special questions as they arose, e.g. the slavery question, the amendment of criminal courts and procedure in Madras. By 1837 they had drafted a Penal Code which was to earn for them the highest praise, and they had prepared voluminous drafts upon other 'titles' of the law. Bethune,[1] who had been brought out from England as Law Member in 1848, had died in 1851 having resisted the passing of the Penal Code in the form Macaulay had given to it and after spending 'much time in attempts to redraft it upon different lines. The projects of codification, of a system of laws which should so far as possible be uniform, of a 'common law' applicable save for stated exceptions to everyone, had not materialized upon the Statute book. In the despatch[2] which accompanied the Act of 1833 and expounded its provisions, the Board of Directors had distinguished between changes in the political constitution which were prospective and those which were immediate; and had elaborated upon the important part to be played by the Law Commissioners. But in 1853 the state of things at which the Act of 1833 had 'aimed in prospect' was still a vision and the first Indian Law Commission had come to an end. Let us remind ourselves of some memorable passages in this great state paper which is known to have been drafted by James Mill. It contains reflections which retained their value long after the discussions of the Indian Legislature ceased to be 'confined to the seclusion of a chamber'.

1 J. E. Drinkwater Bethune. See *Life of Dalhousie*, by Lee Warner, 1904, vol. 1, p. 299.
2 No. 44 of 10 December 1834. Printed in the first (1898) edition of Ilbert's *Government of India*, ch. VIII.

'The state of things at which it aims in prospect is that which is comprehensively described in the preambulary part of the 53rd clause, when a general system of justice and police, and a code of laws common (as far as may be) to the whole people of India, and having its varieties classified and systematised shall be established throughout the country. The preparation of such a system and such a code must be set about immediately; and it is principally with a view to ensure that object, and for the purpose of collecting and arranging the necessary materials and of advising the Government as to the disposition of them, that the law commissioners are to be appointed.... The Act indeed asserts, or rather assumes it to be expedient, that the general system in prospect should be "established in the said territories at an early period" but "early" is a word of relation. No time should be lost by delay; none should be worse than lost by precipitation. The careful observance of these two conditions will practically determine the length of time required.

'5. Thus, however, besides that ultimate state of things to which the Act looks forward, it contemplates an intermediate period: a period of inquiry, of consideration, of preparation, in some degree even of experiment; and it is to this interval that several of its provisions relate. As the labours of the law commissioners are intended to fill up the whole of this interval, one principal care of the Government will be to guide the course and promote the efficiency of those labours; and this is plainly contemplated by the Act....

'8. Although some time may elapse before the whole people of India, native and foreign, can be placed under one common system, yet it is highly desirable that approximations should previously be made to that result. In this view, it will often be advantageous to act on the suggestions of the commissioners partially and experimentally; thus facilitating as well as accelerating the introduction of the system in question.'

The despatch insisted on the need for mature deliberation and discussion in the Legislative Council before any law was enacted, and contrasted Indian conditions with the conditions at home, where the length and publicity of the process and the conflict of opinion constitute a security against rash or thoughtless legislation.

'There may indeed be exceptions, for there are cases in which the pressure of popular feeling forces a law prematurely into existence. To any danger of the latter kind your legislative proceedings will not for some time at least be exposed; but where the discussion is confined to the seclusion of a chamber, it is only the determined prudence of those who are concerned that can guard against the hazard of precipitance. We deem it of great moment, therefore, that you should by positive rules provide that every project or proposal of a law shall travel through a defined succession of stages in council before it is finally adopted....'

Of the 40th section of the Act which authorized the appointment of a fourth councillor and thus brought Macaulay to the shores of India, it was observed in the despatch that this arrangement was more than a substitute for the sanction of the Supreme Courts:

'21. The concurrence of the fourth member of council may be wanting to a law, and the law may be good still; even his absence at the time of enactment will not vitiate the law; but Parliament manifestly intended that the whole of his time and attention, and all the resources of knowledge and ability which he may possess, should be employed in promoting the due discharge of the legislative functions of the council. He has indeed no pre-eminent control over the duties of this department, but he is peculiarly charged with them in all their ramifications. His will naturally be the principal share, not only in the task of giving shape and connexion to the several laws as they pass, but also in the mighty labour of collecting all that local information, and calling into view all those general considerations which belong to each occasion, and of thus enabling the council to embody the abstract and essential principles of good government in regulations adapted to the peculiar habits, character and institutions of the vast and infinitely diversified people under their sway.'

II

THE ACT OF 1853

The Legislature set up in 1833 was expanded at the end of twenty years by the statute which turned out to be the last of the Charter Acts. The Act of 1853 was framed by Sir Charles Wood as President of the Board of Control, without waiting for the reports of any parliamentary committee, upon the lines of an elaborate minute[1] drawn up by Lord Dalhousie who had been Governor-General since 1848; but the provisions for a reconstituted Legislative Council were not so advanced or progressive as Dalhousie had suggested, and the scheme of a Law Commission to sit in England was neither his nor consonant with his opinions. Dalhousie, besides wanting members from the Bombay and Madras services, had desired to include a few non-officials, European or Indian, but this last proposal was not accepted. His idea of local councils had also to wait. He was doubtful about continuing the 'Law Member' from England— a doubt which may perhaps be forgiven to a Governor-General who had had to curb the activities of Bethune by directing that he should not record minutes save on legislative business.[2]

1 Minute of 13 October 1852.　　2 *Life of Dalhousie*, by Lee Warner, vol. I, p. 299.

Dalhousie's proposal to include some judges in the Legislative Council was adopted in the Act of 1853. This was no new proposal, but it had effects which were not foreseen and it lasted only till 1861. Before the Act of 1833 had been framed, the Government of India in Lord William Bentinck's day had at the instance of Sir Charles (afterwards Lord) Metcalfe proposed to the judges of the Supreme Court at Calcutta that a Legislature with jurisdiction over all classes and places in the Company's territory was necessary and should consist of members of the Government and the judges of the Supreme Court. In those days the right of the court to refuse to register any regulation made by the Council and thus to refuse it any effect within Calcutta was felt as a galling restriction upon the Supreme Council's activities, and it must be admitted that the Government had some cause to desire a better system. The court had held that registration could be refused not merely because a proposed regulation was repugnant to English law but also because its expediency was disputed by the court. The judges had held themselves out as ready to hear arguments upon the merits of any proposed regulation.

The Government's letter of 14 July 1829 was answered by Sir Charles Grey, the Chief Justice, and by his puisnes Franks and Ryan in separate minutes—that of the Chief Justice being a very elaborate, able and informative statement containing much of historical interest and value. They all accepted the suggestion that the judges should be members of such a Legislature; but their acceptance was accompanied by the expression of great misgiving on the part of Grey and Ryan; and they all insisted that the court should still retain a power to prevent the passing of regulations which were incompatible fundamentally with English law as administered in Calcutta. Bentinck's reply of 20 October 1829 stated that 'all notion of representation must for the present at least be relinquished', and that on this footing there were no elements in India for a Legislature save the members of the Government and the judges of the court.[1] The draft of a proposed Act of Parliament was got out upon this footing, but in 1833 the device of a 'legal member' and of a Law Commission (to include in addition a barrister from England) was preferred, and the Supreme Court's power to refuse registration came to an end.

1 *Parl. Papers*, 1831, vol. VI.

Under the Act of 1853 the legislative power was no longer exercised by the Governor-General in Council, that is, himself, the three ordinary or executive members and the fourth or 'legal member' now usually referred to as the 'Law Member'. The Act enlarged this body to twelve. It made the Law Member a full member of Council for executive purposes, and for legislative purposes it added the Chief Justice of Bengal, a puisne judge and four representative and paid members from the Presidencies and the North-West Provinces. Instead of being a mere committee its proceedings were held in public and an official report of them was published. Dalhousie started the new Legislature 'with some flourish';[1] it was to be conducted with considerable formality on the lines of the English House of Lords, with a hundred and thirty-six standing orders and a Hansard to itself. When writing to Dalhousie in 1854 as President of the Board of Control and later (6 January 1861) as Secretary of State when introducing in Parliament the Act of 1861, Sir Charles Wood[2] made clear that the Legislative Council was assuming an importance and authority which he had not contemplated.

'I do not want to see a debating society but a working body of committee men.

'I am afraid that you are inclined to place them in a position which I do not think and never intended that they should occupy. I never wished to raise up a great independent body in India. I look to the Governor General.... The Executive Council is to aid him in administering the Legislative Council in law-making. I admit of course that the latter must be more independent but I do not wish to make it a body that is likely to take upon itself more weight or authority than is necessary for the purpose of elaborating laws. I do not look upon it as some of the "young Indians" do as the nucleus and beginning of a Constitutional Parliament in India.' (Wood to Dalhousie, 23 December 1854.)

'The Council, quite contrary to my intention, has become a sort of debating society or petty Parliament. It was certainly a great mistake that a body of twelve members should have been established with all the forms and functions of a Parliament. They have standing orders nearly as numerous as we have and their effect has been, as Lord Canning stated, to impede business.' (Speech in the House of Commons, 6 June 1861.)

'Whatever notions may now prevail, nobody at that time [1853] —and I myself introduced the bill—ever dreamt of a debating body with open doors and even quasi-independence. Lord Dalhousie

1 Lee Warner's *Life of Dalhousie*, vol. II, p. 239.
2 He was President of the Board of Control, 1852–5 and Secretary of State for India, 1859–66.

began wrong and I am afraid that everything since has tended in the same direction. He I believe generally presided and kept things straight. This I believe is not the practice, and everything has gone in the direction of fostering the notion of their being an independent legislative body. It is all wrong and very unfortunate because there is always a sympathy here for independent deliberation.' (Wood to Frere, 18 February 1861.)[1]

By this time, however, Dalhousie was dead.[2] He had never had occasion to overrule his Council. His reply to Wood's comments had been: 'I must be guided by the statute of 1853. Its provisions have given to the Legislative Council the independence which I have ascribed to it. The Governor General cannot help himself' (Dalhousie to Wood, 16 March 1855).[3]

It was owing in large measure to the presence of the judges in the Legislative Council that it claimed a certain independence; Sir Lawrence Peel as Chief Justice and Sir Barnes Peacock as Law Member were particularly difficult persons to override. The Administrator-General's Act (VIII of 1855) allowed of a charge of 3 per cent; the Directors wanted to charge 5 per cent and purported to disallow so much of the Act as was inconsistent with their orders. On 13 October 1855 Peel claimed the right of independent action, maintaining that the Directors could annul the whole Act but could not order the Legislative Council to pass any particular measure. Dalhousie, Peacock and the whole Council agreed in taking this stand (8 December 1855), and Dalhousie wrote to the President of the Board of Control that they were unanimous and twelve successors would be equally unanimous to-morrow. As a result, the Act stood as passed, though in 1860 it was amended on other points.

Canning, who succeeded in 1856, found the Legislative Council embarrassing at times, and Sir Bartle Frere, who became a member in 1859, seems to have agreed with Wood that an independent legislative body was all wrong and to have thought that the judges did the mischief. Peacock had become Chief Justice in 1859. His views on the Arms Act (1860) and his expressed doubts about the right of Government to alienate lands as a reward for services (1861) were thought by Wood, by Canning and by some of their advisers to be particularly tactless and inconvenient. When the Home Government gave to the Mysore family (Tippoo's) a grant which European opinion

1 Martineau's *Life of Frere*, vol. II, p. 336.   2 He died 19 December 1860.
3 *Life of Dalhousie*, by Lee Warner, vol. II, p. 238.

regarded as extravagant, Peacock in December 1860 moved in the Legislative Council for the papers and correspondence. Frere was presiding in Canning's absence and the debate was adjourned. At the next meeting the matter was pressed to a vote and Peacock's motion was carried by his own casting vote. Canning as Governor-General refused to produce the papers.[1] This raised the full claim of the Council to be a legislature having jurisdiction to procure redress of grievances committed by the executive. Sir Lawrence Peel, according to Sir Charles Wood's quotation in his speech in the House of Commons (6 January 1861) on the Act of 1861, did not approve of such a claim, saying that the Legislative Council 'has no jurisdiction in the nature of a grand inquest of the nation. Its functions are purely legislative and are limited even in that respect.'

In this form the claim was definitely negatived by the Act of 1861 and never could have been raised under that Act, or indeed until quite recent constitutional changes provided for it. Thus in a minute of 22 September 1868 Sir Henry Maine[2] had occasion to explain:

'There is a Legislative Branch of the Home Department, and the Legislative Department is officially a sub-department of the Home Office. The strictness with which this subordination was enjoined upon us after the enactment of the India Councils' Act in 1861 was doubtless connected with the desire then prevalent to prevent the new Indian Legislature from imitating the former Legislative Council and (to use a phrase which I have heard and read) "giving itself the airs of a Parliament". It is not necessary to consider here whether the measures taken to ensure that object have or have not been successful. No doubt the vastly preponderant opinion in India is that they have been too successful, and that the present Indian Legislature is wholly wanting in independence.'

If Wood's policy did not coincide with Dalhousie's notion of the Legislative Council set up by the Act of 1853, their views were entirely opposed as regards the provision made by the 28th section of the Act for a Law Commission to sit in England and to report within three years. The statute made public confession of the failure of Macaulay's Law Commission of 1833.

'They have in a series of reports recommended extensive alterations in the judicial establishment, judicial procedure and laws, established and in force in India, and have set forth in detail the

1 Martineau's *Life of Frere*, vol. II, pp. 327, 331–2, 336.
2 Minutes by Sir H. Maine, Calcutta, 1892, p. 206.

provisions which they have proposed to be established by law for giving effect to certain of their recommendations, and such reports have been submitted from time to time to the Court of Directors, but on the greater part of such reports and recommendations no final decision has been had.'

The revision of the laws of India by a body sitting in London was a device in keeping with Wood's notions of the Legislative Council as a mere committee to assist the Governor-General in elaborating laws. Though it represented a sorely needed increase in driving power, and other advantages, it implied that the real or at least the ultimate Legislature of India was to be the Secretary of State with home advisers and with no more resistance or interference than Indian officials or non-officials could apply from afar. The civil and criminal codes of India were to be hammered out in England. The assistance of English judges and practitioners was certainly a great gain; and its importance was not to be denied because of their lack of Indian experience, since they were the only persons who could well be entrusted with the work of stating the English law in a simplified form so as to take the shape of a code. This task was almost certainly beyond the powers of a merely Indian Commission, and lawyers of Indian experience like Sir Edward Ryan were available in England. The influence of the new Commission was first exerted, however, as regards 'the state of the laws of India', not in framing themselves 'such particular enactments as we would propose for the reform of those Laws as we did in respect of Judicial Establishments and Judicial Procedure', but in arriving at a general policy, a plan to meet the wants of India in respect of substantive civil law. They were working to a time limit of three years, and their main declaration of policy (in their report of 13 December 1855) was that 'what India wants is a body of substantive civil law in preparing which the law of England should be used as a basis'. To this they added that 'no portion either of the Mahomedan or of the Hindu law ought to be enacted as such in any form by a British legislature'. So that the Home advisers of the Home Government were responsible for much more than the 'elaboration' of laws or the detailed drafting of Acts on particular subjects; as became apparent when in 1861 a fresh Commission was issued by Her Majesty reciting the advice of 1855 and appointing another Commission to prepare such a body of law as had been recommended. They were also charged with the duty of considering and reporting on such other matters in relation to the reform of the laws of India as might be referred to them by the Secretary of State. It has been observed of the provision of the 28th section of the Act of 1853—

'The Home Government now had to its hand an instrument by which, at more than one period, they hoped to control not merely the general policy but also the detail of legislative enactments. From the first Wood seems to have regarded the new legislative council as a tool for the shaping of his projects.'[1]

Dalhousie took great objection to the new device which had found lodgment in the constitution which his own minute had shaped, and saw that it impaired the standing and authority of the new Legislative Council. He told Wood with some plainness of his sentiments:

'You refer to your Commission at home. You say you "hear rumours from Calcutta of some jealousy of the Commission" and you call upon me to discourage all such feelings. You will perhaps recall to mind that from the first proposal of the measure I expressed freely to you my opinion of its inexpediency, and I was not singular in my opinion. "Jealousy of the Commission" there is not, for all the power is on one side and none on the other. But disapprobation there is, and I do not believe there is a man in India, attending to such things, who did not view the formation of that body with dislike and regret. Its institution to bring forward the measures of the Law Commission was regarded as an unmerited reproach on the former Council of India, as though that body had neglected its duties, when it was morally and physically impossible that such legislative duties should be performed by five men charged besides with the executive administration of this great empire. Further it was regarded as an anomaly that a body, whose only portion having Indian experience was composed of a retired Chief Justice, a retired Councillor and a retired Sadr Judge, who had all left this country years ago, should be thought more capable of preparing Indian legislation, than the actual Chief Justice, Councillor and Sadr Judge, all of them as able as their predecessors, and having the advantage of being on the scene, of sharing in the events, and communicating with the people of this country.…

'You have instituted by law an independent body of ten or twelve English gentlemen, and it is right you should know early that you will find them asserting their legislative independence. They will I am certain receive with respect any reports of the Commission which the Directors may send. They will consider them with care. But they will assuredly not submit their legislation for the previous information of the Commission, nor will they stay their legislation to await indefinitely what the Commission may be expected to bring forth.'[2]

1 Professor H. H. Dodwell in *Cambridge History of India*, vol. VI, p. 18.
2 Lord Dalhousie to Sir Charles Wood, 18 September 1854. Lee Warner's *Life of Dalhousie*, vol. II, p. 235.

How entirely right Dalhousie was in regarding the device of an English Commission as containing a threat of absolutism on the part of the Home Government represented by the President of the Board of Control may be seen from a minute of John Stuart Mill which claims to represent, and which represents very frankly, the standpoint of 1853. It seeks to 'put in their true light' 'the character and consequences of the assertion of independent authority by the Legislative Council of India'.

'But legislation, in many of its parts, is to a great degree an affair of general principles; and the local knowledge which it requires is such as can be obtained from books and records or from a past residence in the country; it is not necessary that the legislators should reside there at the present time; and from the variety of personal endowments it will occasionally happen that the persons or some of the persons best qualified to legislate for India will be resident in England. That this is the opinion of the Act of 1853 is evident from their having confided the task of reforming the Judicial Establishments and Judicial Procedure of India to a Commission in England some of whom had never set foot in India.... It will not be pretended that any of the knowledge, local or general, required for the purpose was not possessed by the Commissioners, nor will anyone doubt their great superiority in the qualifications of legislators to the present or any average Council of India. Now when a great legislative work, whether it be a single complicated enactment or a code, has passed such an ordeal, when it has been deliberately prepared and discussed article by article, by a body of men as competent as any to be procured; the presumption is that the piece of work is as good as there is any reasonable likelihood of making it without trial. The fittest course, therefore, would be, instead of wasting time by inviting premature criticisms, to pass the code exactly as it is, and correct any defects in it hereafter as they disclose themselves in its practical working. This accordingly might be done if the Legislative Council could be ordered to do it. But if their assertion of independent authority is submitted to, the well considered work of men selected for the purpose as the best who could be found, men versed in the great principles of legislation and jurisprudence will be used as mere materials by men in every respect their inferiors...men of whom the lawyers are not as good lawyers nor the thinkers as eminent thinkers as those whose best labours are only to be offered as suggestions for their consideration. What will be enacted will not be the Code of Procedure but that code botched by Mr — and Mr —....

'It is submitted that the only remedy for the mischievous state of things which has arisen is an Act of Parliament declaring that the Home Government of India has legislative power; and either that the Council of India is bound to pass such laws as it shall be directed to pass by the Home Authorities, or else that any enactments sent out by those authorities in their legislative capacity shall be law without being passed by the Legislative Council; such enactments like those passed in India being immediately, or at the earliest possible time, laid before Parliament.'[1]

The 'Memorandum of the Improvements in the Administration of India during the last thirty years', which Mill wrote in 1858 by way of defence of the East India Company after it had been decided in 1857 that the Government of India should be placed under the direct authority of the Crown, had as one of its headings 'Judication and Legislation'. It is much less impressive on this topic than on Revenue Administration, for example. Admitting that the judicial arrangements of Lord Cornwallis's time were totally inadequate, he claimed that by 'the creation of native courts of justice'—'the extensive employment of uncovenanted and native agency'—the policy of Lord William Bentinck had produced the greatest practical improvement. He claimed also that improvement in procedure had been secured, but noted two things as the principal impediments to a good administration of justice—'the complicated and technical system of pleading in the civil courts, and in the criminal courts the character of the police'. Of the Law Commissions of 1833 and 1853 he could record only their labours and their recommendations, mentioning that a Penal Code and codes of civil and criminal procedure had been prepared, and that they were 'in progress through the Legislative Council of India and would probably by this time have been law but for the calamitous events by which the attention of all Indian authorities has of late been engrossed'.[2] In other words, but for the Mutiny. Enlarging on the merits of the civil procedure code, he made an observation in the spirit of the Minute already cited:

'Under the new code, if not materially altered by the Legislative

1 *Parl. Papers*, 1876, vol. LVI, p. 17. The minute was published undated in a command paper of 1876, which contained dispatches of 1861, 1865, 1869–71, 1874. But Mill retired from the Company's service in 1858, and from his references to the 1853 Commission the minute would seem to date from about 1856.

2 It is just possible to blame the Mutiny for some slight delay in the enactment of the Civil Procedure Code, 1859, the Penal Code, 1860, and the Criminal Procedure Code, 1861. The Procedure Codes were drafted by the Commission of 1853 and submitted in their first report (1855). The Penal Code was approved by them in their second report (14 December 1855), and its enactment in 1860 must be attributed to the revision of Macaulay's draft which Sir Barnes Peacock effected as Bethune's successor in the Law Member's office (1852–9). But the principles laid down by Romilly and his colleagues in 1855 for a code of substantive civil law were not accepted till 1861 by the terms of the new Commission to Romilly and others dated 2 December 1861. In truth the Mutiny precipitated the Codes.

Council, India is likely to possess, so far as judicial institutions can secure that blessing, as good and accessible an administration of civil justice as the lights of the age are capable of conferring on it.'

III

HEAVY LEGISLATIVE WORK UNDER THE ACT OF 1861

The Act of 1861, which was also Wood's but was influenced by the opinions of Lord Canning and his Council (including Sir Bartle Frere), added a fifth ordinary or executive member to the Governor-General's Council. For legislative purposes the Council now was given a maximum of twenty members—the Viceroy, Commander-in-Chief, the Governor of the province in which the Council was sitting, five ordinary members, and not less than six or more than twelve additional members of whom half had to be non-official. Frere[1] had pointed out to Wood that, however awkward it might be at times, public opinion made it impossible to lessen the Legislative Council's independence, or to do away with the publicity of its debates. He renewed the suggestion which had been made by Dalhousie before the Act of 1853 that European non-officials and Indians should have places on it.[2] These were not to be representatives in the sense of being chosen by or responsible to those whom they would 'represent', but were to be selected by Government. The proposal was accepted by Wood and found place in the Act of 1861, which put an end to the presence on the Council of the two judges who had come in with the Act of 1853. Local Councils for Bengal, Madras and Bombay were also brought into existence. The first time Indians spoke as members of an Indian legislature was on 29 January 1862, on the bill about Inam lands in Madras. Frere's diary records on 18 February 1862: 'I am glad to see natives and non-officials sit and vote, and to save the principle of publicity—sorely endangered by the want of judgment shown by the judges.'[3]

The contrast which Leslie Stephen draws between British Parliamentary procedure and that of the Legislative Council in his brother's time (1869–72) stands good equally to show the methods and machinery with which Maine, his predecessor (1862–9), had worked for seven years.

1 *Life of Frere*, by Martineau, vol. II, pp. 335–6.
2 *Ibid.*, Letters of March 1860, and 10 April 1861, from Frere to Wood.
3 *Life of Frere*, by Martineau, vol. II, p. 343.

'The Council was composed of men capable on the one hand of judging of the expediency of the general policy involved, and willing on the other hand to trust for details to the official in charge of the measure, without any desire for captious interference with details. It consisted largely of men, each of whom had important duties to discharge and was anxious to facilitate the discharge of duties by his colleagues. It was emphatically a body which meant business and had no temptation to practise the art of "not doing it".

'There is a quaint contrast, therefore, between the reports of the debates in Council and those which fill the multitudinous pages of Hansard. The speeches, instead of being wordy appeals to constituents are (so far as one can judge from the condensed official reports) brief logical expositions of the leading principles involved, packing the essential arguments into the briefest possible space. When a body such as the British Parliament undertakes to legislate, it has certain weaknesses too familiar to require much exposition. If a measure is not adapted to catch the popular ear, it is lucky, however great may be its real importance, in obtaining a hearing at all. It may be thrust aside at any moment by some of the storms of excitement characteristic of a large body agitated by endless party quarrels. Many of the legislators are far less anxious to get business done than to get the doing of business. Everyone who is crotchety, or enthusiastic, or anxious for notoriety, or desirous to serve a party or please a constituency, may set a hand to the work. A man from the best of motives may carry some impulsive suggestion, the measure may be tortured and worried out of shape by any number of alterations, moved without clear apprehension of the effect upon the whole. Trifling details will receive an excessive amount of elaboration, and the most important proposals be passed over with precipitation, because the controversy becomes too heated and too complicated with personal interests to be decided upon reasonable grounds. The two evils of procrastination and haste may thus be ingeniously combined, and the results may be a labyrinth of legislative enactments through which only prolonged technical experience can find its way. I need not enquire what compensations there may be in the English system, or how far its evils may be avoided by judicious arrangements. But it is sufficiently clear what impression will be made upon anyone who tests a piece of legislative machinery by its power of turning out finished and coherent work which will satisfy legal experts rather than reflect the wishes of ignorant masses.'[1]

This, it may be thought, is no more than Macaulay had told the House of Commons in 1833:

'As I believe that India stands more in need of a code than any other country in the world, I believe also that there is no country on which that great benefit can more easily be conferred. A code

---

1 *Life of Fitzjames Stephen*, by Leslie Stephen, 1895, pp. 251–2. Ilbert's *Legislative Methods and Forms* (1901), pp. 225–36, should be read in qualification of Stephen's views.

is almost the only blessing—perhaps it is the only blessing—which absolute governments are better fitted to confer on a nation than popular governments.'

In any view, as the Legislative Council was a body of not more than twenty persons, old-fashioned notions about popular assemblies are hardly needed to point the contrast between it and the British House of Commons or the Indian Legislative Assembly of to-day. But its lack of numbers and the Home Government's right to disallow any measure which it might enact seem in large measure to explain the difficulty which was felt by successive Secretaries of State in regarding it as a body not completely subject to their dictation. The fullest account of its working methods and of the Legislative Department was given by Fitzjames Stephen in the chapter[1] he contributed to Sir William Hunter's *Life of the Earl of Mayo*.[2] To the facts that there was a department superintending all matters concerning the enactment and reform of laws, and that the legislature was a simple and small body having nothing to do with executive government, and to the continuity of its membership and of its sittings, Stephen attributed great advantages—a degree of expedition 'which it is difficult for anyone accustomed only to England even to imagine', 'a degree of vigour and system... unlike anything known in England'. An elaborate process for circulation of proposed measures for opinion to Local Governments, who obtained the advice of district officers and private persons, Indians and others, and a prolonged scrutiny by a Select Committee were normal parts of the procedure.[3]

'I need scarcely state that the real discussion on the drafts of the Commissioners does not take place in the open Legislative Council. ...The true discussion is confined to the Select Committee. The Committee on one of these Bills would ordinarily consist of all the Additional Members of Council who belong to the Civil Service, of such mercantile and native Members as may be supposed to have experience in the subject matter of the Bill, of the Law Member of Council, and of such Members of the Executive Council as can be spared from heavy departmental work....

'The Committees of Council are not so constituted that the difficulties which occur to them can be treated with disregard. So far at all events, as concerns the Civilians who serve as Additional Members of Council, they are selected from the various provinces of British

1 Chapter VIII in vol. II.   2 Viceroy, 1869–72.
3 *Life of Mayo*, vol. II, p. 148. Leslie Stephen's *Life*, p. 269.

India for their large administrative or judicial experience, and this experience is always of the freshest, since, under the present system of constructing our legislative machinery, they are only engaged in legislative work during four or five months, and return to their proper local duties for the rest of the year.' (Maine's minute of 11 September 1868, proposing changes in the Legislative Department. Minutes of Sir H. S. Maine (1892), pp. 146–7.)

Stephen was particularly struck by the care, ability and knowledge of the country and its laws devoted at this stage to the revised Code of Criminal Procedure which became Act X of 1872.[1] But the speed with which legislation could be accomplished in the Legislative Council gave rise in Maine's time to much misgiving in India and to the charge of 'overlegislation'. Maine had no sooner answered this than he had to turn to the Law Commissioners in England who were becoming restive and dissatisfied at the delay in enacting their draft bills. When Stephen in 1872 gave place to Hobhouse, the Government of India was seriously concerned lest legislative projects for the codification of the law should outstrip public opinion in India and overstep the country's requirements. There was to be another Law Commission in 1879 and a further spurt of codification in 1882 under Sir Whitley Stokes, but Sir Courtenay Ilbert who succeeded him in that year has told us of the unanimous advice which he received 'to hold his oars'.[2]

It fell to Maine to organize or reorganize the legislative department,[3] but otherwise he worked with the new legislative machinery of 1861 whose features have now been noticed. The result of the Mutiny was to fill the pages of the Statute Book with measures which had been too long delayed, and the premature death of Ritchie[4] after holding office as Law Member for some six months only had been a real setback. In an appreciative and exceptionally well-informed account of *Seven Years of Indian Legislation*, written by Sir Wm. Hunter in 1869

1 Cf. n. 3, p. 72 above.
2 Ilbert, *Legislative Methods and Forms*, 1901, p. 147.
3 Cf. minute of 22 September 1868. Minutes of Sir H. S. Maine, 1892, p. 204.
4 'Mr Ritchie's name now awakens no chord in the public memory at home, except perhaps some indistinct recollection of the pathetic Roundabout Paper in which his appointment was recorded side by side with the death of his friend. But the little boy who had been Thackeray's playmate is remembered here [i.e. in India] as a hardworking man, who contributed in no insignificant measure towards the legislative reconstruction of the Empire' (Sir Wm. Hunter, *Seven Years of Indian Legislation*, Calcutta, 1870). The reference is to the *Cornhill Magazine*, vol. v, p. 127, Jan. to June 1862. Roundabout Papers, no. XVIII.

upon Maine's leaving office, he describes the task which Maine faced in 1862 as follows:

'The death of the Legal Member of Council had left the Indian Government in the midst of vast legislative enterprises; with a country recently reconquered from a mutinous soldiery and transferred from its former masters to the Crown; with a widely ramified system of codes newly introduced and requiring the most careful watching; with codification still going on upon a scale that finds precedents only in the eras of Justinian and Napoleon; and with demands constantly coming in from ten separate Local Governments for enactments that should give statutory recognition to the altered necessities of the times....'

In the seven years of Maine's tenure of office—from November 1862 to September 1869—Hunter calculates that two hundred and eleven enactments issued from the legislature under his supervision; and he gives a list of thirty of these with the comment that they are destined to wield a permanent influence upon some hundred and fifty millions of men. Maine's speech in Council of 14 December 1866[1] was devoted to the charge of 'overlegislation' which had frequently been brought and had been made with some emphasis by Mr Justice Holloway of the Madras High Court. He had written:

'I regard the rapidity with which legislation is now proceeding as a very great evil. If it continues I do not think that either judges or practitioners, still less the public, will know from day to day the law which governs them. Statutes, unless very carefully constructed, do not afford certainty, but doubt; and litigation is not repressed, but aggravated, by every fresh enactment.'

Maine answered that the annual production of statutes was about thirty, and that they fell into four classes: (1) those affecting the civil usages or religious opinions of the country, (2) those intended to bring up law which was common to England and India to the pitch of improvement which it had reached in the former country, (3) codes, (4) local bills which carried out small judicial or administrative improvements in provinces which had not got Councils of their own. This fourth class was the most numerous of all and was an inevitable concomitant of the country's progress. The first was the class in which incaution or precipitancy would be most harmful; but in four years only two such measures had been passed—the

1 See also his minute of 10 October 1868. Grant Duff's *Memoir*, pp. 227, 237. Minutes of Sir H. S. Maine, p. 211.

Native Christian Marriage Dissolution Act, and the Registration Act—both Acts which had been discussed for years. In the second class only four enactments had of recent years been passed—the two Trustee Acts (XXVII and XXVIII of 1866) which were the work of Lord St Leonards and Lord Justice Turner, the Mercantile Law Amendment Act and the Companies Act. The third class was the Codes. In it were four statutes only—the Penal Code, the Codes of Civil and Criminal Procedure, which had been passed by the previous Council established by the Charter Act of 1853; and the Succession Act, the only code so far passed since 1861, unless indeed the Partnership Amendment Act of 1865 could be counted as another.

This line of defence was sound enough in showing that in the first and third classes few laws were being passed, and these after much deliberation. But the real defence was not that little was being done but that much more required to be done. When Maine was making his defence the Contract Bill had just arrived in India, and as he mentioned this he maintained that Codes enormously reduced the bulk of the law and rendered it for the first time intelligible to the people, saying that the vulgar prejudice against codification had greatly decayed in England. The Council by passing chapters of the Civil Code at the rate of about one in two years would not increase the massiveness or the unintelligibility of the law! In the three years which were left of Maine's period of office the legislative output continued to be heavy and its subject-matters to be of great importance. There was work, too—heavy work—of a negative character as in the case of Act VIII of 1868 when, as Hunter[1] states: 'the entire Regulation Law of Bengal passed under his review, and no less than four hundred and twenty-three enactments being found to have expired or grown obsolete, were formally excised'. Stephen too had in his turn to meet the charge of overlegislation. He did so, fully and clearly, after leaving India in the chapter he wrote for Hunter's *Life of Mayo*.[2] But a trenchant and characteristic reply can be seen in a passage from his speech in Council[3] on 12 May 1871—on which day the Council passed through all its stages a bill to validate the appointment of Sessions Judges in Bengal. This, it seems, had long been done without statutory power.

1 *Op. cit.* p. 20.   2 Vol. II, p. 152.
3 P. 537 of the *Proceedings* for 1871.

'I think it is altogether discreditable that in two of the most important provinces of the Empire, people should have gone on being hung, transported and imprisoned illegally for a period of probably nearly forty years. I can understand those who wish to have no laws at all, I can understand those who wish to have good laws; but people who, because they would prefer personal government to government by law, prefer confused laws to simple ones, and complain of reckless overlegislation when one simple Act is substituted for thirteen bits of Acts enacted at different times and couched in phraseology of very different styles, seem to me to labour under a lamentable confusion of thought. A pettifogging pleader is the only person who can really and logically object to the work of consolidation and re-enactment in which much progress has been made, and which I hope will soon be completed.'

CHAPTER V

SPECIFIC PERFORMANCE IN INDIA

ONE of the first subjects to which Maine's attention was directed when he arrived in India in 1862 was the subject of Specific Performance. The disputes upon this topic are perhaps only to be appreciated by carrying our minds back to the state of ill-feeling which was a consequence of the Mutiny. The European community was for some time in a state of considerable tension, so much so that Sir Barnes Peacock in 1860, as a member of the Legislative Council before its reconstitution in 1861, had attempted though without success to get Europeans exempted from the Arms Act. One of the grievances of the 'planter', especially if he had a factory to keep going, was that though he had settled land with a ryot on the terms that the ryot would cultivate a particular crop, and though he might even have advanced money for the purpose, the ryot might fail or refuse to carry out his bargain, and escape without any greater penalty than a decree for damages which could never be enforced. This was a grievance of special intensity in those parts of Bengal where indigo was cultivated, owing to the fluctuations in its price, though the same thing might occasionally apply to jute or sugar or to other parts of India. On the other hand, that the stipulations made by planters with their ryots for the cultivation of indigo in particular were operating harshly is reasonably plain. Experienced administrators seem to have been practically at one as to the hardship on the ryots, and in any case it was an important matter of agrarian policy on which the Home Government's decision could not be questioned in the interests of law reform. From the minutes of Sir Henry Maine we know that Lord Lawrence was very strong in this opinion.[1] Sir R. Temple,[2] a distinguished Punjab civilian who had seen something of conditions in Bengal, as well as Sir George Campbell, the Lieutenant-Governor, gave strong evidence to that effect in their speeches in Council on the Contract Bill when at long last it came to be passed in 1872. The latter made a provocative suggestion to add as an illustration to section 16 of the Act, which deals with 'undue influence', the following:

[1] Minutes of 15, 23, 25, 27 July 1867. Minutes of Sir H. S. Maine, pp. 126 *et seq.*
[2] He succeeded Campbell as Lieut.-Governor of Bengal in 1874.

'*A*, a rich and powerful zemindar, induces *B*, *C* and *D*, poor and ignorant ryots holding under him, to engage to grow certain produce and to deliver it to him, for a term of 20 years in consideration of an inadequate price for which no independent ryot would have so engaged. *A* employs undue influence over *B*, *C* and *D*.'[1]

A Commission of four under W. S. Seton-Karr (afterwards a Judge) had, in 1860, considered whether in such cases imprisonment should be resorted to as affording a remedy to the planter. The Commissioners were equally divided and the casting vote of the Lieutenant-Governor of Bengal (John Peter Grant) had negatived the proposal. The Government of India under Canning had taken the opposite view, and in 1861 a bill had been introduced into Council by Mr Beadon (Sir Cecil Beadon) providing for the punishment by imprisonment of 'fraudulent breaches' of agricultural contracts. This bill was withdrawn on the orders of Sir Charles Wood who was prepared to veto it. Sir Bartle Frere's letter to Lord de Grey dated 9 June 1861 shows that Canning's Government harboured some grievance over their treatment in this matter. 'You have allowed a section of the community here (with whose views remember I agree in the main) in concert with a few members of the House of Commons to dictate to the Governor-General.'[2]

In 1862 the Law Member (Ritchie), with the approval of Sir Barnes Peacock, had introduced a more general bill for inflicting imprisonment with hard labour on persons who received the consideration but broke their contracts without reasonable excuse. This, too, was withdrawn—Wood and the Select Committee being against it. Maine's first speech in Council (17 December 1862)[3] recommended its withdrawal, but he had no intention of permitting such breaches to go unchecked save by valueless decrees for damages. The Civil Procedure Code of 1859 had given very wide powers to the mofussil courts to order specific performance.

s. 192. 'When the suit is for damages for breach of contract, if it

---

1 This was carrying the war into the enemy's country, and Stephen's riposte was that it would be no more useful or unobjectionable than to say,

'*C*, a rich and powerful Lieutenant-Governor of remarkable force of character, induces *S*, a member of Council of feeble intellect, to sell him a horse for a totally inadequate price. *C* employs undue influence.'

2 *Life of Frere*, by John Martineau, vol. II, p. 358.
3 Grant Duff's *Memoir*, p. 86.

appear that the defendant is able to perform the contract, the Court with the consent of the plaintiff may decree the specific performance of the contract within a time to be fixed by the Court and in such case shall award an amount of damages to be paid as an alternative if the contract is not performed.'

In a draft bill to amend this Code of 1859 Maine had drawn up four sections to amend this provision—sections which never became law. He expressed himself in Council on 11 November 1864 as against a system of perpetually unexecuted decrees for damages[1]—a view which was later adopted by limiting a time within which execution should be completed (C.P.C. 1882 s. 260, 1908 s. 48). He considered that the remedy of specific performance was better for the defendant in many cases, and that this form of remedy was one which would extend and develop in the future. He was not minded to let a particular difficulty about indigo in a part of Bengal dictate a limited rule for the general law. His standpoint was that in a code worked by a simple procedure it was not necessary to exhibit the timidity of the Court of Chancery any more than to exercise the full freedom of the French law which had ordered Dumas to write a novel, or of the Civil Procedure Code of 1859 under which it would seem to be possible to order A to marry B. He regarded India as a land of small contracts and thought specific performance fairer to the poor defendant than damages, that 'the more scientific instrument will inflict the less deadly wound'. If one looks to the English law as a whole, he argued, the performance of small contracts is compelled, not by the civil but by the criminal law. He instanced the Master and Servants Act 1867 (30 & 31 Vic. c. 141), but held that in India civil courts were better agents for the purpose, and that advantage might be taken of this to give further extension to the principles which English civil courts in England had been endeavouring to extend—thus preventing the perpetual recurrence of a demand for the coarse remedies of the criminal law.[2]

Maine's proposals of 1864 came to nothing, Sir Charles Wood having in that year suggested the postponement of the bill to amend the Civil Procedure Code of 1859. Lawrence's Government objected that the Act of 1861 reserved to the Home Government a right to disallow, but did not appear to contem-

1 Grant Duff's *Memoir*, p. 164. See also his minute of 27 July 1867. Minutes of Sir H. S. Maine, p. 133.   2 Grant Duff's *Memoir*, pp. 164–78.

plate that consideration of a bill should be stayed by orders from home. Sir Charles Wood had his answer ready. He laid down that his dispatches and his orders were not addressed to the Legislative Council but to the executive. While saying that extreme claims should not be put forward on one side or extreme rights enforced on the other, he asserted that his full power to control and direct the Executive Council members included the introduction of a bill into the Legislative Council by the Indian Government and the course to be pursued by it in respect of a bill introduced by an additional member (31 March 1865).[1]

In view of the part to be played in 1869 and 1870 by the Duke of Argyll as Secretary of State in taking decisions on the part of the Home Government upon questions arising out of the draft Contract Act prepared by Lord Romilly's commission, we may note that in the *Edinburgh Review* of 1863 the Duke had already written:[2]

'In the special penal legislation, which was unfortunately adopted by the Government of India for the enforcement of indigo-contracts, we have a conclusive proof of the necessity for having a controlling authority at home which shall be competent vigilant and strong. The veto which has been put by the Secretary of State in Council on all legislation tending to entangle the Ryots of Bengal in a virtual serfdom to the European Planters has been universally approved at home.'

1 *Parl. Papers*, 1876, vol. LVI, p. 20, etc.
2 Republished under the title *India Under Dalhousie and Canning*, 1865, p. 126.

CHAPTER VI

THE FETTER DROPS

WE are now in a position to appreciate how matters stood when in 1866 the draft of a code on the subject of Contract was received in India from the hands of Lord Romilly[1] and his distinguished colleagues.[2] As a simplified statement of the law of England its merits were of a high order, but it was not solely a statement of existing law, the Commissioners having thought fit to recommend a departure from the English law as to certain matters. In so doing they were well within the scope of their duty and they called attention by their report to the more important variations. Among a number of useful and acceptable amendments of the English law there were some suggestions which proved to be less happy, since though designed as new rules suitable for India, opinion in India was strongly against them. Of these the two which were to figure most prominently as stumbling blocks when the Select Committee of the Legislative Council came to examine the Commission's draft were in clauses 81 and 50. The former treated all India as 'market overt' for the sale of goods, providing that 'the ownership of goods may be acquired by buying them from any person who is in possession of them provided that the buyer acts in good faith and under circumstances which are not such as to raise a reasonable presumption that the person in possession has no right to sell them'. The latter got over the difficult distinction between penalty and liquidated damages by providing that 'when a contract has been broken, if a sum is named in the contract itself as the amount to be paid in the case of such breach, the amount so named shall be paid accordingly'—thus treating the sum named in every case as liquidated damages and therefore payable, although a much smaller sum might represent the damage actually sustained. Of these two proposals the former provoked the greater opposition: it was considered that it put the onus on the wrong shoulders and that cattle stealing in certain parts of India would get out of all control upon such principles. Maine[3]

1 Sir John Romilly was made a peer in 1865.
2 Sir Edward Ryan, Robert Lowe, John M. Macleod, W. M. James, J. Henderson.
3 Minute of 11 September 1868. Minutes of Sir H. S. Maine, p. 145.

6

was in favour of the rule proposed by the Commissioners but the Select Committee were against it, and on a reference being made to Local Governments it appeared that they and their most experienced administrative officers were 'with hardly an exception' adverse to the Commissioners' proposal. The matter was referred to the Home Government in order that the difficulty might be laid before the Commission. Though the Commissioners and the Secretary of State (the Duke of Argyll) stuck to this proposal[1] the commercial community in India would have none of it. For reasons which in due course were to be explained in Council by Fitzjames Stephen,[2] the Select Committee rejected both proposals. They preferred, upon clause 50, to treat the sum named in the contract as payable in case of breach as a sum stipulated by way of penalty so that the amount recoverable would not exceed the damage sustained—the very converse of the Commissioners' proposal. These, however, were disputes about proposed rules which were new and had no sanction in English law or experience. The greatest controversy which the Commissioners' draft provoked was, however, on the clauses (51–59) in which, at the end of their statement of the English law upon 'contracts in general', they had dealt with the topic of 'specific performance'. In these clauses they had carefully provided that agreements to cultivate land in a particular manner or to grow particular crops should not be enforced specifically—not even as implying negative covenants enforceable by injunction (clauses 52, 55, 59). In this they had—intentionally it would seem—intervened in a controversy of long standing. These provisions were well in consonance with general opinion of experienced Indian administrators, who regarded contracts for the cultivation of indigo as oppressive, and the care taken to prevent such contracts from being enforced specifically was clearly intended to give effect to these views.[3] But the Commissioners, to whom the matter was referred for a second time, maintained in their fourth report (18 December 1867) that their prohibition was required by and was in consonance with the rules of English equity, English courts having refused to order specific performance with regard to any matter which

---

1 Despatch No. 7, 18 March 1869.
2 Speech in Council, 9 April 1872. See pp. 336–9 of the *Proceedings*.
3 'It cannot, I think, be honestly denied that the omitted sections...are in truth directed against indigo planting' (Maine's minute of 15 July 1867).

required a succession of acts or the extra use of skill or the application of personal labour.

Maine, in presenting to the Legislative Council in 1867 the bill which embodied the Commissioners' proposals, excluded altogether their clauses on specific performance, maintaining not only his objections to the narrow scope of these provisions, but also that the rules as to the grant of this form of relief were procedural and not part of the substantive law of contract. On this point too, however, the Commissioners in their fourth report already mentioned stood their ground: they cited in support of their opinion the New York Civil Code of 1862 and the classic works on Jurisprudence of John Austin and Mr Justice Story. This part of the controversy one may regard as logomachy on Maine's part, since rules which relate to the form of the remedy are neither substantive nor merely procedural law, though they may be 'adjective' law in some reasonable sense. The Commissioners in order to produce a statute which might be brought into force at once might well include in it any incidental provisions. The sections which dealt with the measure of damages are equally much or little entitled to be called procedural. Maine does not seem to have contended that the Commissioners' clauses did not express the practice of the Court of Chancery, but he confessed to a strong impression that English lawyers were coming to a tolerably general agreement that their restrictions of the right to specific performance were in a high degree artificial and arbitrary. It does not appear, however, that the reign of Sir George Jessel as Master of the Rolls (1873–83), during which the remedy of specific performance was greatly employed and extended, saw any abandonment of the rule that contracts to grow particular crops would not be enforced. Such contracts if made in England were more likely to take the form of conditions the breach of which might operate a forfeiture.

The Government of India and the Select Committee of the Legislative Council, by taking their duties so seriously as to criticize the Commissioners' work on the Contract law, seem to have displeased both the Commissioners and the Duke of Argyll, who had become Secretary of State in 1868. Early in 1869 the Commissioners complained to the Secretary of State that no progress was being made in India with the enactment of their drafts, which by this time included draft bills on Negotiable Instruments and on Evidence. On 18 March 1869, two despatches were addressed by the Duke to the Indian Government. In one (No. 7) he dealt with the 'market overt' proposal (now become the 75th clause of the bill), saying that he had consulted the Commissioners and that 'when functionaries so eminent in position and knowledge adhere on deliberation to the view which they originally adopted, I should feel it extremely difficult to overrule their judgment. But I am bound to add for my own part that I concur with them in thinking that the section should stand as originally framed.... I trust therefore that you will now adopt the section and procure its being passed into law.'

The second despatch (No. 8) was a hectoring communication in which he laid down how in future the Government of India were to deal with the Commissioners' drafts. They might, he conceded, confidentially consult the judicial authorities and others in India; and if in doubt about the expediency of the measure they were to inform him of their doubt. 'You will then receive back the chapter from me in the shape in which I think it desirable that it should be finally passed into law and (unless in the case of very strong unforeseen objection...) I shall expect that the measure will be introduced by you into the Council.... And while under consideration by the Council I shall further expect that you will employ all the usual and legitimate means to secure its passing as a Government measure.'

In March 1870, Lord Mayo's Government reported that the Select Committee of the Council had made numerous alterations of great importance in the Contract Bill including the omission of clause 75, and that the Government of India concurred in their reasons for omitting it. They objected also that the course which had been laid down for them would deprive the Legislative Council of all real power and would invest the Secretary of State with the character of the legislator for British India and would convert the Legislative Council into a mere instrument to be used by him for that purpose.

On 2 July 1870, the Secretary of State's instructions to the Government of India not having in their view improved matters, the Commissioners resigned their office, complaining of the continued systematic and persistent inaction of the Indian legislature which, as they put it, 'defeats the hope which we entertained that we were laying the foundation of a system which when completed would be alike honourable to the English Government and beneficial to the people of India'.

'Thus expired in a huff', as Ilbert says, 'the third of the Indian Law Commissions. The Indian Government were allowed to take their own course with the Contract Bill....'[1]

Replying to the Indian Government's objections on 24 November 1870, the Secretary of State had no longer any particular matter to discuss, but insisted as a question of constitutional principle that the final control and direction were with the Home Government, that the Indian Government was subordinate, that it made no difference that directions might relate to legislative affairs, and that with a mere veto the Home Government might be helpless to secure legal sanction for any measures however essential. Hence under the Act of 1861 they must hold the power of requiring the Governor-General to introduce a measure and requiring all members of his Government to vote for it. 'The vastness of the Indian dominions in no degree exempts them from the necessary tie of subjection.' The Commissioners had been appointed 'because it was assumed that for the highly scientific work of drawing up codes of substantive law and of procedure there were men and facilities at home such as could not be found in India'.

Lord Mayo's Government on 1 February 1871 wrote a pacific reply enlarging on the expressions in the Secretary of State's despatch which seemed to admit that the principle contended for was not to be applied to 'ordinary procedure' but only 'on rarest occasions'.[2]

The Indian Legislature in the result had its own way with the Contract Act on all disputed points. More important than any matter then disputed was the establishment of the Legislative Council's right to be the legislative body by whose hand the codes for India were in the last resort to be shaped. This was a controversy that had to arise and to be decided at some stage, and it is fortunate that it was quieted before the second of the chapters of a substantive Civil Code was enacted. It had not been raised by the Succession Act of 1865.[3] The intention of

1 *Legislative Methods and Forms*, p. 135.
2 *Parl. Papers*, 1876, vol. LVI.
3 'The Indian Succession Act which follows the Commissioners' draft almost literally, consists nearly entirely of pure Civil Law, but it merely applies to the European and Europeanized natives. For the first time in preparing a contract law for the whole of Her Majesty's subjects in India, the Commissioners address themselves to a subject on which the course of legislation may be strongly affected by native usage, native opinion, and by the local peculiarities of the country' (Maine's minute of 11 September 1868. Minutes of Sir H. S. Maine, p. 148).

1833 had been that such work should be done in India by authority of a Council which had been strengthened for the purpose by the addition of a Law Member and given an Indian Law Commission to advise it. Sir Charles Wood's illiberal conception of a committee engaged in elaborating laws of which the principles were to be dictated from above was soon after 1853 found to imply, or to be at least consistent with, an unlimited amount of interference with the process of elaboration. It cannot be said of the Home authorities at any period that they shirked detail. John Stuart Mill's logic was that 'the Home Government of India' should have legislative power. To anyone who will review the work of the Legislative Council in the time of Lawrence and Mayo (the time of Maine and Stephen as Law Members)—say from 1864 to 1872—it will appear that the nature and quality of the work, its variety and importance, and the special character of the Indian problems, render highly unreasonable such an attitude as seemed correct to the Duke of Argyll; who would have forced upon India not merely well-tried doctrines of English law which were thought by the Legislative Council to be out of place, but even new rules—departures from the English law—which the Commissioners had invented as suitable to Indian conditions and of which, one might suppose, Indian opinion might be allowed to judge. Maine and Stephen might well be right in defending the Council from the charge of overlegislation, but if drafts from the Commission were to be enacted on the principle 'that it is most important that such discussions should not be unduly prolonged',[1] a good deal of doubtful matter might be forced through the legislative machine. The point is not merely that the Indian Government and Legislature were entitled to some say in the rate at which new laws could be considered and digested. It seems to have been overlooked in London that a code when passed is not finished with; that it requires not merely to be left alone but to be amended and kept up to date, all future changes in the law finding their proper place within it. Macaulay's notion of 'successive editions' of the Penal Code and Stephen's suggestion of an annual amending Act for all the codes and that 'once in every five years or so the Acts which had been most frequently amended might be redrawn'[2]—these may have exaggerated the amount of

Despatch No. 7 of 18 March 1869, from the Duke of Argyll to the Government of India.

Minute on Administration of Justice in British India, published by authority, 1872, p. 44.

revision which was necessary or practicable. But a great deal of the success of the Anglo-Indian codes lies in the care and consistency with which the need for revision has been met by the Indian legislature, which in point of fact has since the reforms of 1921 excelled in the vigilance and logic which it has expended on amendment of the codes. Very emphatic was the language held upon this subject by the first Indian Law Commission in their letter to Lord Auckland of 14 October 1837:

'It appears to us also highly desirable that, if the code shall be adopted, all those penal laws which the Indian legislature may from time to time find it necessary to pass should be framed in such a manner as to fit into the code. Their language ought to be that of the code. No word ought to be used in any other sense than that in which it is used in the code. The very part of the code in which the new law is to be inserted ought to be indicated. If the new law rescinds or modifies any provision of the code, that provision ought to be indicated. In fact the new law ought from the day on which it is passed, to be part of the code, and to affect all the other provisions of the code, and to be affected by them as if it were actually a clause of the original code. In the next edition of the code the new law ought to appear in its proper place.'[1]

1 *Parl. Papers*, 1838, vol. XLI. Letter to Lord Auckland, 14 October 1837, by Macaulay, Macleod, Anderson and Millet.

CHAPTER VII

INDIAN CONTRACT ACT

I

ONE of the findings of the Commission appointed under the Charter Act of 1853 had been thus expressed in their report of 13 December 1855:

'We see no reason, however, why, on very many important subjects of Civil Law—we shall only name one, contracts, as an example—such law cannot be prepared and enacted as will be no less applicable to the transactions of Hindoos and Mahomedans, by far the most numerous portions of the population, than to the rest of the inhabitants of India.'

After the draft on the subject of Succession had been submitted in 1863 by the Commission which had been appointed in 1861, a change of personnel was effected in 1864, Messrs William Milbourne James[1] and John Henderson taking the place of Sir William Erle and Mr Justice Willes. The new body produced a draft law of Contract in 1866 which they submitted unanimously, saying that it was the subject which afforded the most frequent occasion for litigation in all parts of India, and that on it they were satisfied that a law could be framed applicable to the whole population.

The Regulations which governed the district courts throughout India contained no mention of the subject of Contracts in the provision that Hindus and Mahomedans were to have their own laws administered to them, but the terms of section 17 of the Act of 1781 clearly embraced the two subjects of Succession and Contract as matters on which these laws were to be dispensed by the Supreme Courts. Sir William Jones's plan for a 'complete digest of the Hindu and Mahomedan laws after the model of Justinian's inestimable pandects' would, he told Cornwallis,[2] require less labour and time than Justinian's, which took three years, since it would be confined to the laws of contract and inheritance. Jagannatha's learned compilation, known in its English translation as Colebrooke's Digest (1798), contained

1 Vice-Chancellor, 1869; Lord Justice, 1870.
2 Letter of 19 March 1788.

a great deal of Hindu law on the subject of Contracts: that subject was prominently mentioned in its title-page and treated as occupying half the book.[1]

Colebrooke in his annotated translation of the Dayabhaga and the chapter on Inheritance from the Mitakshara—'Two Treatises on the Hindu Law of Inheritance' (1810)—had claimed for his subject that it constitutes that part of any national system of laws which is the most peculiar and distinct; saying by way of contrast that 'in the law of contracts the rules of decision observed in the jurisprudence of different countries are in general dictated by reason and good sense; and rise naturally, though not always obviously, from the plain maxims of equity and right'. In 1818, after his retirement from India, Colebrooke finished a treatise upon Contracts which he based not upon the English but the Roman law.

Francis Macnaghten,[2] who, as his son, W. H. Macnaghten, faithfully observes, 'was not by any means disposed to view the Hindu law generally in a favourable light',[3] had a chapter on Contracts, and unbent so far as to concede that 'if a prevalence of common sense is to be discovered in the laws of the Hindus, it must be sought for in that portion of them containing the precepts by which dealings between one man and another are to be regulated'.

Strange,[4] too, had a chapter on this subject dealing with it generally and with particular topics such as bailment, loans, sale and debt. Echoing what Colebrooke had said, he explains that he has confined himself to the peculiarities of the Hindu law of contract, 'considering how much the resolution of every question of the kind depends in all countries upon the dictates of reason and good sense, rather than (as in cases of inheritance) upon conventional rules...'.[5] While Colebrooke in 1816 thought the law of inheritance to be the law of most frequent use and extensive application, Strange found such cases to be in his Court at Madras of rare occurrence among the natives.[6]

'It is respecting their transactions in business principally that they differ. Accordingly actions of assumpsit between Hindus constitute

1 As Strange pointed out it included the topic of marriage.
2 *Considerations upon Hindu Law*, 1824.
3 *Principles of Hindu Law*, Prelim. Remarks, 1829.
4 *Elements of Hindu Law*, 1825.   5 Vol. I, p. 7.
6 *Notes of Cases in the Court of the Recorder and in the Supreme Court*, 1798–1816, Madras, 1816, Preface, p. vi.

a great proportion of the business of the Court. It is observable, however, that allowing for a few peculiarities their law of contracts does not vary materially from our own. Any good English lawyer with the 8th and 9th chapters of Menu in his hand would solve with facility and correctness at once many a dispute between Hindus upon the more ordinary subjects of litigation among them...the Mahomedans engaging seldom in business less frequently resort to the Court.'

W. H. Macnaghten's *Principles* deals very summarily with the law of Contract, referring his readers to the works of his father and Strange.

As the High Courts were obliged to decide disputes between Hindus and Mahomedans by their own laws or by the law of the defendant (the latter a provision which is considered to have special application to cases in Contract), it is surprising that the reports contain so very little evidence of any activity in developing or applying either of these two laws upon this subject. In July 1845, when Sir Henry Hardinge was anxious to obtain from Sir Lawrence Peel, the Chief Justice of Bengal, some assurance that too much technicality, complication and uncertainty would not result from the introduction of 'a digest of English law suited to the conditions of India', the Chief Justice, in giving the assurance in reasoned terms, took occasion to make a statement which has often been referred to and which had considerable effect on policy:

'I may observe in addition that the English law as to contracts, the most fruitful source of litigation, is so much in harmony with the Mahomedan and Hindoo laws as to Contracts that it very rarely happens in our courts, which are bound to administer to Hindoos and Mahomedans their respective law as to contracts, that any question arises on the law peculiar to those people in actions on contracts.'

This statement must certainly be taken as throwing a clear light upon the practice of the Supreme Courts, and goes far to explain the confident decision of 1855 (above noticed) that no classes of the community need be excepted from the general law of contract. We need not conclude that the Hindu, Mahomedan and English laws were found to coalesce into a workable *jus gentium* upon the subject. There is a good deal about contract in Jagannatha which would not square with the English law. We are told by a recent authority that in Hindu law on the whole the largest space is devoted to contract, and that since

Yajnavalkya this has been a still more pronounced feature. A careful presentation of the Hindu law of contract will include much that is special to itself.[1] Many of these teachings are ancient history now, but we have still with us the Hindu law of *dandupat* which traces back to Manu and Yajnavalkya, though it is now given the effect laid down by Medhatithi—namely, that it restricts the amount of interest recoverable at any one time to the same amount as the principal. This rule obtains still in the town of Calcutta and the Presidency of Bombay, and in the latter territory there is a Hindu rule, equivalent to a provision of the Interest Act, making interest run by way of damages after a demand for payment has been made. In parts, indeed, the ancient law is shrewdly modern. The main principles of bailment and agency were fully understood and dealt with.[2]

To present a fair picture of the Mahomedan law of Contract would require a detailed review of the decisions of Aurungzebe's time, of which the *Fatawa Alamgiri* is the repository; but the law of Sale has a chapter to itself in both parts of W. H. Macnaghten's *Principles and Precedents* (1825). In the Digest of Mr Neil B. E. Baillie (2nd edition 1875) a further account of the law of Sale has been added as a Supplement to the first volume; and it is noted that Macnaghten's book 'left unnoticed some of the leading peculiarities of the Mahomedan system' (Preface to Supplement). Sir Abdur Rahim in his *Muhammadan Jurisprudence* (1911)[3] mentions that *hiba* (gift) is like sale a form of contract (*aqd*, literally tie or conjunction), and the doctrine of *iwaz* (return, consideration) has highly special features, gift being treated juristically as a form of contract where there is a proposal or offer to give and an acceptance by the donee.

Maine, defending himself in the Legislative Council from the charge of overlegislation, said (14 December 1866),[4] 'There were great chapters of law on which in India there was no indigenous system of rules of any sort. Contract, for example, was utterly unregulated except by some small portion of Muhammadan jurisprudence.' And the Commissioners in their

1 Jayaswal Tagore Lectures, 1917, *Manu and Yajnavalkya*, Calcutta, 1930, Lectures x and xi.
2 In 1827 Steele, among the customs of sahookdars (money dealers) in the Maratha country, mentions that 'in appointing a mooneem goomastha it is sometimes usual to present him with a cocoa-nut saying "This is my head which I have given into your charge to preserve and to destroy"' (*Hindoo Castes*, p. 292).
3 Pp. 282, 290, 297.   4 Grant Duff, *Memoir of Maine*, p. 232.

second report (28 July 1866) had said that while in the Presidency towns contract suits were practically governed by the law of England, 'everywhere else the judge is to a great extent without the guidance of any positive law beyond the rule that his decision shall be such as he deems to be in accordance with justice, equity and good conscience'. The district courts were not obliged to administer Hindu and Mahomedan law in matters of contract and did so if at all as a matter of 'good conscience'. But in the Supreme Courts it is not altogether surprising that the Hindu and Mahomedan laws of contract failed with a bench and bar manned from England to hold their own against the modern English law. So far as practice is concerned the Hindu law was under the Moghuls in a state of arrested development as it was not enforced in the public tribunals, though doubtless it guided the Hindu panchayets. For modern practice first principles are insufficient without middle principles which guide their application: in these the Hindu and Mahomedan laws as known to British Indian Courts must have proved inadequate. This may be the element of truth in the remarks of Maine and the Commissioners.

The really cogent force was the growth of modern business. The Hindu who took part in modern business as the *banian* or the *gomastha* of an English firm would want the same law applied to his transactions as was applied to his master's. However great an interest in some respects the Hindu and Mahomedan might feel in being given the benefit of his own law, he also had an interest that in other respects there should be a workable common law for all alike. The Hindu's contracts were not always with Hindus; and, to do business, his methods had to fall into line with the business habits and ideas of Europeans and others. The case for a uniform law of contract is overwhelming on its practical merits and depends in no way upon exaggerating the similarity of the different laws or upon depreciating them.

In the Statement of Objects and Reasons dated Simla 9 July 1867, Maine said of this feature of the Contract Bill:

'The recommendation of the Commissioners appears to be justified, not only by the abstract consideration that contract is the branch of the law on which men of all times and races have come most nearly to identical conclusions but also by the actual condition of the law of contract in India....The largeness of the sphere practically occupied in India by the English law of contract is in truth the justification of the course which has been followed by the Commissioners.'

II

The draft which the Commissioners in 1866 produced in their second report contained 269 clauses of which quite a large number were furnished with illustrations in the manner of the Penal Code (1861) and the Succession Act (1865). More trouble had in this draft been taken to give illustrations with local colour, though many of the sections were simple statements of the rule laid down in a particular English case. The first 59 clauses had the heading 'Contract' and dealt with contracts in general, the last nine clauses (51–59) dealing with the topic of specific performance of contracts. These were followed by seven clauses on the topic of quasi-contract which were headed 'On certain obligations resembling those created by contract'. The remainder—some 200 clauses—were devoted to particular contracts: Sale of Goods (68–118); Indemnity and Guarantee (119–46); Law of Bailment (147–79); Agency (180–240); Partnership (241–69). These groups of sections were not further subdivided and, whatever may be said for or against the arrangement of the clauses within each group, there was no declared or express arrangement, still less any parade of classification or logical order. Different minds attach more or less importance to such matters in a Code; but at first sight the main matter was that the Commissioners had reduced to an explicit written form and to a manageable compass a great mass of law which had previously been contained only in text books and reports. This indeed was the merit ultimately to be claimed for the Act of 1872.[1] When the draft was first made public Henry Colebrooke's son was engaged on the memoir which he published of his father in 1873 and welcomed the Commission's work from the standpoint of the Indian Civil Servant:

'One is naturally prompted to ask why was not a similar exposition of lucid principles prepared long ago.... The tardiness with which this boon has been conferred on India is very remarkable. Something may be attributed to the hope which Sir William Jones fostered, that light would come from the East, and that the legal literature of the Hindus would supply the want. More perhaps was owing to the distrust which all laymen and especially Indian officials at that time felt for English law and English lawyers. Mr Colebrooke, groping about for light, turned to the Roman law, and urged its study on his son when he was proceeding to India. The law of England, he considered, was law in disguise; it must be stripped of its techni-

1 Hunter's *Mayo*, vol. II, p. 202, ch. VIII, by Stephen.

calities before it could be made the subject of study. It is a remarkable sequel to his labours, that the Commission now sitting should take the law of England for its basis, deviating boldly from its rules, or borrowing freely from the codes of other nations, wherever they recognised a sounder or simpler rule. But English law and English lawyers have undergone a great change since the period of which I am writing. A work such as this code could not have been produced by English lawyers at the beginning of the present century.'[1]

The Commissioners' draft was an original and expert attempt to present a simplified statement of the English law of contract with some modifications—not a great number, though some were important and indeed remarkable—intended to make it suitable for India. That it swept away the Hindu and Mahomedan law of contract was a feature which incurred no hostility worth mentioning; of its emendations many were approved by general opinion, by the Legislative Council, and by Maine who had introduced the bill with a high encomium in this regard.

'Their draft will be found to consist of the English law of contract much simplified and altered in some particulars so as to accommodate it to the circumstances of this country.... It may be said of these proposed modifications of English law that while all, or nearly all, of them have commended themselves to the approval of enlightened lawyers, not a few are being gradually carried out in England without the aid of the legislature through the direction given of late years to the current of judicial decision.'[2]

Yet so far from being enacted immediately and with little change, like its predecessor in the Law of Succession, it was fated to encounter stiff opposition from Maine because of its nine clauses on the Law of Specific Performance, and to antagonize certain European business interests on other points as well; with results which produced acute dissension, not only in India and between high administrative officials with experience of the country, but between the Home and Indian Governments. It brought about the resignation of Lord Romilly and his colleagues in 1870 and thus brought to an end Sir Charles Wood's scheme of 1853 under which a Commission sitting in London was to draft the Indian codes. These incidents of the controversy which kept the Contract Bill before the Legislative Council from 1867 to 1872 have an interest which in some respects exceeds that of the particular provisions of the Act as ultimately passed. It is however with the latter that we are now solely concerned.

1 *Life of Colebrooke*, 1873, p. 279.
2 Statement of Objects and Reasons, 9 July 1867.

The Commissioners' work, as we have seen, fell into four parts, of which the most important were the first and fourth. The first comprises the fifty clauses on contracts in general giving the fundamentals of the subject, and the fourth has the 200 clauses devoted to particular contracts. The bulk of these 200 clauses became law without much serious alteration, though on one or two important points the Indian Legislature differed from the Commissioners. Some improvement was made in arrangement by grouping the sections on Sale of Goods and on Agency so as to make their sequence clearer and one or two clauses were omitted for one reason or another. Thus the provisions which since 1872 have become the daily law of British India as defining the rules which govern particular contracts are in substance the work of Lord Romilly[1] and his colleagues. Certain matters must now be noticed as showing the modifications made in consequence of discussion in India and as indicating special features of their draft.

The Chapter (VII) on the Sale of Goods, as Stephen said in Council, 'represents the English law on the subject disembarrassed of the inexpressible confusion and intricacy which is thrown on every part of it by the vague language of the Statute of Frauds'. This branch of the law was much extended in its application, being made to apply not only to 'goods' in the ordinary sense but to 'every kind of moveable property', thus including what in English law would be called choses in action. Hence stocks, shares and debentures of every kind come within its scope—a great gain in simplicity and intelligibility to the commercial world, as it substitutes familiar rules and ways of thinking for doctrines of equity which might or might not arrive at the same result. The Commissioners had proposed (clause 81) that 'the ownership of goods may be acquired by buying them from any person who is in possession of them provided that the buyer acts in good faith and under circumstances which are not such as to raise a reasonable presumption that the person in possession has no right to sell them'. This was strongly opposed by the Select Committee of the Legislative Council. The Act, rejecting this proposal to make the whole of India 'market overt', set forth (section 108) as a governing principle that no seller could give to a buyer a better title to the goods than he had himself, but by way of exception to this rule gave full effect

1 He was made a peer in 1865.

to the principle of the Factors Acts and gave every protection to the honest buyer from one of a number of joint owners or from one in possession under a voidable contract. It also included as section 109 a provision, which the Commissioners thought new but which they recommended, that the seller should be responsible for invalidity of his title if the buyer be deprived of the thing sold.

A few other useful changes may be noticed. In the law of Suretyship an agreement by the creditor to give time to the principal debtor, or to take a composition from him, or not to sue him, was to release the surety (sections 134, 135); and the Commissioners intended that the creditor should not be able to avoid this result by reserving his rights against the surety. The release of one surety was not to discharge the others or free him from responsibility to them (section 138). The equity doctrine was rejected in favour of the common law view in the case of two persons liable as principal debtors, and it was declared that an arrangement between themselves that one should be liable only on default of the other should not affect the creditor merely by reason that he knew of it (section 132).

As to Bailment, it was provided that the same degree of care should be exigible in all cases (section 151)—that which a man of ordinary prudence would take of his own goods. An endeavour was made to improve the law applicable to cases where the bailee had mixed his own goods with the bailor's.

As to Partners, the Commission's proposals had both good and bad fortune. They proposed that a continuing guarantee given to a firm or in respect of a firm's transactions should not be revoked as to future transactions by any change in the firm, but the opposite view was taken in India; and section 266 of the Act declared that it should be revoked by any change in the constitution of the firm, in the absence of agreement to the contrary. So too the Commissioners' proposal (clause 262, borrowed from the German and Italian commercial codes) that a new partner should become liable for all past debts of the firm found no place in the Act. But their view was accepted that whether or not there is any partnership property, the separate property of the partner is to be applied first to his separate debts (section 262).

As to Agency, they proposed a clause which was accepted and enacted as section 236—though its meaning is not very clear nor its desirability very evident—viz. that a person with whom a contract has been entered into in the character of agent is not entitled to require performance of it if he was in fact acting on his own account. Another clause—not to be found in the Act—was concerned with a master's responsibility for things done by his agent to third persons. On this 'we have stopped a little short of the limit assigned to it by the English law. We think that the responsibility ought to cease as soon as the misconduct assumes the character of intentional wrong doing.' The text of the clause excluded 'wilful misconduct'. The matter is outside the scope of the Act as passed, but the suggestion is interesting.

With the modifications which we have noticed the Commissioners' draft clauses upon special contracts have in substance, as Chapters VII to IX of the Indian Contract Act 1872, been the law of British India upon these subjects for over half a century. With the aid of the illustrations they have been found reasonably clear and satisfactory. But where they fall short they have in general been supplemented by reference to the English law, and as time has gone on they have been found less adequate to modern business requirements. The Commissioners repeated the hope, which they had expressed in connection with the Succession Act of 1865, that judges 'will not resort to any other system of law for an authoritative solution of an ambiguity or supply of an omission, but will in such cases be entirely guided by regard to justice, equity and good conscience'. In practice, as the decisions show, the proposed exclusion of the law of England has hardly been seriously taken; nor is there much reason why it should be, since the law of the Act is basically English law and the Act purports only 'to define and amend certain parts of the law relating to contracts'. In 1930 and 1932 separate Acts were passed restating more fully and minutely the law on Sale of Goods (III of 1930) and Partnership (IX of 1932) on the lines of the English statutes which codified the law upon these subjects in 1893 and 1890. The distinction between conditions and mere warranties—a specially valuable feature introduced into the law by the English Act of 1893—was not to be found in the Indian Act of 1872 and has now been adopted into India; indeed the Indian Sale of Goods Act 1930 keeps close to the English Act of 1893. The new Partnership Act takes like advantage from the work done in England. Sir Frederick Pollock had before him the Commission's draft of 1866 when drawing out the clauses which became the Partnership Act of 1890, but the Indian Act of 1932 departs more freely from the English model, putting more emphasis on the firm (or body of persons) as distinct from the partnership (or relation between the persons). It has introduced an improved arrangement by collecting in a separate chapter sections upon Incoming and Outgoing Partners and has made some provision for dealing with Goodwill. Both of these new Acts are at once clearer and fuller, more thorough and 'thought out', if the phrase may be permitted, than the work of 1866. But that the Commissioners' draft served so long and so well is proof of its great worth—first attempt though it was to codify the English law of contract. When the Contract Act was before the Legislative Council in 1872 Stephen said, 'Such re-enactment will in my judgment be as necessary as repairs to a railway. I do not think that any Act of importance ought to last more than ten or twelve years.' His estimate of the exact time may be a trifle pessimistic. 'The Government', he said on another occasion, 'ought to re-enact its Codes as often as a law bookseller would bring out a new edition of them.' But he is at least right in saying[1] that: 'It is nearly impossible, when an Act is first drawn, to foresee every case which can arise in reference to the subject, unless it has already been exhausted by judicial decisions. Judicial decisions are the material from which codifying acts should be drawn and it cannot I think be expected that a really important Act of this sort should reach its full maturity till after several re-enactments.'

Ilbert somewhat impatiently observes that 'it would seem as if Indian codifiers built not with brass or stone, but with materials more nearly resembling the brick or stucco of Lower Bengal. Their structures soon show signs of weathering, and require to be patched or pulled down and rebuilt.'[2] One might emphasize in reply Sir Frederick Pollock's dictum that the Contract Act's 'more practical defects are evidently due to the acceptance by the original framers of unsatisfactory statements which, coming to India with a show of authority, naturally escaped minute criticism amid the varied business of the legislative department'. But the subjects of Sale of Goods and Partnership are not static; time reveals defects and the methods of business alter. No code could reasonably last longer without

1 *Minute on Administration of Justice in British India*, published by authority, 1872.
2 *Legislative Methods and Forms*, 1901, p. 154.

revision than the clauses upon special contracts which were 'put together in 1866 as clauses 68–269 and which in the Act are sections 76–266. There is every reason for thinking that the Acts of 1930 and 1932 will serve a succeeding generation equally well and that it will acknowledge its great indebtedness to Sir B. L. Mitter, who was the Law Member in charge of these measures.

III

The dispute over the Commissioners' clauses as to specific performance was the main cause of the delay in passing any Contract Act. When it came finally to be passed in 1872 it had been under the consideration of the Legislative Council in various forms for the long period of five years, Maine's chief minutes on the subject having been written in 1867 and his 'statement of objects and reasons' for the bill having been dated 9 July 1867. By 1871 the Home Government had recognized the necessity, if not the desirability, of permitting the Government and Legislature of India to have an effective voice in the framing of the Indian Codes. Thus in the end the clauses about specific performance which Maine had excluded from the bill remained excluded from the Act and found no place in the Statute Book till 1877. In that year Mr Hobhouse (afterwards Lord Hobhouse) carried a Specific Relief Act which Whitley Stokes had drafted on the lines of the draft New York Code of 1862. In that Act sections 14 and 15, which deal with the conditions under which specific performance of part of a contract can be obtained, are taken from the Commissioners' draft Contract Bill (clauses 53 and 54). It may be noted also that the principle stressed by the Commission that a succession of acts of continued performance will not be decreed has been adopted in a limited form by clauses (*b*) and (*g*) of section 21 of the Act of 1877.

Stephen, speaking in Council on 9 April 1872 on the Contract bill, said:

'The final result was that the Secretary of State left the Government of India to deal with the matters under discussion as they thought proper, but expressed a very decided wish that the Bill should be disposed of as early as possible. The dispatch arrived in India about a year ago...advantage was taken of the delay which thus arose to subject the Bill to another and a final revision. It was compared with the standard text books...and various alterations were introduced into the arrangement of that part of the Bill which deals with contract in general.'

It was at this stage that certain borrowings were made from Dudley Field's New York Code of 1862 which never became law in New York though it did in other States of America. Stephen himself redrafted the preliminary sections defining 'the fundamental terms of the subject' and stating the elements of which a Contract is composed (proposal, acceptance, promise, agreement, contract). He explained and defended these amendments in Council as being 'alterations in form rather than in substance though I do not by that remark mean to say that I regard them as unimportant'. The Commission's draft had many merits but 'form' was not one of them; though it may be too severe to say with Whitley Stokes that 'it had been sent out to India in a very crude form; it never underwent the patient penetrating revision by a skilled draftsman necessary in the case of such a measure'.[1]

Sir Frederick Pollock on the other hand describes the draft in 1905 as 'uniform in style and possessing great merit as an elementary statement of the combined effect of common law and equity doctrine as understood about forty years ago'.[2] To Fitzjames Stephen who succeeded Maine as Law Member in December 1869 it appeared that the first fifty clauses needed revision in respect of form and arrangement; whereas the Commissioners' treatment of particular contracts in the 200 clauses which treated of Sale of Goods, Agency, Partnership, etc.—though not to be accepted upon some particular points—was in no need of such general revision. Hence, as he put it, 'I redrew the whole of the first part'.[3]

It is to this first part of the Act that criticism on the score of draftsmanship has generally been directed. Lord Bryce, recalling opinions gathered by him in India in 1888–9, wrote:

'It was with regard to the merits of the Contract Code that the widest difference of opinion existed. Anyone who reads it can see that its workmanship is defective. It is neither exact nor subtle and its language is often far from lucid. Everyone agreed that Sir J. F. Stephen (afterwards Mr Justice Stephen) who put it into the shape in which it was passed during his term of office as Legal Member of Council, and was also the author of the Evidence Act, was a man

1 *Anglo-Indian Codes*, vol. i, p. 554.
2 Pollock and Mulla's *Indian Contract Act*, Preface to 1st ed.
3 Hunter's *Mayo*, vol. ii, ch. viii, p. 202.

of great industry, much intellectual force, and a warm zeal for codification. But his capacity for the work of drafting was deemed not equal to his fondness for it. He did not shine either in fineness of discrimination or in delicacy of expression.... These criticisms may need to be discounted a little, in view of the profound conservatism of the legal profession, and of the dislike of men trained at the Temple or Lincoln's Inn to have anything laid down or applied on the Hooghly which is not being done at the same moment on the Thames.'[1]

Sir Frederick Pollock's opinion[2] too is not wholly in praise of Stephen's revision. 'Lastly Sir James Stephen made or supervised the final revision, and added the introductory definitions, which are in a wholly different style and not altogether in harmony with the body of the work.' This learned critic has further noted as 'a source of unequal workmanship, and sometimes of positive error', that the framers of the Indian Codes and of the Contract Act in particular 'were tempted to borrow a section here and a section there from the draft Civil Code of New York, an infliction which the sounder lawyers of that State have been happily successful so far in averting from its citizens'. Of this the clauses on fraud and misrepresentation (which are sections 17 and 18 of the Act) are instanced as particularly bad examples. The inclination to make use of the draft code of 1862 intended for New York is traceable I think to Whitley Stokes but the work was done in 1871 under Stephen's superintendence.[3]

While the Commissioners' draft was certainly free from oversubtlety or from any parade of logical processes or methods, one can hardly disagree with Stephen's view that 'the fundamental terms of the subject were not defined with complete precision by its learned authors'.[4] The first clause had defined 'contract' by saying that 'a contract is an agreement between parties whereby a party engages to do a thing or engages not to do a thing. A contract may contain several engagements; and they may be either by the same party or by different parties.' Stephen very correctly asked, What is the use of this definition? Why should it not run 'an agreement is a contract by which people engage...' or 'an engagement is an agreement by which people contract?' Contract engagement and agreement are used in

1 *Studies in History and Jurisprudence*, vol. I, pp. 128–30.
2 Pollock and Mulla's *Indian Contract Act*, Preface to the 1st ed.
3 Stephen's speech in Council 8 December 1871; *Proceedings*, p. 756.
4 Speech in Council 9 April 1872; *Proceedings*, p. 334.

ordinary English as having much the same meaning and very little is gained by ringing the changes on them. Stephen considered that it was necessary to set forth the elements of which a contract is composed and his analysis is exhibited in section 2 of the Act. A proposal when accepted becomes a promise; and when there is consideration for the promise there is an agreement; an agreement if not enforceable by law is void; if enforceable by law it is a contract; if enforceable by law at the option of one party but not of another it is a voidable contract. This logical structure may be assailed with certain criticisms, but does at least recognize that there is a fundamental question to be asked—viz. upon what conditions does the law regard a promise by one person as giving rise in another to a right that it should be fulfilled? We may prefer different language to express the question; one may talk of offer, of obligation, of cause of action, of promises being or not being enforceable at law, but the matter for analysis and the need of analysis are not in doubt. That Stephen did not shirk a problem which the Commission had not wrestled with is perhaps specially significant since, as his brother states, 'If there was one thing which Fitzjames hated it was needless subtlety—and the technicalities which are the product of such subtlety—the provision of a superfluous logical apparatus, which, while it gives scope for ingenuity, distracts the mind from the ends for which it is ostensibly designed'.[1] But the fact that the analysis was an afterthought cannot be hidden from any careful student of the Act, and the terms in which the analysis is expressed are not clearly and consistently employed. These defects do not always impart any real ambiguity; no one is seriously hurt by the statute speaking of 'agreement' when it should say 'promise', or of 'void contract' when consistently with section 2 it should have said 'void agreement'. But grave difficulty of a practical character is at times presented to the courts as when they had to answer upon the terms of the Act the question whether a contract is 'voidable' when one party becomes entitled by reason of the other's default to 'put an end to' or 'rescind' it, and whether when that is done the contract 'becomes void' (sections 2, 39, 64, 65) so as to give a right of restitution to the party in default.[2] Stephen's use of language is not always that

---

1 *Life of Sir J. F. Stephen*, by Leslie Stephen, 1895, p. 280.
2 *Muralhidhar Chatterjee* v. *International Film Co.* (1942), L.R. 70 I.A. 35.

of the Commissioners and in places he trips over his own language or employs it with results which are far from clear.

The requirement of consideration is in India affected by the law's refusal to attribute any special character to documents which are under seal as distinct from those which are executed by signature in the ordinary way. The Commissioners had proposed to make promises given without consideration binding if given in writing and registered with the permission of the promisor. This they thought would be sufficient to secure that they were given 'with due deliberation'. The requirement of registration was a new suggestion, otherwise their standpoint was much the same as that of Lord Mansfield in *Pillans* v. *van Mierop* 1765 Burr, 1663, who for commercial transactions would have been content to regard the fact that the promise was in writing as sufficient proof that it was given with serious intentions.[1] Agreements in writing registered, however, if without consideration are not made binding by the Act unless entered into on account of natural love and affection between parties standing in a near relation to each other. The Act (section 25) follows the draft in treating as exceptions to the requirement of consideration promises to compensate a person who has already done something which the promisor was legally compellable to do; also promises to pay a debt due from the promisor but barred by limitation. It includes also a section (section 63) based upon a clause (32) of the draft which gets rid of the doctrine of *Cumber* v. *Wane* (1 Smith's Leading Cases)—reaffirmed by the House of Lords in *Foakes* v. *Beer* (1884) 9 A.C. 605—that a less sum of money cannot be taken in satisfaction of a greater sum already due. A promisee may dispense with or remit performance in whole or in part, or may accept instead of it any satisfaction which he thinks fit. Perhaps the most noticeable innovation upon English principles is introduced by the interpretation clause (*d*) of section 2 which applies the word consideration 'when at the desire of the promisor the promisee *or any other person* has done, or abstained from doing or promises to do or abstain from doing something....'. In other words, consideration need not move from the promisee but may proceed from any other person. This follows the wording of the Commissioners'

---

[1] Sir William Holdsworth has renewed this proposal as regards all contracts (*History of English Laws*, vol. VIII, p. 47). See Lord Wright's *Essays and Addresses*, p. 325.

draft (clause 10), but neither in their report nor in their illustrations does it appear that they had given any special consideration to this particular point. There is nothing in either clause to suggest that a person who is not a party to a contract can sue upon it and the act must be done or promise given 'at the desire of the promisor'. The rule as laid down in the Act is probably not quite the same as that of *Dutton* v. *Poole* 2 Lev. 210, which was set aside in *Tweddle* v. *Atkinson* (1861) 1 B. and S. 393. Having regard to the date of this last-mentioned decision, it is difficult to doubt that the Commissioners had it well in mind and that it had overruled previous decisions. 'The modern cases', said Crompton J., 'have in effect over-ruled the old decisions, they show that the consideration must move from the party entitled to sue upon the contract. It would be a monstrous proposition to say that a person was a party to the contract for the purpose of suing upon it for his own advantage, and not a party to it for the purpose of being sued' (p. 398). It cannot, however, be said that Indian experience since 1872 shows that the extended meaning given to 'consideration' by the Act is a valuable or even a workable improvement in the law.

On another question affecting the essentials of a valid contract the Commissioners' language has been followed by the Act so as to effect a departure from the common law without any clear indication that the departure was an intentional and considered step. The Commissioners provided that 'every person who is of the age of majority according to the law to which he is subject and who is of sound mind may enter into a contract' (clause 2). By section 10 of the Act it is a condition of an agreement being a contract that it be made by the free consent of parties competent to contract, and section 11 follows the Commissioners' clause. The result did not become apparent till 1903. It never was law in England that infants are absolutely incompetent to contract and in many cases certain types of contract have been held to be voidable at the infant's option. Hence the Indian High Courts endeavoured to avoid a construction of the Act which would make all contracts with a minor void, and it was not until 1903 that the Judicial Committee declared that the Act had this effect.[1]

'The general current of decision in India certainly is that ever since the passing of the Indian Contract Act (IX of 1872) the con-

[1] *Mohori Bibee* v. *Dhurmodas Ghose* (1903) L.R. 30 I.A. 114.

tracts of infants are voidable only. This conclusion, however, has not been arrived at without vigorous protests by various judges from time to time; nor indeed without decisions to a contrary effect.... But in their Lordships' opinion the Act, so far as it goes, is exhaustive and imperative, and does provide in clear language that an infant is not a person competent to bind himself by a contract of this description' (*per* Sir Ford North).

The Judicial Committee suggested that it may have been intended to give effect to the rule of Hindu law upon the subject. There is no mention of this matter in the Commissioners' report although it purports 'to specify the most important' of the departures from the English law. That it was an important matter becomes very plain when it is considered that 'a minor's agreement being void' there can be no question of ratifying it. The Commissioners note that in accordance with the principles upon which they had prepared the rules of Succession (Indian Succession Act, 1865) they did not think it necessary to place married women under any disability to contract.

Undue influence is an important ground of defence in cases upon Indian contracts. The Commissioners' draft referred to it summarily in a clause (clause 5) which said that 'any engagement which a contracting party has been induced to form by deceit or coercion, or by such influence as impedes or interferes with the freedom of his agency renders the contract voidable at the option of that party'. As redrawn by Stephen, the Act devoted a separate section (16) to undue influence—separating it from fraud and misrepresentation—but this section was found to be too narrow, notwithstanding a provision (section 111) of the Evidence Act of the same year (1872) which put the burden of proving good faith upon the party who is 'in a position of active confidence'. In 1899 a new section was substituted for Stephen's and this set forth two elements—that one party (*a*) is in a position to dominate the will of the other, and (*b*) uses that position to obtain an unfair advantage over the other. It brought within (*a*) cases where one party holds real or apparent authority over the other, and stands in a fiduciary relation to the other, and where the other's mental capacity is affected by age, illness or mental or bodily distress. The burden of proving that the contract was not induced by undue influence was put upon the party who was shown to be in a dominant position if the transaction appeared to be unconscionable and the Evidence Act provision as to good faith was retained as an additional provision.

It should here be noticed that the courts give to *pardanishin* women a protection which is not restricted to the provisions of the Act but is warranted by a line of decisions which date back to an earlier period. The mere fact that such a woman has executed a transfer does not *prima facie* import such understanding of the transaction as makes it her act. 'Proof must go so far as to shew affirmatively and conclusively that the deed was not only executed by, but was explained to and was really understood by the grantor. In such cases it must also of course be established that the deed was not signed under duress but arose from the free and independent will of the grantor.'[1] The doctrine applies to women who are completely secluded from ordinary social intercourse and the phrase *quasi pardanishin* is rejected: outside the class to which the doctrine applies—'a well known and easily ascertained class of women'—'it must depend in each case on the character and position of the individual woman whether those who deal with her are or are not bound to take special precautions that her action shall be intelligent and voluntary, and to prove that it was so in case of dispute'.[2]

The Commissioners had said nothing of contracts in restraint of marriage or in restraint of trade, but the Act on these subjects borrowed from the draft New York Code provisions which are very widely expressed (sections 26 and 27). It also made void (section 28) all agreements by which a party was restricted absolutely from enforcing his rights in respect of a contract by the usual legal proceedings in the ordinary tribunals, but provided exceptions to cover arbitration clauses. 'Agreements by way of wager are void' by section 30, but the section does not render unlawful agreements to subscribe to a purse of Rs. 500 or upwards to be awarded to the winner or winners of a horse race. The Act did not make void agreements collateral to wagering contracts, though in the Bombay Presidency these were struck at by Bombay Act III of 1865.

The Contract Act changes the English law applicable where two or more persons are liable upon a promise or are entitled to the benefit of a promise. 'In regulating the devolution of rights and liabilities we propose', said the Commissioners, 'in accordance with the rule of English Courts of Equity and of the Indian Code of Civil Procedure that joint liabilities and rights

---

1 *Kali Bakhsh* v. *Ram Gopal* (1913) L.R. 41, I.A. 23, 28–9.
2 *Hodges* v. *The Delhi and London Bank Ltd.* (1901) L.R. 27, I.A. 168.

shall after the death of one of the persons liable or entitled go to his representative jointly with the survivor, and after the death of the survivor to the representatives of both jointly.' This is effected by sections 42 and 45 of the Act. But the Act goes further and by section 43 makes all joint contracts joint and several as far as the liability is concerned. 'When two or more persons make a joint promise the promises may in the absence of express agreement to the contrary compel any one or more of such joint promisors to perform the whole of the promise.' And section 249 carries out this principle in the case of partnerships by making every partner liable for debts incurred while he is a partner in the usual course of business by or on behalf of the partnership. This was in agreement with what was thought to be the rule of equity in England until 1879 when the House of Lords in *Kendall* v. *Hamilton*[1] held that during his life a partner's liability is only joint and that he is not liable to be sued separately.

The Contract Act thus raised the question: What is to happen when a decree is obtained against one of the promisors but is unsatisfied? Can another suit be brought against the other promisor? The courts in India have differed upon this but the answer of Strachey C.J.[2] that he can is approved by Pollock and Mulla. The Act provides expressly that the release of one joint promisor does not discharge another and does not free the promisor released from his obligations towards the others to contribute; and that the right of contribution, where one of the joint promisors makes default, includes the right to make the others share in the loss by such default.

The law as to damages for breach of contract is laid down in the three sections (73–5) which compose Chapter VI of the Act. The first two of these reproduce a single clause (50) of the Commissioners' draft to which they had appended a specially large number of illustrations lettered (*a*) to (*x*), of which all but the first two are illustrations of the rule in *Hadley* v. *Baxendale* (1854) 9 Ex. 341. This measures the damages by the standard set by asking what may reasonably be supposed to have been in the contemplation of both parties at the time they made the contract as the probable result of the breach of it. The explanation to section 73 affirms the duty of the wronged party to

1 1879, L.R. 4, A.C. 504.
2 *Muhammad Askari* v. *Radhi Ram Singh* (1900) I. L.R. 22 All. 604.

'mitigate his damages'. This section is unique as an instance of the use of illustrations to bring home the meaning of a general principle, in that the great variety in the applications of this rule was clearly relied upon by the Commissioners as a better means of eliciting its meaning than any further refinement in the rule itself. Section 75 is careful to state that a person who rightly rescinds a contract is entitled to be compensated for any damage he has sustained through non-fulfilment. Section 74 as it now stands is the result of an amendment made in 1899, but the section itself is the result of a pronounced difference of opinion between the Commissioners and the European business community in India as represented on the Select Committee of the Legislative Council. The Commissioners' clause had simply provided that 'when a contract has been broken, if a sum is named in the contract itself as the amount to be paid in case of such breach, the amount so named shall be paid accordingly'. In their report they explained that 'in order to avoid the litigation which arises under the English law on the subject of the distinction between penalty and liquidated damages...we propose that the rule of law shall have no regard to that distinction but simply require payment of the specified sum'. Stephen and the Calcutta business men whose opinions fortified his own (R. Stewart and J. R. Bullen Smith) favoured the 'converse operation'—that such specified sums should be in all cases regarded as specified by way of penalty, and that such damages only should be payable as was commensurate with the loss, the sum named being treated as a maximum. This was one of the less fortunate suggestions of the Commission for a departure from the English law: the proposal to make all India a 'market overt' for the sale of goods was the most unfortunate instance; but the proposed rule as to liquidated damages, like the proposed rules that an incoming partner should be liable for the firm's previous debts, and that a continuing guarantee given by or to a firm should not be rendered invalid by a change in the firm, was not thought by Indian opinion to be suitable for India, though recommended by the Commissioners as more suitable than the English law.

The Act contains in Chapter III (sections 31–36) a careful treatment of contingent contracts, and section 56 provides expressly that a contract to do an act which, after the contract is made, becomes impossible, or by reason of some event which the promisor could not prevent, unlawful, becomes void when the act becomes impossible or unlawful. Under section 65 when an agreement is discovered to be void, or when a contract becomes void, any person who has received any advantage under such agreement or contract is bound to restore it or to make compensation for it to the person from whom he received it. Section 56 deals with impossibility of performance not by making assumptions as to the intention of the parties in the particular case but by positive rules. That this method, though not in accordance with the rules observed in England, is to be commended may perhaps be thought established by the statement in Pollock and Mulla that 'there is no reason to suppose that a broad simplification of the English rules was not intended nor does it appear that any inconvenience has ensued or is to be expected'.[1] If one were inclined to seek a test of Stephen's draft by asking how under it the Coronation cases, or the cases of 'frustration of adventure' arising out of the war of 1914–18 would fall to be determined, I think it might be claimed for the Indian statute that on the whole it would have provided better justice and greater certainty than have been achieved in the English decisions. The principle which has come to be signalized by the word 'restitution' is writ large in the Act. Its application is obscured to some small extent by the language used as to contracts being 'voidable', 'rescinded', 'put an end to', but the principle is expressly asserted in sections 64 and 65 with regard to contracts rescinded, agreements discovered to be void, and contracts which become void. The principle, however, also finds its place in the group of sections upon quasi-contract which may here be noticed.

In the Commissioners' draft a group of seven clauses (60–7) dealt with 'certain obligations resembling those created by contract'. This topic of 'quasi-contract' was thought by the Commissioners to include the liability to make good a representation if made with the intention that the other party should act on it in a transaction between the parties, or made fraudulently to induce another to enter into a contract with a third party. Three of the seven clauses dealt with these matters; but the former is a question of estoppel dealt with in 1872 by section 115 of the Indian Evidence Act, and the latter is a question of tort and of the law of deceit. These clauses were very properly

1 6th ed. p. 329.

omitted from the Act, but the remaining five clauses are Chapter v of the Act (sections 68–72) and have so far as India is concerned avoided the difficulty—frequently encountered and discussed of recent years in England—which cases of 'unjust enrichment' present. The terms of section 70 are:

'Where a person lawfully does anything for another person, or delivers anything to him, not intending to do so gratuitously, and such other person enjoys the benefit thereof, the latter is bound to make compensation to the former in respect of or to restore the thing so done or delivered.'

To this the Commissioners had added in their draft:

'This rule shall apply notwithstanding that there shall have been a larger contract between the parties, which has been put an end to by reason of a breach thereof.'

These words were not enacted, however, but the principle of 'restitution' in such cases was laid down in sections 64–65. Thus in substance the third part of the Commissioners' draft became law in 1872 and has justified itself.

CHAPTER VIII

INDIAN EVIDENCE ACT

THE Indian Evidence Act of 1872, like the Indian Penal Code of 1860, has in substance become the law of many places outside British India. ,It was drawn, as is well known, by James Fitzjames Stephen and is nearer to being the work of one man than any of the other Indian codes. It has all the more interest on that account since it makes a new beginning by repealing 'all rules of evidence not contained in any Statute Act or Regulation'. The Courts in the Presidency towns had governed themselves by the English law of evidence as part of the English law which they administered. Thus Chief Justice Impey at the trial of Nuncomar in 1775 read over to the jury with comments certain written observations of Mr Farrer the prisoner's counsel upon the evidence, telling them:

'By the laws of England the counsel for prisoners charged with felony are not allowed to observe on the evidence to the jury but are to confine themselves to matters of law: but I told them that if they would deliver to me any observations they wished to be made to the jury, I would submit them to you, and give them their full force; by which means they will have the same advantage as they would have had in a civil case.'

But so far as regards the rules of law which limit the matters which may be laid before a court for its consideration the English law of evidence had assumed no precise or systematic form until late in the eighteenth century,[1] after Lord Chief Baron Gilbert's book was published in 1761. Stephen in his *General View of the Criminal Law of England* (1863) said of the law of evidence (p. 70):

'The construction of a whole department of law, of such intricacy, such extent, and such vast importance, in little more than a century

---

1 In *Nuncomar and Impey*, 1885, vol. I, p. 121, Stephen says that 'After much study of the law of evidence my opinion is that the greater part of the present law came into definite existence (after being for an unascertainable period the practice of the courts, differing by the way to some extent on different circuits) just about a hundred years ago'. This appears to be in line with what is said by Wigmore, *Select Essays on Anglo-American Legal History*, 1908, vol. II, p. 691. He points out that at the trial of Warren Hastings (1794) Burke tried to 'argue down' the rules of evidence, and to ridicule them as petty and inconsiderable: 'As to rules of law and evidence he did not know what they meant;...it was true, something had been written on the law of evidence, but very general, very abstract, and comprised in so small a compass that a parrot he had known might get them by rote in one half-hour and repeat them in five minutes.'

is the most remarkable instance which the law affords of the importance of the legislative powers which the judges possess in virtue of their right to declare with authority what the law is.'

LAW BEFORE THE ACT

In the middle of the nineteenth century a number of Indian Acts had been passed to amend the law of evidence as administered in the Supreme Courts by introducing reforms taken from English Acts. These reforms made witnesses both competent and compellable notwithstanding that they might have committed a crime, or were interested, or were parties, or the husbands or wives of parties to the case.

Outside the Presidency towns the Regulations of each of the three Presidencies had provided some rules regarding evidence, and there was in certain parts a customary law upon the subject, but neither the English law of evidence nor the Hindu or Mahomedan laws of evidence were as such binding in the Company's courts. This emerged very clearly from the Full Bench decision in the High Court at Calcutta in a criminal case of 1866 *R. v. Khairulla (Khyroolla)* 6 W.R. Cr. 21 where the question was whether the wife of an accused was a competent witness for the prosecution. It was held that she was competent. Though Norman J. dissented from this conclusion it was agreed by all the judges—Peacock C.J., Norman, Campbell,[1] Seton-Karr and Kemp J.J.—that the law of England was not the law of evidence in mofussil courts. The same was held in Bombay in 1869.[2]

Although the English rules had no authority as such in the country courts, certain Indian Acts applied English reforms to all courts in British India—e.g. Act XIX of 1837, declaring that no one should be incompetent as a witness by reason of conviction for any offence. Act XIX of 1853 extended to the civil courts in Bengal the principles which enabled persons to be witnesses notwithstanding that they were parties or were related to parties or were interested, etc. etc. It also made provision for production of documents subject to exception for title deeds and for privileged communications with a professional adviser. Lastly by Act II of 1855 (for the further improvement of the law of evidence), there had been enacted for all courts in British

---

1 Sir George Campbell, author of *Modern India* (1852) and Lieut.-Governor of Bengal (1872).
2 *R. v. Ramswami Mudaliar* 6 B.H.C.R. 47, 49.

India a great many provisions of a useful character, modifying the English law but conceived upon English lines. This Act belongs to the period when the Legislative Council had as members the Chief Justice of Bengal and a puisne judge: it was introduced by Sir Lawrence Peel and carried by Sir James Colvile. There were certain provisions in the Civil (1839) and Criminal (1861) Procedure Codes which dealt with the summoning and examination of witnesses. The most noticeable among these were the provisions in the latter code which dealt with the thorny topic of confessions. It was in this that there first appeared the rules which excluded confessions made to the police or while in custody of the police.

The position of the Company's courts—that is of all the courts outside the towns of Calcutta, Madras and Bombay—was rendered very difficult, since while the English law of evidence was not binding on them certain amendments of that law had been prescribed. The judicial officers, whether Indian or members of the Civil Service, could not claim to have had any training in the conduct of cases at *nisi prius* and no library of English decisions was available to them. The lawyers who practised before them, however, very naturally insisted upon some compliance with the rules of evidence. 'As to evidence, knowledge of it and skill in appreciating and manipulating it are probably more widely diffused among the English Bar than any other legal accomplishments.'[1] They cited English textbooks and used the English decisions as their arsenal. The result as it appeared to Sir Henry Maine in 1868 was expressed by him to the Legislative Council[2] thus:

'On looking, however, at the two Indian Evidence Acts,[3] it would seem that they implied that the English law of evidence, except where they modified it, was in force in the bulk of India, the Mofussil. During the last ten or fifteen years the doctrine that the English law of evidence was *vi propria* in force throughout the whole of the country had certainly gained strength, and the habit of applying that law with increasing strictness was gaining ground. No doubt much evidence was received by the Mofussil Courts which the English Courts would not regard as strictly admissible. But Mr Maine would appeal to Members of Council who had more experience in the Mofussil than he had...whether the Judges of those Courts did

1 Maine, Minute of 10 September 1857 on the Judge Advocate-General's Office. Grant Duff's *Memoir*, p. 350. Minutes of Sir H. S. Maine, p. 154.
2 4 December 1868.
3 Act XIX of 1853 and II of 1855.

not, as a matter of fact, believe that it was their duty to administer
the English law of evidence as modified by the Evidence Acts. In
particular Mr Maine was informed that when a case was argued by
a barrister before a Mofussil Judge, and when the English rules of
evidence were pressed on his attention, he did practically accept those
rules, and admit or reject evidence according to his construction of
them.'

The inevitability of the English law of evidence and the
Judges' acceptance of a duty to administer a law in which they
were not skilled produced different reactions from people of
different temperament and training. The Lieutenant-Governor
of Bengal was Sir George Campbell, who had been one of the
Charter judges of the Calcutta High Court when in 1861 it was
established to combine the old Supreme Court and the Sudder
Dewani Adalat. He had had much experience of the Upper Provinces and the Punjab as well as of Bengal, and stoutly represented the civilian Judges and magistrates who felt it unfair and
unreasonable that they should be expected to apply a body of
rules which they did not know and which were not really
available to them.

Like many other officers of experience he was inclined to
depreciate systematic rules as theoretical and to coquette with
the notion that the best Evidence Act would consist of a sentence
abolishing all rules of evidence. The other course—the only other
course—was that which the Indian Law Commission in London
had proposed and which Maine summed up.[1]

'The Commissioners would appear to be right in supposing that
what was wanted for the greatest part of India was a liberalised
version of the English law of evidence enacted with authority and
thus excluding caprice and superseding the use of textbooks by
compactness and precision.'

When at last in 1872 Stephen as Maine's successor was in a
position to move that the Evidence Act as we now know it be
passed, Campbell, agreeing that it was now hopeless to avoid
some law of evidence, conceded the great merit of this other
policy:

'He hoped and believed that a law of evidence freed from intri-
cacies and technicalities, had this very great advantage to the Courts
of the country, that it at least put them, in respect of the law, on an
equal footing with the Advocates practising before them. It enabled

1 Speech in Council 4 December 1868.

the Judge to say to the Advocate, "I am as good a man as you; if you raise a question of evidence, there is the law by which your question can be decided" It would put a stop to the practice hitherto prevalent, of an Advocate shaking in the face of the Court a mysterious law of evidence, which was not to be found codified anywhere as substantive law or otherwise in any shape admitting of its being easily referred to by our Judges and judicial officers of all grades.'[1]

The provision of the second section, which made away with all rules not imposed by positive enactment, was a pivotal feature of the Act, which but for this might well have operated to let a flood of English case law into the Mofussil. There was even room for apprehension that 'Taylor on Evidence' might come to be regarded as a special depository of the law of India owing to the use avowedly made of that work by Stephen in framing the Act. As Campbell put it—successfully combining for the moment the roles of Lieutenant-Governor and *enfant terrible*—'It was not desirable to take any dictionary of English law as the basis of a law of evidence in this country. If he could find any ground for objecting to any part of the bill, it was that in some parts it somewhat smelt of the English law of evidence; but he hoped that most of the sting of Taylor had been taken out of him.'

The exclusion of evidence not authorized by the Act was insisted upon by the Judicial Committee in *Rani Lekraj Kuar* v. *Baboo Mahpal Singh* (1879 L.R. 7 I.A. 63, 70). Later, in a very curious case in which a woman's dying declaration had taken the form of answers given by signs to questions orally put to her,[2] the High Court at Allahabad had some difficulty in agreeing on the particular section under which it could be admitted; and it was said by Mahmood J. that while the principle of exclusion adopted by the Act was the safest guide, 'yet it should not be so applied as to exclude matters which may be essential for the ascertainment of truth'. This dictum, however, has recently been disapproved by the Privy Council (*Maharaja Sris Chandra Nandy* v. *Rakhalananda Thakur* 1941 L.R. 68 I.A. 34). By Act I of 1938—a statute law revision measure—section 2 of the Evidence Act has been repealed, but it is not thought that this has revived or reintroduced any new principles of evidence.

---

1 Speech in Council 12 March 1872.
2 *R.* v. *Abdullah* (1885) I.L.R. 7 All. 385.

LAW COMMISSIONERS' DRAFT, 1868

The Indian Law Commissioners, Lord Romilly and his col-leagues,[1] having presented a draft code of Negotiable Instruments in July 1867 proceeded to deal with Evidence as their next subject; though as they themselves remark in their report 'it may perhaps be made a question how far the subject of evidence falls under the head of Substantive Law and some of the sections of the draft now submitted certainly border closely on Procedure'. Their report was dated 3 August 1868 and their draft bill was very short, comprising only thirty-nine clauses, of which about a dozen were furnished with illustrations. It dealt with a number of matters clearly and well, e.g. with judgments, and the method of proving writings, including secondary evidence of documents. It excluded oral evidence of the terms of written contracts, grants or other dispositions of property. It dispensed with the proof of certain classes of documents. It made certain communications privileged, including those made by one of a married couple to the other. It laid down certain rules as to cross-examining witnesses to credit. All persons were made competent to testify save those who from tender years, unsoundness of mind or other cause appeared to the judge to be incapable of understanding the questions. A court might be satisfied with and act on the testimony of one witness.

The Commissioners observed upon the Act of 1855 that it contained many valuable provisions but that it 'bears reference in many places to the existing law and it appears to have been designed, not as a complete body of rules, but as supplementary to and corrective of the English law, and also of the customary law of evidence prevailing in those parts of British India where the English law is not administered'. They notice that the Country Courts had in fact no fixed rules of evidence except those contained in that Act; that, though they were not required to follow the English law as such, they were not debarred from so doing where they regarded it as the most equitable. The Commissioners' opinion of the system which had grown up in England was that it was too artificial to be suited to India, having been 'moulded in a great degree by our social and legal institutions and our form of procedure': that in England much useful evidence was excluded, and some evidence admitted which was

1 Lord Romilly, Sir Edward Ryan, Robert Lowe (Lord Sherbrooke), Sir Robert Lush, Sir John M. Macleod, W. M. James (afterwards Lord Justice).

at least as dangerous as that which was shut out: e.g. parent and child could not refuse to give evidence against each other in a criminal case, while a wife was not allowed to give evidence at her husband's trial unless the trial be for an offence against herself. They considered that in India the danger was greater that the Court would be insufficiently informed than that it would be unduly influenced by anything laid before it. Hence they provided (clause 2) that 'anything which has a bearing upon any question in issue in a cause, the determination of which question is material to the decision of the cause is admissible unless it is excluded by the rules contained in this chapter'. They explain that the judge must form his own opinion regarding the relevancy of any evidence which the parties may desire to submit to him, but that they had included some provisions to guard against the trial of collateral issues arising out of questions asked to impugn a witness's credit; and that they had also made some relevant evidence inadmissible— chiefly that of the kind called 'hearsay', though their draft avoids the word. On this subject they relaxed the English rules still further than the Act of 1853 had done. But as compared with the Indian Evidence Act as passed in 1872, their draft and their report contain no strained attempt to equate the notions 'relevant' and 'admissible'. They say expressly that

'the exclusion even of relevant evidence may be desirable, when the evidence is such that people are naturally inclined to attach undue importance to it; when it is such as cannot be admitted without the danger of encouraging forgery; or when it is such as cannot be received, or at least cannot be extorted, without injury to interests which are even more important than the judicial investigation of truth'.

The Commissioners' draft was introduced into the Legislative Council and referred to a Select Committee in 1868 during Maine's period of office as Law Member. His speeches on the bill had contained nothing but praise: in particular he considered that there was probably no subject upon which a codified law was more wanted. His general view was that the English law was a model of good sense but made no claim to be scientific; that some evidence must be excluded, since if all relevant evidence was admitted the courts would be overwhelmed; and that the Commissioners had been wise in modifying the English rules so as not to exclude too much. When Stephen in December

1869 succeeded Maine, the Legislative Council gained, as their leader upon legal matters, one who had already paid special attention to the theory of evidence and to the English rules for criminal trials. In his *General View of the Criminal Law of England* published in 1863, Stephen had devoted chapter VII to the 'Principles of Evidence'—a chapter which may perhaps be said to discuss the philosophy of the subject. It contains something of logic, of psychology, and of the theory of probability; and if not very profound or even very useful, its shrewdness and its good sense are undeniable. A sentence may be quoted (p. 268) as stating shortly what the Indian Evidence Act was afterwards to set forth at large and with precision:

'The evidence at a criminal trial is almost invariably directed to prove something suggested to be either motive or act of preparation for the design, or something done in carrying it into execution, or subsequent conduct having reference to it and being caused by it—all of which form parts of the criminal transaction....All the evidence ...given against Palmer, Smethurst and Donellan might be classed under one or other of these heads: yet these are just the sort of cases which would be selected as illustrations of circumstantial evidence.'

Of chapter VIII upon the English rules of evidence in criminal cases, it may be noted that the main rules are stated as five: (1) The burden of proof is on the prosecution; (2) Evidence must be confined to the points in issue; (3) The best evidence must always be given; (4) Hearsay is no evidence; (5) Confessions under certain circumstances are no evidence (p. 302).

CRITICISM IN INDIA: STEPHEN'S PROPOSALS, 1871, 1872

Stephen found soon after his arrival in India that the Commissioners' bill had met with much objection. The result of its circulation for opinion to local governments was that 'it was pronounced by every legal authority to which it was submitted to be unsuitable to the wants of the country'.[1] In a speech of 6 September 1870 he observed that the object of the English rules was rather to bring the proceedings to a point than to aid inquiry into truth, and that he doubted whether such a system should be introduced without great modifications. In 1871 the Select Committee reported that the Commissioners' draft 'is not suited to the wants of this country', giving reasons in detail which they summarized by saying that it was not suffi-

1 Stephen, speech of 31 March 1871.

ciently elementary, that it was incomplete and that it assumed an acquaintance with the law of England which could scarcely be expected from officers in India. On the other hand, they stated that their own draft though based on a different principle embodied most of the Commissioners' provisions, and that it was based on the English law with certain modifications—most, though not all, of which were suggested by the Commissioners. The Committee's report—which was really Stephen's work—discloses that his real quarrel was not so much with the Commissioners as with the law of England, which is described as totally destitute of arrangement and reproached because 'its leading terms are continually used in different senses'. Not without a certain boldness the Committee claimed to have 'discarded altogether the phraseology in which the English text writers usually express themselves' and to have 'attempted first to ascertain and then to arrange in their natural order the principles which underlie the numerous cases and fragmentary rules which they [i.e. the text writers] have collected together'. Their report and draft bill were to be circulated to local governments for opinion and considered at a later session in the light of criticism received. It was in presenting this first report[1] that Stephen made his often quoted remark about 'justice, equity and good conscience' that 'practically speaking these attractive words mean little more than an imperfect understanding of imperfect collections of not very recent editions of the English text books'. He restated as five the main rules of evidence thus: (1) that evidence must be confined to the issue, (2) that hearsay is no evidence, (3) that the best evidence must be given, (4) rules as to confessions and admissions, (5) rules as to documentary evidence. He showed that these rules would not teach a judge whether a particular witness was to be believed, or what inferences he could safely draw from the particular facts which he accepted as proved; but that their real use is that they supply reliable negative tests as to two great points—the relevancy of facts to the question to be decided and the sort of evidence by which facts ought to be proved. The main claim made by Stephen in this speech is that the bill stated specifically and in a positive form what sort of facts are relevant as being sufficiently connected with the facts in issue to afford ground for an inference as to their existence or non-existence.

1 31 March 1871.

This is the part of the Indian Evidence Act which may fairly claim to be called original and which Stephen so regarded. They are sections 5–11 inclusive.

When the Select Committee made its second report, 30 January 1872, substantial changes had been made in the draft, which included new sections dealing with presumptions. Stephen summarized the main criticisms received by saying that the bill was charged with being very incomplete as regards its provisions concerning judgments and presumptions. The charge had been made by Mr J. B. Norton—at one time Advocate General of Madras and himself the author of a textbook on the law of evidence[1]—that the bill consisted of portions arbitrarily selected from 'Taylor on Evidence'; but Stephen was able to reply that the arrangement of the bill was unlike anything in Taylor or in any other textbook, that there was a reason why each section stood where it did, and that every principle applicable to British India in the 1598 pages of Taylor and in Norton's book was contained in the 167 sections of the bill. The criticism of the treatment of judgments was mostly that the law of *res judicata* had been left to the procedure codes; but the question of presumptions was more important, and the bill had been altered to meet certain criticisms on this point. Stephen was determined on both topics to exclude much that had found its way into books on evidence but which did not really belong to the subject. Chapter VI of the bill as amended dealt with the burden of proof in 14 sections (101–14). These cover specifically the question of burden of proof as regards general and special exceptions contained in the definition of an offence (105), facts especially within the knowledge of any person (106), whether a man is alive or dead (107–8), relationship as partner landlord principal (109), possessor being owner (110), good faith of person in a position of active confidence (111). Certain facts are conditionally made 'conclusive proof' of legitimacy by section 112. Section 113 (which was *ultra vires* of the Indian legislature[2] under the Act of 1861) was meant to cure a doubt with which Maine had been troubled upon the legality of a cession of British territory.[3] These topics are disposed of by

---

1 Published Madras 1858, 7th ed. 1869.
2 *Damodhar Goodhan* v. *Deoram Kanji* (1876) L.R. 31 A at 152–3.
3 Minutes of Sir H. S. Maine, p. 193. Minute of 11 August 1868 on the Rampore Cession case.

their respective sections, but a further and more general section (114) had been added by the Select Committee and furnished with illustrations:

'114. The Court may presume the existence of any fact which it thinks likely to have happened, regard being had to the common course of natural events, human conduct and public and private business in their relation to the facts of the particular case.'

As illustrations are given what in England would be regarded as well-known presumptions made by the law in the case of persons in possession of goods soon after they were stolen; accomplices unless corroborated; evidence which could be, but is not, produced; judicial and official acts being regularly performed, and in certain other cases. Stephen's desire was to refuse admission into the law of India to the distinction between a presumption of law and a presumption of fact, and to put all such matters as these in the position of mere presumptions of fact with which the court could deal at its discretion. In this connection the abrogation by section 2 of all non-statutory rules of evidence was thought by him to be specially important. 'The effect of this provision, coupled with the general repealing clause at the beginning of the bill, is to make it perfectly clear that courts of justice are to use their own common sense and experience in judging of the effect of particular facts, and that they are to be subject to no technical rules whatever on the subject.' He went on to emphasize as an illustration that the court was to be at perfect liberty to act on the uncorroborated testimony of an accomplice if in its discretion it thought fit to do so: 'every one I think must have met with instances in which it is practically impossible to doubt the truth of such evidence.'[1]

To revert to the special provisions in the sections which precede this general rule as to presumptions of fact, we must note that the Act expressly lays upon the accused by section 105 the burden of bringing himself within any of the general exceptions or any special exception or proviso in the Penal Code or other law defining the offence, 'and the Court shall presume the absence of such circumstance'. It would seem to be beside the mark to cite *R. v. Woolmington* 1935 A.C. 462 in such cases. On the other hand the doctrine laid down in *R. v. Schama and Abramovitch* 24 Cox's C.C. 591 as to 'recent possession' being evidence on a charge of receiving stolen goods seems to be quite

[1] Speech in Council 12 March 1872.

in consonance with section 114 illustration (*a*): the court may presume but is not obliged to presume guilt on any view of the matter. Section 106, however, is an unfortunate and misguided section though it has had its admirers. It runs: 'When any fact is especially within the knowledge of any person the burden of proving it is upon him.' It is an outstanding instance of the regard paid by Stephen to Taylor on Evidence. The doctrine it embodies is found in the edition of 1868 (5th) and in all later editions until the last—viz. the 12th ed. 1931 when it is modified and partially retracted. To the general rule that the onus is on the party who substantially alleges the affirmative, Taylor admits an exception which in some cases the legislature has enacted but which he says the common law also recognizes— 'that where the subject matter of the allegation lies peculiarly within the knowledge of one of the parties that party must prove it whether it be of an affirmative or negative character and even though there be a presumption of law in his favour'. There is some support in the English decisions for such a rule in cases where a man is charged with doing acts which are not permitted unless the doer is qualified or licensed in a certain manner, or even more broadly in cases where the prosecution's case involves a negative. Thus, as Taylor noted,[1] in *R.* v. *Turner* 5 M. & Sel. 206 Bayley J. said, 'I have always understood it to be a general rule that if a negative averment be made by one party, which is peculiarly within the knowledge of the other, the party within whose knowledge it lies and who asserts the affirmative is to prove it and not he who avers the negative'. But in *Elkin* v. *Janson* 13 M. & W. 662 Alderson B. commenting on this passage observed, 'I doubt whether as a general rule those expressions are not too strong. They are right as to the *weight* of the evidence but there should be some evidence to start it, in order to cast the onus on the other side.' Bowen L.J. challenged the doctrines of Bayley J. in *Abrath* v. *N.E. Rail. Co.* 1883 11 Q.B.D. at 457 saying, 'I think a proposition of that kind cannot be maintained and that the exception supposed to be found among cases relating to the game laws may be explained on special grounds'. And the proposition is reduced by Taylor's latest edition to this—that when the facts lie peculiarly within the knowledge of one of the parties very slight evidence may be sufficient to discharge the burden of proof resting on the opposite

1 5th ed. 1868, vol. 1, p. 380.

party. Section 106 is part of the law of Ceylon under the Ceylon Evidence Ordinance 14 of 1895, and in *Attygalle* v. *The King* 1930 A.C. 338 the relevant passage was quoted from the eleventh edition of Taylor. The charge was of performing an illegal operation, and the judge had told the jury to apply the principle, but the Judicial Committee rejected this application of the doctrine. 'It is not the law of Ceylon that the burden is cast upon an accused person of proving that no crime has been committed.' No such provision as that of section 106 is admitted by Stephen into his *Digest of the Law of Evidence*: the rule of the law of England is stated very moderately: 'in considering the amount of evidence necessary to shift the burden of proof the Court has regard to the opportunities of knowledge with respect to the fact to be proved which may be possessed by the parties respectively'.[1] It seems a pity that the law on this subject was not left as stated in section 114 (g): the Court may presume that evidence which could be and is not produced would if produced be unfavourable to the person who withholds it.

STEPHEN'S SUMMARY

In retrospect Stephen's own view of the Act was given in the chapter which he contributed to Hunter's *Life of the Earl of Mayo*:

'The Evidence Act (I of 1872) compresses into a very short compass the whole of the English and Indian law of evidence. I had charge of this Act, and drew it in its present shape, though in such a manner as to include the provisions of a bill previously drawn by the Indian Law Commissioners. It forms a good illustration of the justice of the charge of over-legislation, and an undue fondness for English law, so often brought against the Government of India. The truth is that the English Law of Evidence was inevitably introduced into India to an uncertain and indefinite extent as soon as English lawyers began to exercise any influence over the administration of justice in India. Nor was this all. In order to avoid refinements which would have been most injurious to India, legislation was necessary which, by declaring that particular parts of the English Law of Evidence should not apply to India, gives an implied sanction to the rest of it. The general result was, that the Law of Evidence before the Evidence Act was passed had a sort of dead-alive existence in India, and was the bugbear of civilian judges, who were placed by it much at the mercy of every English barrister who might appear before them. The Evidence Act reduced the whole subject to a plain short and explicit form.'[2]

1 *Digest*, 1881, art. 96, p. 105; 1936, art. 104, pp. 128–9.
2 Hunter's *Life of the Earl of Mayo*, vol. II, ch. VIII, p. 201, by Stephen.

STEPHEN'S PHILOSOPHICAL THEORY

So great was his interest in and so thorough his work upon the law of evidence that Stephen at once prepared a short treatise on the 'principles of judicial evidence' by way of commentary on or introduction to the Act. This *Introduction to the Indian Evidence Act* was published in the same year (1872) after his return to England.[1] The main feature of this work was the second chapter which contains 'a statement of the principles of induction and deduction, and a comparison of their application to scientific and judicial enquiries'. The professed object of this logical dissertation was to explain what facts are relevant: 'relevant facts' being the phrase used in the Act for facts which, though not themselves in issue, affect the probability of facts in issue and which can be used as a foundation of inferences respecting them. While comparing and contrasting scientific and judicial enquiries in an instructive manner, Stephen gives, as exhibiting the nature of the reasoning in both, an exposition of the four methods of induction which John Stuart Mill had described, in his *System of Logic* published in 1843, as methods by which facts may be exhibited as standing to one another in the relation of cause and effect. Stephen's view is that reasoning from cause to effect or from effect to cause is the basis of the nature of 'relevancy' in judicial enquiries; though probability rather than certainty is the best which can be expected under the conditions to which they are subject, and 'moral certainty' is rather a question of prudence than of calculation. He had not failed to appreciate that even in scientific enquiries the results obtained by the Method of Agreement, at least, were most useful as suggesting a general truth which could be regarded as an hypothesis, and verified or discarded according as particular instances are found to be consistent with it or not—that is, as something to be tested by resort to deductive reasoning. But this attempt to give a philosophical exposition of the basis of 'relevancy' met with criticism,[2] and did not long satisfy its author. In the introduction to his *Digest of the Law of Evidence*, of which the first edition was published in 1876, Stephen repeats that when the nature of relevancy has to be considered in itself

---

1 He was in India as Law Member for some 2½ years only—from 12 December 1869 to 18 April 1872—only half the usual period of five years as against Maine's seven years' tenure of office.

2 *Theory of Relevancy for the purpose of Judicial Evidence*, by G. C. Whitworth, Bombay, 1875.

we are led to inductive logic, and that the ultimate answer is that judicial evidence is only one case of the general problem of science—inferring the unknown from the known. In stating the meaning of the word 'relevant', however, Stephen gave an expanded definition not entirely limited to the cause-and-effect relationship between facts—thereby accepting correction from his critics; and by 1881 his definition was made still more general —applying the word 'relevant' whenever, according to the common course of events, one fact taken by itself or with others proves or renders probable the past, present or future existence or non-existence of the other.

Not only does it appear that relevancy is not a pure question of causal connection, but it may even be suggested that Stephen somewhat misconceived matters when he imagined that the arguments by which a crime or the authorship of a book is brought home to an individual are instances of the methods of Agreement or Difference as these were stated by Mill. The argument of Macaulay[1] that five facts may be predicated of Junius and these may also be predicated of Sir Philip Francis is given by Stephen as an instance of the kind of reasoning employed in law courts. But with all respect, this is not Mill's 'Method of Agreement': if one adds that the five facts can be predicated of no one else, that is not Mill's 'Method of Difference'. Such an argument infers identity from a number of marks or 'notes' each having some claim to be distinctive and the sum of them all having strong claim to be distinctive: this is not like the inductive process which from particular experiences concludes that 'fire burns'. Philosophies moreover are perishable articles, and one of the greatest of the German philosophers addressed to them 'the words which the apostle Peter spoke to Ananias: "Behold, the feet of them that shall carry thee out are at the door!"'[2] It was very natural in one whose Cambridge days began in 1847 to pride himself[3] on having been in 1872 the first to notice 'the very close resemblance which exists between Mr Mill's theory and the existing state of the law'. But since F. H. Bradley's *Principles of Logic*[4] appeared in

1 Introduction, p. 48.
2 Hegel's *History of Philosophy*, trans. E. S. Haldane, vol. 1, p. 17. The words are not literally quoted and were spoken to Sapphira; cf. Acts v, 9.
3 *Digest of the Law of Evidence*, Introd.
4 'I shall endeavour to show three things: first that the Four Inductive Methods cannot be used if we start from mere facts, that the Canons presuppose universal truths as the materials upon which the work is to be done; and that, therefore, if valid the Methods are not inductive at all in the sense of generalising from

1883 a generation has grown up to whom Mill's methods carry little conviction.

Sir Frederick Pollock sums up by saying:

'The Evidence Act...was entirely Stephen's own. It not only consolidated the rules of judicial proof but endeavoured to connect them by legislative authority with a logical theory of probability set forth in the Act itself. This part of the Act has been criticised both as to the principle (which indeed seems open to much doubt) and as to the success of the draftsman in applying it. At any rate, it is characteristic of Stephen's anxiety never to shirk a difficulty.'[1]

One may here note that Lord Chief Baron Gilbert, who died in 1726 and whose book on the Law of Evidence was published long afterwards (1761), begins with a reference to John Locke[2] on the different degrees of certainty and assent and employs Locke's language and ideas to some extent in his exposition. He did this, one may confidently hold, without perilling the value of his work upon the truth of the 'Sensationalist' philosophy. So too it would be a mistake to assume that defects in Stephen's theories about the nature of the reasoning employed in judicial proceedings have had much effect in reducing the usefulness or clouding the meaning of the Act. The wide rules of exclusion made familiar in English law by the 'best evidence' rule or the rule against 'hearsay' had each its attendant list of exceptions or apparent exceptions. From these in Stephen's view it was possible to collect the positive rules upon which evidence was admitted by the courts—'positive rules as to the relevancy of facts to the issue, which will admit every fact which a rational man could wish to have before him in investigating any question of fact'.

'The object of drawing the Act in this manner was that the general ground on which facts are relevant might be stated in as many and

particulars. In the second place I shall briefly exhibit the real nature of the reasoning used in the above Four Methods and shall point out that its essence is not thus inductive. And finally I shall show that not one of the Canons is a test of proof, and that by every one you can bring out what is false... (p. 358).

'I do not mean to say that for all the purposes of discovery, the flaws in the Methods amount to serious mistakes. Such a contention would be beyond the scope of my volume. It is certain, however, that independent logicians such as Dr Whewell and Professor Jevons in our own country, and Professors Lotze and Sigwart in Germany, have taken a view of the process of scientific discovery which is not favourable to the claims of the Four Methods' (p. 364). *Principles of Logic*, by F. H. Bradley, 2nd ed. 1922.

1 *Encyc. Brit.* 11th ed. Article on Stephen by Sir Frederick Pollock.
2 *Essay on the Human Understanding*, 1690.

as popular forms as possible, so that if a fact is relevant its relevancy may be easily ascertained. These sections are by far the most important, as they are the most original part of the Evidence Act, as they affirm positively what facts may be proved, whereas the English law assumes this to be known, and merely declares negatively that certain facts shall not be proved.'[1]

RELEVANCY

Considering the stress laid on the distinction between (1) what facts may be proved; (2) how any particular fact may be proved, one may indeed be surprised to find how the notion of 'relevancy' is made to serve as a test in both respects. The Act declares by section 5 that evidence may be given 'of every fact in issue and of such other facts as are hereinafter declared to be relevant and of no others'. The 'other' facts are 'listed' so to say, the quality of 'relevancy' being conferred, in the course of the fifty sections which follow, not only upon certain classes of facts (in the primary sense), but under carefully expressed conditions upon 'admissions' and upon 'statements' by third parties upon 'opinions' of experts and other persons with special knowledge and upon 'judgments'. Sections 6 to 11 bear the brunt of the difficulties encountered by this method. It is not of much service to say that 'collateral' facts are only to be proved if they are declared 'relevant' if the sections which confer or recognize relevancy are loosely drawn. Facts are made relevant by these sections if they are 'part of the same transaction' (section 6), the occasion, cause or effect of relevant facts or facts in issue or constitute the state of things under which they happened or afforded an opportunity for their occurrence (section 7), show motive or preparation or are conduct influencing or influenced by any such fact (section 8), are necessary to explain or introduce such facts or to establish identity or fix time or place (section 9), things said or done by a conspirator in reference to the common design (section 10), if inconsistent with any fact in issue or relevant fact or make the existence or non-existence of any such fact highly probable or improbable (section 11). These provisions, as Stephen has told us, 'are designedly worded very widely and in such a way as to overlap each other'. The language employed by section 11 in its second paragraph is too wide, moreover, by Stephen's own admission. 'The sort of facts which the section was intended to include are facts which either

1 Stephen's *Introduction to the Indian Evidence Act*, 1872, p. 55.

exclude or imply more or less distinctly the existence of the facts sought to be proved. Some degree of latitude was designedly left in the wording of the section....' The meaning of the section would have been more fully expressed, it would seem, if 'statements' had been excluded from it so as to leave their admissibility to be governed by other sections. Upon the whole, since Sir Raymond West's judgement in *R.* v. *Parbhudas* 1874 11 Bom. H.C. Rep. 90, the decisions in India have restricted the effect of section 11 in the sense indicated by Stephen and the illustrations seem to show that sufficient meaning can be given to it without abrogating the careful restrictions imposed on the admissibility of statements by other sections of the Act. The terms of section 7 may also be said to be unduly wide, especially the phrase 'which constitute the state of things under which they happened'. The result can hardly be said to be precise, simple, tidy or scientific, but to be a series of working rules which will keep judicial enquiries from leaving the proper track and becoming bogged. That they can be made serviceable to this end is very well brought out by Stephen's statement of the evidence in the cases of Donellan (1781), Belaney (1844), Richardson (1786), Patch (1805) and Palmer (1856). Of these his remarks in Patch's case throw a particularly clear light upon his views—he regards it as illustrating the 'method of difference': as a 'very complete illustration of section 11': and as showing 'that it is impossible to draw a line between relevant and irrelevant facts otherwise than by enumerating as completely as possible the more common forms in which the relation of cause and effect displays itself'.[1]

Stephen considered—very correctly—that sections 6 to 11 did not make admissible (1) statements made by persons not called as witnesses; (2) transactions similar to but unconnected with facts in issue, or (3) opinions as to facts in issue or relevant facts, and that other sections must be relied on to establish the relevancy of any of these matters. Section 32, which deals with statements, is very wide as it applies not only to persons who are dead or cannot be found, or are incapable of giving evidence, but also to those whose attendance cannot be procured without an unreasonable amount of delay or expense.

So, too, entries in books kept in the ordinary course of business are admissible if made by a person to whom the section applies.

1 Introduction, p. 80.

The Act does not restrict their admissibility by requiring the entry to have been made at the time or by excluding collateral matters. The Act accepts as evidence the statements made in published maps or charts generally offered for sale or made under authority of government. And on questions of custom or public right the Act is particularly liberal in the admission of evidence of opinion and admits upon questions of relationship the opinion of anyone who, as a member of the family or otherwise, has special means of knowledge.

What are called dying declarations as to cause of death are received in England only in trials for murder or manslaughter of the declarant, and only when the declarant is shown to have been in actual danger of death and to have given up all hope of recovery. Certain theological implications lie at the back of this last requirement. In India it has been thought that they do not hold good universally as a matter of received opinion. The Act abolishes the requirement of 'expectation of death' and even the requirement of 'danger of death'; and it makes such evidence admissible in any proceeding in which the cause of death comes into question.

Sir Whitley Stokes[1] says that dying declarations are not to be regarded as if they were made in England and quotes from an article by Sir W. Rattigan—the well-known Punjab lawyer—who said in 1885: 'Very often the murdered man before his death implicates every male member of his supposed murderer's family, or of the supposed instigator of the murder, hoping by this means to drink the cup of revenge to its last dregs and to rid his own family of all future annoyance.' Such cases undoubtedly occur and not only in the Punjab. But the sanction implied in an immediately expected death is not by the Act dispensed with because it has no force—in general it would have force as a matter of opinion or sentiment among Indians, and in any case the motive to speak falsely is often removed by the prospect of immediate death. Section 32 is not meant to be so narrow as the English law or to introduce all possible safeguards. But in disengaging Indian law and practice from the religious presuppositions of the common law the section is in line with section 6 of the Oaths Act (X of 1873) and section 118 of the Evidence Act itself. The former provides that if a witness interpreter or juror is a Hindu or Mahomedan, or has an objection

1 *Anglo-Indian Codes,* vol. II, p. 841.

to making an oath he shall make an affirmation. Under certain strict conditions a witness may, in modification of this rule, take an oath in a form offered by himself and a party may agree to be bound by the statement of a particular witness made on oath taken in a particular form. In the early days of the Mayor's Court at Madras[1] there was much dispute over the question whether a party should be required to swear to his case at the Triplicane pagoda or only 'by mint and water'.[2]

Shore in his *Notes of Indian Affairs* (1836) says, 'the Koran or a bottle of dirty water (supposed to be that of the Ganges) was placed in their hands'. Hindus were at times sworn by the solemnity of touching a Brahmin or the eldest son of the witness. The case of *Omichand* v. *Barker* 1744, 1 Atkins 21, which was argued by Mansfield when he was Solicitor General, is instructive on this point. The forms of oath formerly imposed on Indian witnesses were a long-standing grievance.[3]

Section 118 of the Act makes all persons competent to testify, unless the court considers that they are prevented from understanding the questions or giving rational answers by tender years, extreme old age, disease, etc. There is of course no practice of insisting on a condition that a child must believe that he would be punished in a future state if he gave false evidence— a condition which the law of England seems to have given up.[4]

1 *Records of Fort St George, Mayor's Court Minutes*, 1736–7, vol. III (publ. 1937), p. 18.
2 'The Evidence, Sidoo Yellaree and Poterause, all three Lascars,...were sworn to speak the whole truth and nothing but the truth, according to the rights of their own religion, by a Braminy, who put a sprig of Mint into each of their hands and power'd water upon it; they eat the Mint, and power'd the water out of their hands upon their heads: which ceremony being performed, each of them severally gave in a full relation of the Fact, their evidence agreeing even in the minutest circumstances.' Trial of Richard Seale by the Council for murder of a lascar, 23 June 1718, Madras (Indian Records Series, *Vestiges of Old Madras*, 1640–1800, by Henry Davison Love, 1913, vol. II, pp. 174–5).
   Form of an oath for Mahadew. You are first to wash your body in the Tank at Triplicane, and with a garland about your neck you are to go to the Pagoda and swear that Sunca Rama obliged you to pay him Pagodas 446....In Confirmation of all which you are to put out the Lamps according to Custom.' 4 May 1724 (*Ibid.* vol. II, pp. 233–4).
3 They were first abolished by section 1 of Act V of 1840, which prohibited the use of the Koran and Ganges water and enacted that all Hindus and Mahomedans must affirm. Mahmood J., the learned Muslim judge, thought that the Act went too far. *R.* v. *Maru* (1888) I.L.R. 10 All 207.
4 Stephen, *Digest*, 12th ed. 1936, art. 116, p. 142.

PARTICULAR PROVISIONS

More than half a century has now elapsed since Sir Whitley Stokes[1] detailed the principal differences between the Act and the English law. No attempt to do this again will be made here, but some of the most interesting features of the Act were new and were intended to provide more conveniently for Indian conditions.

Section 157 (in principle suggested by Lord Romilly's Commission) permits of proof, in corroboration of the testimony of a witness, of a former statement made by him if made at or about the time when the fact spoken of took place, or before any legal authority competent to investigate the fact. This often strikes the English practitioner as an unfortunate novelty but it is expressly permitted by Gilbert in his *Law of Evidence*.[2]

'Though hearsay be not allowed as direct evidence yet it may be in corroboration of a witness's testimony to show that he affirmed the same thing before on other occasions, and that the witness is still consistent with himself.'

In his book on *Nuncomar and Impey*,[3] Stephen in 1885 noticed that such evidence was given in confirmation of the witness Commaul o' Dien[4] and was not objected to.

It had been doubted by the Judicial Committee in 1871[5] whether the judgments of Indian courts other than High Courts could have the effect of determining the legitimacy of a party as against all the world, but Sir Barnes Peacock in *Kanhya Lal v. Radha Charan*[6] had recognized that certain types of judgment though not technically *in rem* were for some purposes admissible against third parties, e.g. judgments of divorce. The first report of the Select Committee stated that 'for the sake of simplicity, and in order to avoid the difficulty of defining or enumerating judgments *in rem* we have adopted the statement of the law of Sir Barnes Peacock in that case'. This accounts for the terms of section 41. In a recent case, owing to somewhat pronounced variations in the current of authority as to adoptions in Bombay, it became important to notice that a decision upon the validity of an adoption was not a judgment *in rem*.[7]

---

1 *Anglo-Indian Codes*, 1888, vol. II, p. 827.
2 3rd ed. 1769, p. 153; 6th ed. 1801, pp. 135-6.
3 Vol. I, p. 116.
4 Kamaluddin.
5 11 Ben. 247, *Jogendro* v. *Funindro*.
6 1867, 7 W.R. 338.
7 *Appa Trimbak* v. *Waman Govind* (1941) 69 I.A. 64.

A proposal made by Lord Romilly's Commission is given effect by section 122, which not only prevents husband or wife being compelled even after the marriage has ended to disclose a communication made to him or her during marriage by the other, but says that neither is to be *permitted* to disclose such a communication without the consent of the other except in certain cases—that is in litigation between themselves. This latter form of privilege appears to extend considerably the English rule (Evidence Amendment Act 1853, and Criminal Evidence Act 1898) and it is capable of creating problems which English law has not presented. On a joint trial of man and wife it might be important to the wife's defence that she should give in evidence some communication made to her by her husband and it might not be to the husband's interest to consent.

By the law of India certain transactions, e.g. a lease for more than a year, can be entered into only by means of a registered document and certain classes of documents are required to be registered, but there are no rules of evidence requiring particular facts to be proved by more than one witness or by the oath of a particular person, and no rules on the lines of the English Statute of Frauds. But there are two matters which are placed by the Act in the ambiguous position of being evidence but not in the full sense.[1] The first is that by section 34 entries in books of account regularly kept in the course of business are made relevant but 'shall not alone be sufficient evidence to charge any person with liability': thus there must be other evidence of the debt sued for besides the plaintiff's books. The second is that by section 30, where more persons than one are being tried jointly for the same offence, the court 'may take into consideration' as against one of them a confession proved to have been made by another. In England the judge would direct the jury that the confession was not evidence at all against anyone other than the person who made it, and that as against co-accused it must be put out of sight. Illustration (*a*) to section 30 says on the contrary: 'The Court may consider the effect of this confession as against *B*', but the section does not in terms give such a confession the status of evidence against *B* and it could not by itself ground a conviction.

The Act by section 54 provides that in criminal proceedings

---

1 Section 165 may be considered to provide a third—'indicative evidence'. See *post.*

the fact that the accused has been previously convicted of any offence is relevant. The fact that he has a bad character is irrelevant unless evidence has been given that he has a good character. There is nothing in the Act to suggest that evidence of previous convictions is to be admitted only for purposes of sentence. Courts disagreeing with the policy of the Act on this point have at times distorted it. The Select Committee in its first report (1 July 1871) were at pains to make the matter clear: 'we include under the word "character" both reputation and disposition, and we permit evidence to be given of previous convictions against a prisoner for the purpose of prejudicing him. We do not see why he should not be prejudiced by such evidence if it is true.' There seems here to be some ambiguity in the notion of 'prejudice', but the question of policy need not now be argued. Whitley Stokes was strongly against this provision.[1]

The Act takes a strong line for the protection of accused persons in the sections which make confessions irrelevant if they are induced by threat or promise proceeding from a person in authority, or are made to a police officer, or made by a person in custody of a police officer and not in the immediate presence of a magistrate (sections 24–6). By section 27, if a fact is discovered in consequence of information received from a person accused while in custody of a police officer, so much of the information as relates distinctly to the fact thereby discovered may be proved whether it amounts to a confession or not. Before the Parliamentary committees which took evidence just before the Charter Act of 1853 was passed, there was much evidence to show that the police had not seldom obtained confessions by torture or violence; and Lord Romilly's Commission, which was appointed under that Act, proposed to forbid the police to record in writing any statement made by them. This, however, was not thought to be sufficient and in the Criminal Procedure Code of 1861 the sections now numbered 25–7 of the Evidence Act first found place as sections 148–50. These provisions have now to be read with section 162 of the Criminal Procedure Code as amended in 1923, which prohibits any statement made to a police officer in the course of any investigation into an offence from being used for any purpose at any inquiry or trial in respect of any offence under investigation at the time. The question

1 *Anglo-Indian Codes*, vol. II, p. 830.

whether the provision of section 27 can in any case have effect in view of section 162 has been settled in the affirmative by a recent Act (XV of 1941).

The concluding sections of the Act are of great importance. By section 165 the Judge 'may in order to discover or to obtain proper proof of relevant facts, ask any question he pleases, in any form, at any time, of any witness, or of the parties, about any fact relevant or irrelevant' and the parties can only cross-examine upon the answers so obtained if he gives them leave, but the judgment must be based upon facts which are relevant and duly proved. This power is given to the Judge in order that he may secure what has been called 'indicative' evidence. Under the Procedure Codes the Judge is given power to call a witness not called by any party and to examine him as a court witness, but such a witness may be cross-examined as of right by any party. The effect of section 165 was described by Stephen as being 'that in order to get at the bottom of the matter before it the Court will be able to look at and inquire into every fact whatever'. The Act parts company with the view that the Judge is only to receive and adjudicate upon the evidence submitted to him by the parties.

The last section is 167, which re-enacts what was formerly provided by section 57 of Act II of 1855. 'The improper admission or rejection of evidence in India, has no effect at all unless the Court thinks that the evidence improperly dealt with either turned or ought to have turned the scale'—so Stephen put the effect of this section which has a central function in the Act. Because of this provision Stephen's clauses about relevancy could, he thought,[1] without inconvenience be framed in popular form and so as to overlap without having to take account of nice distinctions. He said in Council:[2]

'The fact that the opposite is the rule in England is the great cause of the enormous intricacy and technicality of the English law upon this point. If in the Tichborne case, one single question has been permitted after being objected to, and if the Court had afterwards been of opinion that it had been wrongly permitted, then however trifling the matter might have been, the party whose objection had been wrongly over-ruled would have been by law entitled to a new trial and the whole enormous expense of the first trial would have been thrown away. This never was the law in India nor will it be so now.'

1 Introduction, p. 55.   2 12 March 1872.

CHAPTER IX

CODIFICATION OR DEVELOPMENT

I

THE fifty-third section of the Charter Act of 1833 (3 & 4 W. IV, Ch. 85) was the legislative mainspring of law reform in India so far as regards policy, though principles and ideas were still to seek. It is a prolix section whose cumbrous expressions and vain repetitions seem almost to forbid quotation.[1] The repeated references which it makes to laws and usages peculiar to the Indian peoples are not there because such matters were to be outside the Commission's scope, but because they would be special centres of resistance to the principle of uniformity and to projects of amendment. They are among the things into which the Commission 'shall fully enquire' and 'from time to time suggest such alterations as may in their opinion be beneficially made... due regard being had to the distinction of castes, differences of religion, and the manners and opinions prevailing among different races in different parts of the said territories'. But the main purpose of the Commission was to provide, so far as possible, a common law—'that such laws as may be applicable in common to all classes of the inhabitants of the said territories, due regard being had to the rights, feelings and peculiar usages of the people, should be enacted'. Outside the Presidency towns

---

1 53. 'And whereas it is expedient...that such laws as may be applicable in common to all classes of the inhabitants of the said territories due regard being had to the rights feelings and peculiar usages of the people should be enacted and that all laws and customs having the force of law within the same territories should be ascertained and consolidated and as occasion may require amended. Be it therefore enacted....

'and the said Commission shall fully inquire into the jurisdiction powers and rules of the existing courts of justice and police establishments in the said territories and all existing forms of judicial procedure and into the nature and operation of all laws whether civil or criminal written or customary prevailing and in force in any part of the said territories and whereto any inhabitants of the said territories whether Europeans or others are now subject

'and the said Commission shall from time to time make reports in which they shall fully set forth the result of their said enquiries and shall from time to time suggest such alterations as may in their opinion be beneficially made in the said courts of justice and police establishments forms of judicial procedure and laws due regard being had to the distinction of castes difference of religion and the manners and opinions prevailing among different races and in different parts of the said territories.'

there was need for a general law applicable *prima facie* to every-one in British India by reason of the territorial jurisdiction of the government established therein, though in certain respects particular classes of persons might be exempted from its rules and governed by rules more appropriate to them.

The provisions of section 53 take on a very plain meaning from Macaulay's speech of 10 July 1833, upon the second reading of the bill which became the Charter Act. His speech betrays the limited character of his acquaintance with the Hindu and Mahomedan laws—the 'native laws'—if we may acquiesce in a phrase used by old-fashioned writers but which is far from happy and seems to ignore the fact that Arabia and not India was the birthplace of Islam. But the superficiality of his remarks was perhaps inescapable from the newness and the difficulty of the subject and the limited character of the knowledge then available to Englishmen in general.

He explained to the House of Commons that the only Mahomedan book in the nature of a code is the Koran, the only Hindu book, the Institutes—meaning the Manu of Sir William Jones's translation. Everybody who knows these books, he says, knows that they provide for a very small part of the cases which must arise in every community: all beyond them is comment and tradition. Our Regulations in civil matters do not define rights; they merely establish remedies. If a point of Hindu law arises the judge calls on the pundit for an opinion: if a point of Mahomedan law, he applies to the *kazi*. That the integrity of these functionaries is doubtful he proves by citation of the well-known passage from Sir William Jones's letter to Lord Cornwallis (19 March 1788) and the remarks of Sir Thomas Strange in his textbook on the Hindu law. Sir Francis Macnaghten is also cited for the warning—'that the first lesson to be impressed on a functionary who has to administer Hindu law is that it is vain to think of extracting certainty from the books of the jurists'. The consequence is that in practice the decisions of the tribunals are altogether arbitrary. What is administered is not law but a kind of rude and capricious equity. It is time, he exclaims, that the magistrate should know what law he is to administer, that the subject should know under what law he is to live. 'We do not mean that all the people of India should live under the same law: far from it. We know how desirable that object is but we also know that it is unattainable....But whether we assimilate those systems or not, let us ascertain them, let us digest them.... Our principle is simply this—uniformity where you can have it —diversity where you must have it—but in all cases certainty.'

Such is the outlook and the standpoint of the Charter Act and its authors.[1] That the Hindu and Mahomedan laws were so vague and uncertain that they needed to be codified seems to-day a statement of two doubtful premises and of a conclusion which does not necessarily follow. In 1833 it was doubtless a very natural opinion—perhaps no more than Warren Hastings himself had implied in admitting the need for 'a well digested code of laws compiled agreeably to the laws and tenets of the Mahomedans and Gentoos'. But Macaulay was at pains to disclose a poor opinion of Hindu and Mahomedan law alike. In maintaining that all the law needed to be modified—Hindu law, Mahomedan law and all the other kinds of law—he was a good Benthamite, following though at a distance a master who found all laws to be utterly defective when tried by the standard of utility or the greatest good of the greatest number. He had no particular tenderness for the law of England and none at all for the primitive usages or subtle distinctions of an Oriental system. For a great historian he was singularly little under a temptation to 'throw off the censor and put on the antiquarian' when dealing with them. This for the purposes of law reform in 1833 was no disqualification of itself. On the contrary it was an attribute of mind which the new despotic legislature in India must needs adopt if it was to produce any results commensurate with its opportunities or with the needs of the country.

The process to which the 53rd section looked forward had three phases—ascertainment, consolidation and amendment. If the first of the three aims was sincerely and efficiently pursued the extent to which the other two might profitably be carried out might become apparent; but the prospects might be different in the case of Hindu law and in the case of Mahomedan or any other law. If from the first the intention was to make a code,

---

[1] James Mill was a devoted disciple of Bentham. He was examiner of Indian correspondence when Macaulay was sent out with instructions to draw up a code or codes for British India; and it is to the pen of James Mill that is attributed by tradition the despatch in which those instructions were emphasized and developed. Ilbert, *Legislative Methods and Forms*, 1901, p. 126. The despatch (No. 44, dated 10 December 1834) is printed in Ilbert's *Government of India*, ch. VIII, p. 492 (1898). See p. 493.

which should in practice supersede the *shasters* or the *shariat* though claiming to have their authority and to be their embodiment, a very moderate exploration of the unwieldy material about to be superseded would be all that it was likely to get from practical reformers. Again if the new legislature with authority over the whole of British India and over all persons within that country was to take seriously the task of providing a common law, it would be unduly cumbrous as a method to codify the Hindu or the Mahomedan law as a whole without first deciding upon what subject-matters either or both of them should give way to a common law. On certain matters no interest could be greater for a Hindu or a Mahomedan than to be given the benefit of his own law—'the private laws which they severally hold sacred', as Sir William Jones had put it in his letter to Lord Cornwallis in 1788—but the time had come when on other matters to have a uniform or common law was in the interest of all. How were these subject-matters to be selected?

CODIFICATION OMITS INDIAN TOPICS

Looking back over a hundred years to the provisions of the Act of 1833 as a project to apply the principles of Bentham to the heterogeneous laws of India, we see that so far what can rightly be claimed for Bentham is that he provided the method and the direction necessary for giving principles of the English law to the peoples of India.

'Here at least Bentham's teaching has borne fruit. Had Bentham done nothing more than point out the way in which the law of England could best be applied to the needs of India, he would have rendered a distinguished service to his country and to mankind.... Should the English Empire in India prove durable, the Indian codes will do much to transform Indian civilisation. Even should that Empire pass away these codes will remain the first successful essays towards the recasting of English law.'[1]

This has had effect to enable the laws of England to provide for India a common law superseding the Hindu and Mahomedan laws, e.g. in the sphere of contract. But as a project for the codification of these Indian laws we have to observe with interest but without regret that the Act of 1833 came to nothing.[2]

[1] F. C. Montague, *Introduction to Bentham's Fragment on Government*, pp. 56, 57 (1891).
[2] 'Bentham', wrote J. S. Mill in 1838, 'demonstrated the necessity and practicability of codification, or the conversion of all law into a written and systematically arranged code.' 'In truth, he demonstrated neither the one nor the

Indeed, of the Indian statutory Code of substantive law—impressive as it has now become—the observation made by Mr Justice Field in 1883 still holds good in essentials: that 'there is nothing Indian or Oriental about it' and that its topics are 'all in the table of contents to Smith's and Kent's books'.

'The experienced Indian Civil Servant finds in it nothing about those subjects with which he is practically conversant—Zemindars and Ryots—Revenue Board and Commissioners—Collectors and Deputies—Settled and Waste Lands—Mal and Lakhiraj—Khas and Malguzari—Revenue and Rent—Pottahs and Kabulyats—Talookdars and Putnidars—Tenures and Undertenures—Mukarrari and Istemrari—Khudkhast and Paikasht—Howlas and Karshas—Lumberdars and Pattidars—Polliems and Kanoms—Nankar and Shankalap—Jagirs and Chakran—Khamar and Nijabad—Bastoo and Ooahbastoo—Ejaras and Gatwals—Jangalboori and Abadkari—Malikana and Mahtoot—Abwabs and Enhancement—Ladavi and Lawaris—Koolachar and Desachar—Kanungoes and Patwaris—Record of Rights—Rights of Occupancy—Permanent and Temporary Settlements—Julkars and Phulkars—Sebaits and Mutawallis—Kazis and Kartas.'[1]

This list is rather a *tour de force* and if it be intended as a complaint, certain matters must be omitted as being provincial in character and in some case covered, in part at least, by provincial enactment. But it may rightly serve to show that a great number of important matters peculiar to India are untouched by the Indian Codes—matters not of Hindu or Mahomedan law only, but also many which are characteristic of the land laws.

PANDITS

It is necessary to arrive at a clearer and fairer notion of the pandits than Macaulay had attained. The pandits and maulavis who began to act as 'law officers' in 1772 continued as an official class till their office was abolished by Act XI of 1864, by which time they had outlived much, if not all, of their usefulness. The Mahomedan law officers for many years played a great part under the British administration in the criminal courts

other.... We no longer believe either in the practicability or the desirability of a code which shall be complete and self-sufficing, which shall absolve from the necessity of researches into the case law or statute law of the past, which shall preclude the judicial development of law in the future, and which shall provide a simple rule applicable to every case with which the practical man may have to deal.' Ilbert, *Legislative Methods and Forms*, 1901, p. 125.

1 *Some Observations on Codification in India*, 1883, by C. D. Field, Judge of the High Court at Calcutta, 1880–6. Author of *Regulations of the Bengal Code*, 1875.

where Mahomedan law was enforced. Their *futwas* (opinions) were the pivot of the system which was set up by Bengal Regulation IX of 1793—a part of the 'Cornwallis Code'. Amended from time to time by Regulations, the Mahomedan criminal law came to turn less upon the *futwa* of the *mufti* or *kazi* associated with the British court and more upon the judge and the courts of appeal. The object of many legislative changes was to bye-pass the 'law officer' and his *futwa* in order to elide provisions of the Mahomedan law which were regarded as unsuited to the times and to the country. These law officers played a great part in their country's history and were on the whole conscientious expositors of the law in which they were skilled and stout defenders of its principles in practice.[1] But in the case of Hindu law officers we may confine ourselves to the civil law, as they played little part in the administration of criminal law, except indeed in the Bombay Province. As regards the Hindu civil law, the judges both of the Sudder and the Supreme Courts had long before 1864 become, so to say, masters in their own house, having been enabled by English textbooks and translations to check and criticize the conclusions of the pandits and to apply Hindu principles to the facts which came before them. Not without reason, they had been sensitive and uneasy so long as they felt themselves to be wholly in the pandit's hands as regards the Hindu law. Jones, in his letter to Cornwallis of 19 March 1788, had given reasons (repeated afterwards by W. H. Macnaghten in the Preliminary Remarks to his book on Hindu law (1829)) for thinking that it was not difficult for them to mislead the judges: and had declared in language long remembered: 'I could not with an easy conscience concur in a decision merely on the written opinion of native lawyers in any cause in which they would have the remotest interest in misleading the Court.' Sir Francis Macnaghten in his sententious and biting Preface said, 'Native lawyers may not be deserving of the blame which is imputed to them, but there are instances of their partiality and tergiversation which cannot be palliated or denied; nothing but

1 Cf. Abdur Rahim, *Muhammadan Jurisprudence*, 1911, pp. 37–8: 'But whatever may have been the merits of the condemned system, it should in fairness be admitted that the futwas of the Maulavis so far as they can be found in the pages of the old law reports are a faithful exposition of the Mohammadan law on the points covered by them.' A very good *futwa* by the chief *kazi* at Benares declaring the Mahomedan law in a case of murder by strangling is given in his *Observations on Malabar* (1793) by Jonathan Duncan (section 46).

an ascertainment of the law can prove a corrective of this evil.'[1]
W. H. Macnaghten's view was 'that the Hindu law in its pure
and original state does not furnish many instances of uncertainty
or confusion. The speculations of commentators have done much
to unsettle it and the venality of the Pundits has done more.'
'To the Pundits is chiefly attributable the perplexity of the
system which it is their province to expound.'[2] Strange, in his
milder manner, had in 1825 followed Jones, observing of the
opinions which he was publishing in his second volume that

'considering the infancy of the judicial establishment provided for
the dependencies of the Madras Government, at the time when the
collection was made, the authority of many cannot be looked upon
as very great. The most competent (it may be presumed) were
appointed. But in that part of India and at the time in question,
little if any encouragement having been begun to be given to the
cultivation of learning among natives, the field for selection could
not be ample. Allowance is also to be made for the possibility of
corruption in particular instances.'[3]

These were the strictures which Macaulay repeated in his speech
on the Charter Act of 1833. Considering the newness of their
judicial office, the smallness of their pay, the get-rich-quick
atmosphere which the British adventurer had introduced into
India, the character of the questions which arose, the ignorance
of the British judges and the difficulties of detection, it can hardly
be supposed that the suspicion of venality and prejudice was
without some foundation.[4]

> pudet haec opprobria nobis
> et dici potuisse et non potuisse refelli.[5]

It may be doubted, however, if the best and fairest of the critics
of the pandits—people like Jones or Strange—appreciated fully
their position and their difficulties. The subject of civil law and
justice—*vyavahara*—plays no more than a part, and a minor
part, in the total area of the Hindu scriptures. The customs and
practice followed in any part of India may not be accurately

---

1 *Considerations on the Hindoo Law*, 1824, Preface, p. xi.
2 *Hindu Law*, 1829, Preface, pp. iii, iv.
3 *Elements of Hindu Law*, 1825, Preface, p. xxi.
4 But it still comes as a shock to find a learned Bengali authority (Golapchandra
 Sarkar) in his Tagore Lectures of 1888 on *Adoption* (p. 124) and in his book on
 Hindu Law (7th ed. pp. 196–8) seriously entertaining the suggestion that the
 Dattaka Chandrika was a forgery (c. 1800) by Colebrooke's pandit—a learned
 Brahmin presumably of the same social class and attainments as the 'law officers'.
5 Ovid, *Metamorphoses*, 1, 758.

represented by any particular text and it will be impossible to find a text for everything. Mandlik's account of the pandits' work shows how even a knowledge of Hindu texts might work towards an unjust disparagement of their opinions.

'Up to the year 1863, when the Sastris were attached to our courts, they used to consult all current works and usages: and yet they would often naturally quote those which were either printed or lithographed, especially those under the orders of Government. Works like the Mitakshara, the Mayukha, the Vira-mitrodaya, the Bhagavata, Manu-Smriti and the Dharma Sindhu and the Nirnayasindhu and such like were more often brought into requisition than others, but the currents of popular usage were as a rule kept up by a staff of men who were displaced in the establishment of the High Courts on grounds which do not appear to me to be sound and sufficient. To say that the Mitakshara or any other similar Treatise is decisive of Hindu law is in my opinion completely to ignore the history and growth of the Hindu law itself.'[1]

The pandit was a religious teacher, a moralist or casuist rather than a lawyer, and as Strange pointedly observed he was given no training for his official duties. There was no organization or supervision of their work throughout the many different courts. Sutherland, in his translation of the *Dattaka Mimansa* and *Dattaka Chandrika* published in 1821,[2] observed that 'much collision of decisions would be obviated and the accuracy of undeviating principles attained' if the opinions of the subordinate pandits on any contested question or dubious point were submitted for verification to the pandits of the Sudder Diwani. When on a difficult point opinion had been collected over a series of years from many pandits in different parts of India the result might well be confusion. The courts who had to state the question put to them for their opinion were in many cases far from diligent, perspicuous or clever in stating the facts sufficiently or the question clearly: in *Myna Boyee* v. *Ootaram* (1861) 8 M.I.A. 401, 422 the Judicial Committee can be seen making complaint upon this score.

In *Collector of Madura* v. *Mootto Ramalinga* (1868) 12 M.I.A. 397, the widow's competence in Madras to adopt a son to her husband without his express authority was affirmed by the High Court, proceeding on the strength of their own examination of the Hindu texts, and declining somewhat ostentatiously 'to attach

---

1 *Introduction to Vyavahara Mayukha*, p. lxx, 1880.
2 Preface, p. iv.

any weight to Pandits' opinion'. But the Judicial Committee (per Sir James Colvile) said,

'The evidence that the doctrine for which the respondents contend has been sanctioned by usage in the South of India consists partly of the opinions of pandits, partly of decided cases. Their Lordships cannot but think that the former have been too summarily dealt with by the Judges of the High Court. These opinions at one time enjoined to be followed, and long directed to be taken by the Courts, were official and could not be shaken without weakening the foundation of much that is now received as the Hindu law in various parts of British India. Upon such materials the earlier works of European writers on the Hindu law and the earlier decisions of our own Courts were mainly founded. The opinion of a Pundit which is found to be in conflict with the translated works of authority may reasonably be rejected; but those which are consistent with such works should be accepted as evidence that the doctrine which they embody has not become obsolete, but is still received as part of the customary law of the country.'

On this view the widow was held competent to adopt with the consent of her husband's *sapindas* or relations; but only because she was governed by a particular school of Hindu law prevailing in Southern India.

In 1873, in the case which raised the question of the liability of a Hindu widow who had succeeded to her husband's estate to forfeit her interest by reason of subsequent unchastity, pandits made an appearance before the Division Bench (Bayley and Dwarkanath Mitter JJ.), which heard the special appeal and which referred the question to a Full Bench. In making the order of reference Mitter J. stated:

'In order to arrive at a solution of this question we thought it proper to consult some learned Pundits in Court; and we accordingly summoned [4 names]. Pundit — however could not attend on account of ill-health. The three other Pundits appeared, and orally stated unanimously that the question under our consideration ought to be answered in the affirmative, each giving his separate opinion and the authority on which it rested, also orally.'[1]

As 'law officers' had been abolished in 1864, the provisions of law authorizing this procedure are not readily discernible and are not mentioned by Mitter J. In the judgment of the Judicial Committee which overruled the view taken by him and by the pundits no mention of the pandits or their reasoning was made. This seems to have been the swan song of the pandits, at least in Bengal.

1 *Moniram Kolita* v. *Kerry Kolitany* L.R. 7 I.A. 115 at 117.

In 1879, long after 'law officers' had been abolished, in *Hari Das Dabi* v. *Secretary of State* I.L.R. 5 Cal. 228 counsel had by consent put in as part of his argument a printed paper said to be the composition of one learned in the *shastras*. On this Mr Justice Louis Jackson said:

'I confess it seems to me to be among the advantages for which the people of this country have in these days to be thankful that their legal controversies, the determination of their rights and their status have passed into the domain of lawyers instead of pundits and casuists: and in my opinion the case before us may very well be decided on the authority of cases without following Sreenath, Achyatanund and others through the mazes of their speculations on the origin and theory of gift.'

This, however, seems to depreciate texts as well as pandits; and it is perhaps significant that the passage was in 1892 appropriated by Mr Justice Trevelyan to a consideration of the Mahomedan law of Wakfs in the Full Bench case of *Bikani Mian* v. *Suklal Poddar* I.L.R. 20 Cal. 116—one of the few subject-matters on which there is substantial ground for thinking that the British Indian courts failed to appreciate the Oriental law.

INDIAN LAWS A NEW STUDY

Sir William Jones in his day had talked about Justinian and Tribonian and the Pandects, and had set on foot the first great scheme to clarify 'the native laws' and present them in an orderly and logical form. By 1833 the most important of the ancient texts had been translated into English either directly or through a Persian translation. Jones himself had translated the *Institutes of Manu* and two Arabic treatises on the Mahomedan law of inheritance. The *Hedaya* had been translated into English from the Persian by Charles Hamilton. The *Dayabhaga* and the *Mitakshara* had been made available by Colebrooke and W. H. Macnaghten; Sutherland in 1821 had translated the *Dattaka Mimansa* and *Dattaka Chandrika*—authoritative treatises on adoption. The Pandit Jagannatha had, by 1797, worked over large tracts of the Hindu law and his work was available in Colebrooke's translation of that year. It certainly presented many difficulties.

'The author's method of discussing together the discordant opinions maintained by the lawyers of the several schools, without distinguishing in an intelligible manner which of them is the received doctrine of each school, but on the contrary leaving it uncertain whether any of the opinions stated by him do actually prevail, or which doctrine must now be considered to be in force and which obsolete, renders his work of little utility to persons conversant with the law, and of still less service to those who are not versed in Indian jurisprudence, especially to the English readers for whose use through the medium of translation the work was particularly intended.'[1]

Francis Macnaghten followed with severer criticism:

'The plan of Sir William Jones may have been excellent but the execution of it fell to the share of Jagannatha. He has given us the contents of all books indiscriminately. That he should have reconciled contradictions or made anomalies consistent, was not to be expected: but we are often the worse for his sophistry, and seldom the better for his reasoning. His incessant attempts to display proficiency in logic and promptitude in subtilty, he might have spared without the regret of his readers' (p. viii).

'Of Jagannatha's *digest* it is enough in this place to say that the labourer might have given a more appropriate appellation to his work' (p. xvi).

It is fair to note, however, that much of the defect pointed to in these criticisms was probably due to the scheme of the work as designed by Jones which was to be 'after the model of Justinian's inestimable Pandects'. As Jones did not die till 1794, more than five years after his plan had been approved and accepted by Cornwallis in 1788, it is difficult to think that the general method of the *Digest* was not his. Mr Justice Dwarkanath Mitter thought Jagannatha's authority to be higher in respect of the Bengal school than any writer living or dead save Jimutavahana, Raghunandana and the author of the *Daya-krama-sangraha*; higher even than that of Henry Colebrooke himself. But it may be doubted whether he had Colebrooke's mastery or grasp of what he knew, and on the point then before Mitter J. Colebrooke's view prevailed.[2]

It was all very well for Macaulay to repeat in 1833 the strictures of Jones and the Macnaghtens on the pandits and maulavis upon whom the courts were dependent for the rules of law which they applied. But, as we have seen, English text-books on the Hindu law had only begun to appear some ten years before. Sir Francis Macnaghten's *Considerations* was the first in 1824: it related only to Bengal; its Preface spoke in the

1 Colebrooke, *Two Treatises*, 1810.
2 *Kerri Kolitany* v. *Moneeram* (1873) 13 B.L.R. 50: 19 W.R. 394.

most disparaging terms of Hindu law—'unjust depreciation' as Morley rightly says.[1]

Sir Thomas Strange's book on Hindu law published in 1825, and Sir W. H. Macnaghten's books on the Mahomedan and Hindu laws (1825 and 1829 respectively) were admirable works of the greatest practical utility, real guides to the courts and to the profession, of a class greatly superior to Halhed's *Gentoo Code* or Hamilton's *Hedaya*, the former of which had contained little about Contract and the latter had omitted the topic of Inheritance. Strange's book has been praised by all authorities: it is open-minded, balanced, well informed—dealing reasonably alike with the proper statement of accepted principles and with points of doubt or difficulty. Of Macnaghten's books that on Mahomedan law was perhaps the better of the two. It 'remained for at least half a century the standard textbook for English readers'.[2] Of the book on Hindu law a large portion is occupied by a translation of those parts of the *Mitakshara* which are not concerned with Inheritance: the book was accepted as a high authority. These books of Strange and Macnaghten were the earliest attempts to make systematic use of the answers of the 'law officers' and the decisions of the courts thereon. Macnaghten, in the preface to his work on Hindu law, claimed to have examined all the opinions delivered in Bengal courts from 1811 to 1829, and to have found nine-tenths of them to be 'erroneous, doubtful, unsupported by proof or otherwise unfit for publication'. In 1829 he published a series of reports of the decisions of the Sudder Court dating back to 1791—decisions based on the opinions of the 'law officers'.[3] More than half a century later a learned Tagore Lecturer, Dr Jolly, thought it necessary to remind his readers that—

'the task of understanding a whole fabric of ancient law such as the Sanskrit Law of India, cannot be accomplished in a day, and much more patient absorption in the habit of mind and expression of the Sanskrit lawyers, and a careful investigation of all their compositions will be required before a full insight into the nature and history of Sanskrit Law can be obtained.'[4]

---

1 *Digest*, vol. i, p. ccxxiv.   2 Wilson, *Anglo-Mahomedan Law*, 6th ed. p. 42.
3 By Act XII of 1843 the decisions of the Sudder Courts at Calcutta and Agra were ordered to be published monthly.
4 *History of the Hindu Law*, 1885; Tagore Lectures, 1883, p. 29.

MODERN PRACTICE

The new textbooks were all the more welcome that they were a dawning light upon the principles of the Hindu law; but as a systematic effort the practical study of the Hindu and Mahomedan laws was only beginning in 1833; and on the threshold of the study a new feature was becoming clear:—that the ancient texts—remote, venerable and even sacred—were not the last word for modern practice. The time was past when it could be assumed with confidence in Madras or in Bombay that because a man was a Hindu his family arrangements were those of the *Mitakshara* or that all Mahomedans would be Sunnis who followed the Hanafi law as laid down in the *Fatawa Alamgiri*. Elphinstone, when in 1819 he became Governor of Bombay, had emphasized the discrepancy between modern practice and the ancient texts, and had appointed a committee not only to reduce to system the Regulations which the Bombay Council had passed but to investigate thoroughly the legal customs and usages of the people. He was mostly concerned with Hindu law, but had aimed at a complete code—written and unwritten law together. In an admirable Minute of 22 July 1823 he had proposed as the first step 'to ascertain in each district whether there is any book of acknowledged authority either for the whole or any branch of the law'; and as the second step 'to ascertain what exceptions there are to the written authorities and what customs and conditions exist independent of them'. Writing in 1892, Mr J. S. Cotton, in his book on Elphinstone in the 'Rulers of India' series, said that his project 'still remains unaccomplished, being as far in advance of our time as it was of his'. I venture to think it wrong to identify the views of Elphinstone upon native laws, or even the terms of section 26 of Bombay Regulation IV of 1827, with the system which in 1872 was applied to the Punjab.[1] Certainly it would be untrue to suggest that *deshachar* (local custom) plays the same part in both provinces. But Elphinstone did insist with effect that the law actually obtaining among Hindus was not to be neglected for a study of the ancient texts. He set on foot investigations which disclosed the modern usages. The results did not appear till he was about to retire from India (1827), when Arthur Steele's *Summary of the Law and Customs of Hindoo Castes within the Dekhan* was added to Harry

[1] As is done by Professor van Vollenhoven, *Asiatic Review*, 1927, vol. XXIII, p. 117, etc.

Borradaile's *Reports* and translation of the *Vyavahara Mayukha*. Steele's inquiry appears to have been limited to the Poona and Sattara localities, and though it showed that most of the castes purported to follow 'ancient usage' and that custom had sanctioned many things in opposition to the *Sastra*, nevertheless in the result 'a general uniformity is observable with the leading principles of the Hindu system'. The chief points on which law and custom were observed to be at variance were thus stated:

1. The great variety of castes and sects.

2. The custom of a second and inferior marriage allowed to wives and widows in many castes.

3. The small or irregular punishments in some cases enforced by caste assemblies.

4. The disregard to legal restrictions as to caste, in trading and taking interest; besides an infinity of local usages which have become established, unwarranted by *Sastra* if not opposed to its rules.

THE LAW COMMISSIONERS' REPORT, 1855

When in 1853 the time came for a new Charter Act the labours of the Law Commission and the projects outlined in section 53 were unrepresented by results in the statute book of the Indian legislature at whose inauguration in 1833 they had played so prominent a part. The Commission had done brilliant work in drafting a penal code and much detailed, valuable but unpublished work on chapters of the civil law; but the times were not propitious for law reform and the Law Commission was withering and losing influence for lack of success. Accordingly the Charter Act of 1853 set up a new and different Commission with a distinguished English judge at its head and members of English and of Indian experience. They were required to do their work in England and to make their report within three years. This change of method proceeded upon or at least involved two principles—first, that knowledge of Indian conditions was not of itself a sufficient qualification for judging a code of law for India; second, that the Indian legislature could properly be required by the Home authorities to enact what the latter should decide.[1] But apart from any question of principle,

---

[1] On these points difficulties arose and came to a head in 1870 with the resignation of the Commission which had prepared a draft Contract Act in London. A minute written by John Stuart Mill gives an explicit statement of the implications of the course adopted by Parliament in 1853 (cf. *Parl. Papers*, 1876, vol. LVI, p. 17). See page 68 *supra*.

important results attended the transfer to England of the centre of activity in matters of Indian law reform. While the first Commission, under the presidency of Macaulay's successor Andrew Amos, in its report of 31 October 1840 (the *Lex Loci* Report) is to be found looking forward to the making of three Codes—one for the Hindu, one for the Mahomedan and one for the English law—the second report of the new Commission dated 13 December 1855 recommended that 'no portion either of the Mahomedan or of the Hindu Law ought to be enacted as such in any form by a British Legislature'. The decision to leave these laws alone lightened enormously the task of law reform at a time when the Home authorities were taking charge of the movement; and after 1857 the task assumed a new urgency. 'Then came the Mutiny,' says Stephen, 'which in its essence was the breakdown of an old system; the renunciation of an attempt to effect an impossible compromise between the Asiatic and the European view of things, legal, military and administrative. The effect of the Mutiny on the Statute Book was unmistakable.'[1] On two classes of subjects the British in India could hardly be expected to succeed in applying legal principles not fundamentally their own—procedure and the criminal law. Legislation on these subjects came off the stocks in some volume —the Code of Civil Procedure and the Limitation Act of 1859, the Penal Code of 1860, the Criminal Procedure Code and the High Courts Act of 1861. The Succession Act of 1865 was the first of the codes of substantive law—the second was the Contract Act of 1872. But to this day, as we have already noticed, the Hindu and the Mahomedan laws have been left uncodified. They have been by no means left untouched; indeed, a learned Hindu textbook tells us that 'there is scarcely any principle of the orthodox law that has not been eaten into either completely or partially by the Legislature or by the Codes'.[2] This, however, is a little strong, and we can think of no single subject of these laws which has been codified, save indeed for the Mahomedan subject of Pre-emption which in the United Provinces and the Punjab has been made statute law.

That in the state of knowledge possible in 1833 codification was about the worst service that could have been done to the Hindu or to the Mahomedan law, their development during the century which has followed has sufficiently shown; and that the

1 Trevelyan's *Life of Macaulay*, vol. I, p. 417.
2 Gour's *Hindu Code*, 4th ed. p. 42.

preparation of complete codes of these laws would have over-weighted the scheme of 1855 and imposed a burden which could not have been sustained by an English commission operating in London is an obvious practical consideration which justifies the decision taken in that year. But it is time to regard the Hindu and the Mahomedan laws as presenting quite distinct and different problems in respect of codification; as in many other matters error is almost inescapable if we bracket them together. Let us concentrate then for the present on the Hindu law, not attempting for the moment to describe in detail its development at the hands of British Indian courts, but intent to see whether development by the process of judicial decision has been misguided.

II

SANSKRIT LEARNING IN THE SEVENTIES

In the seventies of the last century Sanskrit studies were making progress and the researches of Goldstücker, Bühler, Burnell, Jolly, Mandlik, Sarvadhikari and others entailed considerable heart-searching as to the methods and conclusions of the courts. Dr Burnell, in publishing the *Dayadasasloki* (Mangalore, 1875), gave an account of the study of Hindu law which was certainly depressing.

'There have been three periods in the study of Hindu law by foreigners: *First*, that of enquiry from the middle of the seventeenth century to 1820. The earlier works by Baldaeus, Halhed and others are forgotten, and Sir William Jones is only remembered by his having drawn attention to the subject. Colebrooke and his followers are the only ones who rendered real service to the science. The second period began when Colebrooke had left India and lasted till recently. In it, English lawyers, without any preparation for the task, attempted to systematise the materials they could find (whether good or bad, they did not seem to care); these they interpreted by European notions and introduced incongruous ideas whenever they could. All that did not square with the preconceived notions of these "elegant" jurists was denounced as imposture and corrupt forgery, and this period is marked by a vigorous but entirely unfounded denunciation of the Pandits. The third and last period has only commenced quite lately, and was promoted by the late Professor Goldstücker. It is marked by critical new editions of the old standard translations by Colebrooke and others, and by critical editions of texts and an enquiry into the sources and growth of Hindu Law. The progress of this new school is slow but sure, and for the sake of the people of the country it is to be earnestly desired that the false science of what

I have termed the "second period" may soon become a matter of history.'

The strictures passed upon the period after 1820 may be meant to apply to the English writers of textbooks, Strange and the Macnaghtens, or as a general characterization of the decisions of the courts. In either case they need hardly be seriously taken. It has long been accepted on all hands that, as Sir Robert Phillimore put it in 1870 when delivering the judgment of the Judicial Committee:

'The Hindu law contains in itself the principles of its own exposition. The Digest[1] subordinates in more than one place the language of texts to custom and approved usage. Nothing from any foreign source should be introduced into it nor should Courts interpret the text by the application to the language of strained analogies.'[2]

Mayne[3], who had as full knowledge of the decisions as anyone of his time, had summed up the matter thus:

'A great deal has been said, often by no means in a flattering spirit, of the decisions upon Native Law of our Courts, whether presided over by civilian, or by professional, judges. It seems to be supposed that they imported European notions into the questions discussed before them, and that the divergencies between the law, which they administered, and that which is to be found in the Sanskrit law-books, are to be ascribed to their influence. In one or two remarkable instances no doubt this was the case; but those instances are rare. My belief is that their influence was exerted in the opposite direction, and that it rather showed itself in the pedantic maintenance of doctrines whose letter was still existing but whose spirit was dying away.'

On the whole it cannot be said that the effect of modern researches has been to alter fundamentally the methods or conclusions of the courts, though it is recognized by the Privy Council and the courts that 'the greater attention paid of late years to the study of Sanskrit has brought with it more translations of sacred Hindu books and closer examinations of texts previously translated'.[4]

NELSON'S STRICTURES

Mr J. H. Nelson, a civilian District Judge in the Madras province, in his *View of the Hindu Law* (1877) and *Prospectus of the Scientific Study of the Hindu Law* (1881) made vigorous and far-

---

1 Colebrooke's translation of *Jagannatha*.
2 *Bhyah Ram Singh v. Bhyah Ugur Singh* (1870) 13 M.I.A. 373.
3 *Hindu Law and Usage*, 6th ed. 1900, pp. 42–3.
4 *per* Lord Hobhouse in *Sri Balusu Gurulingaswami's* case (1899) L.R. 26 I.A. 113, 129.

reaching criticisms imputing some of them as faults to the High Court of Madras, though they were in fact covered by decisions of other High Courts and of the Privy Council; and jibing at the accepted Hindu law as the work of 'Sanskritists without law and lawyers without Sanskrit'. He would seem to have been disturbed at the complacency with which Mr H. J. Cunningham —then Advocate-General of Madras and later a Judge of the Calcutta High Court—had ventured upon the compilation of a *Digest of Hindu Law* (1877) in the form of 392 numbered sections —'in such a form as may indicate the possibility of enactment in a Code if at any time hereafter the Government should consider this desirable'. Mr Nelson objected to the practice by which the non-Mahomedan inhabitants of the Madras province were treated generally as Hindus. He appears to have considered that Hindu law could only be applicable to descendants of Aryan tribes or families who had at one time inhabited the Punjab: and that while this might be true of Brahmins it was improbable that they had preserved intact the laws or most of the laws by which the Aryans of the Punjab had guided themselves. He was convinced that the Tamils of the province, as a body, did not possess and never had possessed a body of positive laws. He derided the attempt to apply the very strictest Sanskrit law to rude tribes and castes—'the semi-barbarous races of the extreme South of India'; holding that 'the various tribes and castes which constitute the population of the Madras Province in fact guide themselves each in its own rude manner by customs of which many are most widely and radically different from the rules supposed to have obtained in the Punjab, and indeed for the most part wholly inconsistent and incompatible therewith'. He made much of the observation of Holloway J. in *Kattama Nachiar* v. *Dorasinga Tevar* (1868) 6 M.H.C.R. 310 about Maravans.

> 'I must be allowed to add that I feel the grotesque absurdity of applying to these Maravans the doctrine of Hindu law. It would be just as reasonable to give them the benefit of the Feudal Law of real property. At this late day it is, however, impossible to act upon one's consciousness of the absurdity. I would not, however, be supposed to be unconscious of it.'

He explains that the learned judge in saying this was under the apprehension that 'these Maravans' were a very low caste, whereas in fact they are no worse than their neighbours.

Mr Nelson quarrelled with the view which had Colebrooke's authority that the *Mitakshara* was a work of paramount authority on the law of partition and succession, suggesting that 'the conduct of an ordinary Chetti or Maravan or Reddi of the Madras Province, unless indeed he happens to come into our Courts as a litigant, is no more affected by precepts contained in the Mitakshara than it is by precepts contained in the Psalms of David'. Following Burnell he disputed the existence of schools of law in different parts of India and in particular the division of Southern India into three—the Karnataka Kingdom, the Andhra country, the Dravada country. He emphasized the provision of section 16 of the Madras Civil Courts Act 1873 giving effect to 'any custom having the force of law and governing the parties or property concerned', and he criticized the reluctance of the Madras High Court in cases not coming from the west of the province to accept customs when proved as good customs enforceable as such. His view of the duty of the Madras Government was that they ought to make adequate efforts to ascertain what are the customs and usages of the various tribes and castes subject to its will and to require the High Court to recognize them judicially. He suggested in his later work (*Scientific Study*, Chapter IX) a commission to report upon Sanskrit books that are generally supposed to contain Hindu law—in particular to report whether there is evidence that they are regarded as authorities obligatory on men's consciences.

'I have searched in vain for such evidence; I honestly believe that not a particle of it can anywhere be found. If a properly appointed commission were to report that no such evidence is forthcoming the monster called "Hindoo Law" would be quietly slain and buried without delay and Government would begin the task of collecting and arranging in a simple form the few primitive usages and customs that are common to all or most Indian castes.'

To this over-trenchant critic a detailed answer was made by Mr Justice Innes of the Madras High Court in 1882. Some of the criticisms were refuted by Sarvadhikari in his Tagore Lectures of 1880 on the *Hindu Law of Inheritance*, who observes unkindly that the original treatises of Hindu law were not accessible to Mr Nelson as he was not a Sanskritist. Others were answered by Mr J. D. Mayne in *Hindu Law and Usage*, 1st edition, 1878. The doubt thrown on the authority of the *Mitakshara* and the attempt made to deny the existence of different 'schools' of Hindu law are sufficiently refuted by Sarvadhikari (Lecture VII) and Mayne's Preface to his third edition of 1883. Indeed on the former point the testimony of competent inquirers has been consistent. Thus Steele in his *Summary* of 1827 says specifically, when giving a list of 'the books chiefly referred to in *wywustas* in the Dekhun' (Preface, p. vi), 'The Mitakshara is preferred on account of its comparative clearness and decision, and is the work most usually quoted by the *sastrees* of Poona.' To Nelson's main assumption—that Hindu law could not be applied to anyone in Southern India who was not descended from an original Aryan family which emigrated from the Punjab into Southern India—it is answered by Mayne in effect that those parts of the Sanskrit law which are of any practical importance are mainly based upon usage which in substance, though not in detail, is common both to Aryan and non-Aryan tribes; and that Nelson underestimated the influence which the Sanskrit law has exercised in moulding to its own model the somewhat similar usages even of non-Aryan races. 'This influence', he adds, 'has been exercised throughout the whole of Southern India during the present century by means of our Courts and Pandits, by vakils and officials, both judicial and revenue, almost all of whom till very lately were Brahmans.' Mayne recognizes very clearly, however, that the courts in their endeavour to 'maintain the integrity' of the Hindu law have not seldom applied the *Mitakshara* to matters upon which the general law had in the intervening centuries outgrown the old authorities. In an arresting passage which has been repeated by later writers he voices the complaint:

'But in Southern India it came to be accepted that Mitakshara was the last word that would be listened to on Hindu law. The consequence was a state of arrested progress in which no voices were heard unless they came from the tomb. It was as if a German were to administer English law from the resources of a library furnished with Fleta Glanville and Bracton and terminating with Lord Coke.'[1]

It is true, moreover, that until the Madras Civil Courts Act of 1873 made plain that customs were to be given effect, there was some confusion on this head. The Bengal Regulations of 1793 did not expressly provide for custom and the Madras Regulation III of 1802, section 16, only followed them. Indeed,

[1] *Hindu Law and Usage*, 6th ed. 1900, p. 44.

so far as regards Mahomedan law, it was not decided that the courts under the Bengal etc. Civil Courts Act (XII of 1887) were entitled to give effect to special custom in derogation of the Islamic law until 1913 when the Judicial Committee so determined reversing the Allahabad High Court.[1] It would seem from one judgment of the Madras High Court[2] and from what was said by Mr Justice Innes in his reply to Mr Nelson that before 1873 custom was not given its proper place and to some extent Mr Nelson's criticism on that score can be justified.

CUNNINGHAM'S *DIGEST*

Cunningham's *Digest* of 1877 did not claim to be a code but only to arrange the material so that the codifier of the future might find it ready to his hand. The distinction, however, was a little thin, and the Preface contained the usual arguments in favour of a code as the only way of attaining certainty. 'The moment a Judge is left without his lawful rations in the shape of express enactment he is constrained to go out foraging for supplies, and the more learned and diligent he is the further he is likely to go.' Cunningham objected that judicial legislation in Hindu law took the form of deciding not what the law *ought to be* but what it is according to the correct interpretation of primitive texts or forgotten phases of society unmodified by contemporaneous opinion. Referring to certain decisions which appeared to hold that the consent of any one *sapinda* was sufficient to authorize a Hindu widow to adopt—a view not in the end accepted by the Privy Council—he asked,

'Can anyone seriously contend that "judicial legislation" of this order is preferable to the deliberate, well-weighed, well-informed action of the Legislature, grounded solely on consideration of the public welfare, guided by the wishes and opinions of the best educated, most thoughtful and most intelligent among those whose interests are in question.'[3]

That at least is the question to be answered: though it is as well to remember that the answer has to be given by people who regard their *sastras* with a certain religious veneration. Cunningham's attempt of 1877 received little encouragement— less indeed than a first attempt deserved. Mr Nelson poked fun

---

1 *Mahammad Ismail* v. *Lale Shevmukh* (1913) 17 Cal. W.N. 97.
2 *Narasammal* v. *Bavalamacharlu* M.H.C.R. 420.
3 Preface, p. xvii.

at it as a 'codelet' not free from errors, and Mayne in his Preface observed that Mr Cunningham appeared to look upon the entire law with a mixture of wonder and pity.

'The age of miracles has passed, and I hardly expect to see a code of Hindu Law which shall satisfy the trader, the agriculturist, the Punjabi and the Bengali, the Pandits of Benares and Ramaiswaram of Umritsur and of Poona. But I can easily imagine a very beautiful and specious code, which should produce much more dissatisfaction and expense than the law as at present administered.'

CUSTOM AND LAW

After the Punjab Laws Act of 1872 had introduced into that region a system under which custom, carefully ascertained by inquiry in each locality, was made the primary rule of decision, a tendency became noticeable to regard any general system of law as inapplicable to Indian conditions. The village community of the Punjab, and the fact that the province had in different ages been the corridor through which many different types of immigrant had entered India from the North, had pushed into the background the general or religious laws of Hindus and Mahomedans. It was thought by some that these laws should have no higher place in other parts of India than they were entitled to in the Punjab. When in 1879 the scheme for providing British India with a statutory civil code was threatening to break down in mid-career, a small commission was appointed to consider the position. Its members were Sir Whitley Stokes, Sir Charles Turner and Sir Raymond West, and in their report (15 November 1879) they dealt with an objection to any attempt at scientific legislation. This took the form: 'Collect and group the existing facts of custom and practice and leave the future wholly to natural development.' They replied that,

'the answer is that essential as an exact ascertainment of the facts of the society and of their true relations is to the legislator, a sound theory is just as essential.... The contempt for theory which is felt by some men of considerable observing powers is in truth a contempt for all that makes their observations valuable.'

This is not the place to attempt an estimate of the merits of the Punjab system which has recently been modified for Muslims by the Shariat Act (XXVI of 1937); but that it is no ideal system is very plain: however difficult it might be to provide one more workable in the conditions of that Province. So far as regards the great bulk of the non-Mahomedan population of India, the endeavour to ascertain what is received as Hindu law by the people who claim to be Hindu for purposes of law has not followed the same purely empirical method. Custom at variance with the Hindu law is freely recognized when proved. But the general law as represented by such a digest as the *Mitakshara* is itself subject to modification not only by particular custom but by later commentaries which have in particular parts of India acquired a predominant influence on the usage and opinions of the people. This is well illustrated by the *Vyavahara Mayukha* of Nilkantha in Bombay; and the method outlined by Elphinstone in the minute of 22 July 1823 already cited allows fully for the authority of such a work. It was open to Nelson to say that Steele's enquiry into caste customs was fragmentary and incomplete, and to opine that a full inquiry into the customs of the castes of Southern India would show a wider discrepancy between the Hindu law and the usages of the people. Though the right to allege and prove a special custom has now long been clear under the Madras Civil Courts Act of 1873 and the practice of the courts thereunder does not seem to disclose any grievance that Hindu law is forced upon unwilling litigants who repudiate its authority in principle—nevertheless it may be that their usages represent what Mayne has called 'laxity',[1] rather than any divergence in important principle. If so it may be that in some matters the rule of the general law might be relaxed with advantage—*in favorem libertatis*. In all provinces this might well be done as regards the classes of persons who may not be taken in adoption.[2] This would be more reasonable than Nelson's suggestion of a short enabling Act which 'should recognise and proclaim the general right of the Indian to consult his own inclination in all matters of marriage, adoption, alienation, testation and the like'.[3]

While these concessions must be allowed, the main argument of Nelson is not made out. It is not established that the bulk of the people of Southern India have always been guided by customary law alone and that the Sanskrit law is applicable only to a small minority. What may fairly be said, as Dr Jolly has noticed, is that before the British rule most disputes were decided

[1] 6th ed. p. 44.
[2] Sarkar Nelson and Mandlik agree that usage among the regenerate classes is contrary to prohibitions of the law.   [3] *Scientific Study*, p. 182.

by panchayets and not by public tribunals which, as he notes, were 'excessively corruptible'; and that in consequence custom played a more prominent part than the written law. This, he agrees, was changed under British rule so far that custom in order to acquire the force of law must be proved to be continuous and ancient. But in his view there is no sufficient reason for questioning the wisdom of those who have established the principles on which the administration of law to the Hindus has been based ever since.[1]

<h1 style="text-align:center">III</h1>

The reasons given in 1855 by the Commission against codifying the Hindu or the Mahomedan law were two:

'Such legislation we think might tend to obstruct rather than to promote the gradual progress of improvement in the state of the population. It is open to another objection too which seems to us decisive. The Hindoo law and the Mahomedan law derive their authority respectively from the Hindoo and Mahomedan religion. It follows that as a British legislature cannot make Mahomedan or Hindoo religion so neither can it make Mahomedan or Hindoo law. A Code of Mahomedan law or a digest of any part of that law, if it were enacted as such by the Legislative Council of India, would not be entitled to be regarded by Mahomedans as very law itself but merely as an exposition of law, which might possibly be incorrect. We think it clear that it is not advisable to make any enactment which would stand on such a footing.'

The first reason given is, in effect, that a code would stereotype the law making development more difficult. Confining ourselves to the case of the Hindu law—the concluding part of the passage quoted refers, it will be noted, to the Mahomedan law—we must admit that there was great force one hundred years ago in the consideration that a code would stereotype the law and make development more difficult. To-day far-reaching changes as regards the rights of women to inherit, the right of widows to adopt, and many other matters, threaten to give a new aspect to important doctrines. The rights of the individual member as regards joint family property and the right to make a will are signalized by Sir Francis Oldfield[2] as two subjects upon which the Hindu law developed, not without difficulty, in the nineteenth century. Hindu law, with exceptions for par-

1 *History of Hindu Law*, 1885; Tagore Lectures, 1883, pp. 32–3.
2 *Cambridge History of India*, vol. VI, ch. XXI.

ticular customs, has been received by and is at least applied
throughout India to many different races who have become
more or less deeply imbued with Hindu principles. A code of
Hindu law giving form to the principles, which derive from
Manu, Yajnavalkya or Narada and their commentators might
tend to give a false pre-eminence to these principles, unless
indeed the exceptions and exemptions were among its most
important feature. This might exaggerate and reinforce a defect
in the British administration of justice of which, as we have seen,
complaint has been made by Mayne and others—that so much
stress is laid upon ancient authorities like the *Mitakshara*, that
the intervening law and practice are ignored. But it would not
seem to be accepted by Hindus to-day that their law should
remain uncodified much longer. The advent of representative
institutions has made possible the amendment and definition of
the Hindu law by legislation which is free from the objection
that it represents the mind of Europeans and not of Hindus.
Recently a committee of the Legislative Assembly has recommended the preparation in gradual stages of a complete code of
Hindu law beginning with the law of succession, on which
certain draft rules have already been prepared for the whole of
India.[1] This, if one may say so, points the difference between
Benthamism good and bad, between codification with knowledge and without. The second reason of the Commission—that
the law is a religious law—seems as an argument against codification to have less and less force as regards Hindus as the years
go past. Doubtless a summary attempt made in the grand
manner to express the whole of the Hindu law could still arouse
hostility which might take the form of an appeal to the Hindu
religion. But in a question of this kind everything depends on
the actual sentiments of the community concerned, and there
seems to be no reason at the present time to think that a successful
attempt to codify the Hindu law *paulatim et gradatim* by careful
choice of subjects and scrupulous regard to existing rules would
be decried on religious grounds. The wide scope permitted to
special custom absolves the Hindu law from any bigoted attach-
ment to the particular expression given to its principles by its
most venerated writers, many of whom belong to a very remote
past. It is the English judge and legislator whose idea of first
principles requires him to hark back to Manu and to force

1 Cf. *Cal. Weekly Notes*, vol. XLVI (1 December 1941).

outworn ideas on a modern, if Eastern, world. The Indian
public and the Hindus, as much as any other people, are by
now thoroughly accustomed to codes[1] and appreciative of their
practical advantages, though they might, of course, be very
critical indeed both of the method of preparation and of the
contents of a Hindu code. They might well be trusted to dis-
criminate between different subject-matters of the Hindu law,
finding by trial and error which 'titles' lend themselves best to
codification and which might best be left untouched for a time.
The work of British Indian courts since 1772 would find its
fulfilment in that way.

1 'So far as I am aware, the native public has never raised its voice against
codification. To them codified laws mean the introduction of certainty where
there is uncertainty, precision where there is vagueness. Nor can it be said that
codification is unpopular, even among the most conservative sections of my
countrymen' (Sir Sayyid Ahmad quoted in Grant Duff's *Memoir of Sir Henry
Maine*, 1892).

PART II: CRIMINAL LAW

CHAPTER X

CRIMINAL LAW BEFORE THE PENAL CODE: BENGAL, AGRA AND MADRAS

I

THE Indian Penal Code has so entirely obliterated the criminal law which preceded it that the efforts of the British to retain and improve the criminal law which they found in India have fallen out of sight. To-day one reflects with some surprise that not until 1862 did the criminal law obtaining over the greater part of British India become detached from its base in Mahomedan jurisprudence. Had it not been extensively amended to adapt it to modern and western notions of policy and behaviour, Mahomedan criminal law could not have lasted so long. Before 1833 all the main topics had been dealt with by the Regulations. In 1832 non-Muslims ceased to be subjected in Bengal to the Mahomedan criminal law and in 1827 Bombay had been given a statutory criminal code. But the Mahomedan criminal law had never been cast aside altogether till the Penal Code of 1860 and the Criminal Procedure Code of 1861 came into force. To the extent and reality of its sway throughout the first half of the nineteenth century, over all except European British subjects, abundant testimony is borne by British administrators.

Galloway,[1] in his *Observations on the Law, etc. of India*,[2] speaks of 'the Mahomedan criminal law which has long prevailed to the exclusion of the Hindoo criminal law and which has brought the Brahmin and the Bhungee within the same scale of punishments'. He is perhaps suspect as being rather a champion of Mahomedan law, holding like James Mill and others that the value of Hindu law was not great and objecting to the 'ashes' of the Hindu civil law being 'raked up'. But his account of the judicial administration of the country brings it vividly before us.

---

1 Sir Archibald Galloway, *circa* 1780–1850, Major-General, 1841; Chairman of the E.I. Company, 1849.
2 First edition anonymously published in London, 1825. Second edition London, 1832, p. 127. A reference to his long residence in the Upper Provinces, p. 196.

Sleeman,[1] well known as the expert on *thuggee* and for his picture of Oude in 1850 (before its annexation), sheds in his *Rambles and Recollections* many interesting sidelights derived from his experience on the Nerbudda. Campbell, whose *Modern India* was written with a view to the impending Charter Act of 1853, gives us a carefully drawn picture of the last stage before the Code:

'The foundation of our criminal law is still the Mahomedan code; but so altered and added to by our regulations that it is hardly to be recognised; and there has, in fact, by practice and continual emendative enactments, grown up a system of our own, well understood by those whose profession it is, and towards which the original Mahomedan law and Mahomedan lawyers are really little consulted. Still the hidden substructure on which the whole building rests is this Mahomedan law, take which away and we should have no definition of or authority for punishing many of the most common crimes.'[2]

But the fullest and most systematic account of the criminal law applied in India before the Code is to be found in the very large volume known as Beaufort's *Digest*,[3] where its complexity, its lack of system, and its different sources are exhibited in detail for the benefit of the practising lawyer.

British India before 1833 is the India of the 'Regulations'—laws passed by the separate legislatures of Bengal, Madras and Bombay, before the Charter Act of 1833 had set up one legislature for the whole of India, having authority over all the inhabitants whether European British subjects, Indians or others. This reform made it possible for Parliament to aim at a common law for India, and brought about Macaulay's membership of Council, the Indian Law Commission over which he presided and the Penal Code, of which he was the draftsman. His draft was completed in 1837, though the Code did not find its way to the statute book till, like a number of other legal reforms which had long been held in suspense, it was at length precipitated by the Mutiny.

1 Major-General Sir W. H. Sleeman. His book was first published in 1844 but was mostly written soon after 1836. It was republished in 1893 in Constable's *Oriental Miscellany*, 2 vols. See vol. I, pp. 80, 97, 240–3, 367–9; vol. II, pp. 20, 209–10, 214, 220. He was influential in getting the offence of adultery retained as a crime in the Penal Code, vol. I, p. 240.
2 Sir George Campbell's *Modern India* (1852), ch. XI, p. 464.
3 Beaufort, *Digest of the Criminal Law*, 1849.

THE COMPANY'S CLAIM TO ADMINISTER
CRIMINAL JUSTICE

Under the Moguls, the *nizamat*—the military power and the right
to administer criminal justice—was distinguished from the *diwani*
or right to administer the revenue and civil justice. But in
Bengal, though not in other provinces, both rights were united
in the Subadar. By the middle of the eighteenth century, however, the Mogul Empire was breaking up and the vice-gerents
of the Emperor were in practice discarding their allegiance to
him. In his *Essay on Clive*, Macaulay has drawn a parallel
between the break up of the Mogul Empire after the death of
Aurungzebe (1707) and that of the Roman Empire in the fifth
century after the death of Theodosius (A.D. 395). In his day
such parallels could be mentioned in the House of Commons
and he brought it into his speech on the second reading of the
Charter Act (10 July 1833). It is enough here to notice that in
effect, if not in form, British rule throughout the territories of
Bengal, Bihar and Orissa began when in 1765 as a result of the
battles of Plassey (1757) and of Buxar (1764) Clive took from
a powerless claimant to the Mogul throne, who called himself
Shah Alum the Second, a grant of the *diwani*. Till 1772, when
Hastings was made Governor, the Company did not 'stand
forth as diwan' or exercise authority as such by its own servants.
If the grant of the *diwani* had been more than a mask for the
assumption of complete sovereign power,[1] it would be of greater
interest to inquire how the Company came to claim the *nizamat*.

1 'The grant of the Dewanny included not only the holding of Dewanny Courts,
but virtually the Nizamut also, the right of superintending the whole administration of law in Bengal, Bihar and Orissa, as it was vested in Shah Aulum in
1765. This is avowed in the letters of Lord Clive, and this is only a part of the
claim of the Company themselves in the case made for them upon the appeal of
Mr Buckingham against the press regulation. There were motives, however,
which were very intelligibly explained in Lord Clive's letter of 30 September 1765
which had made it convenient for a time that the Nuwaub should appear to
retain the Nizamut, or superintendence of the administration of justice, and
accordingly when Shah Aulum gave the Dewanny to the Company, it had been
agreed at their request that he should put the Nizamut into the hands of the
Nuwaub, who at the same time entered into an agreement to take a fixed annual
allowance from the Company to enable him to carry it on. He was, in fact, from
thenceforth, no other than a native officer of the Company; he held his courts
only at their will and pleasure, and they exercised the power of regulating and
altering them. Something had been done in this way between 1768 and 1772.'
(Minute of Sir Charles Grey C.J. 2 October 1829; *Parl. Papers*, 1831, vol. VI,
p. 54. Clive's letter of 30 September 1765 is printed in the *Third Report on the
Nature etc. of the East India Co.* 1773 at pp. 391, 394.)

The facts are that in February 1765, Nujm-ul-Dowla, the titular Subadar, entered into a treaty with the Company enabling them to exercise his authority; so that they could claim to hold the *diwani* from the Emperor and the *nizamat* from the Subadar.[1] Though some supervision was meanwhile exercised over the criminal courts by servants of the Company, it was not until 1790 that criminal jurisdiction was withdrawn from the Naib Nazim, whose chief criminal court (*nizamat adalat*) sat at Murshedabad. From 1790,[2] however, the Company took criminal jurisdiction into its own hands, continuing the Mahomedan criminal law as part of the public law of the land as it had been theretofore. It was applied in Bengal, in Madras and, later on, in other parts of India, though not in Bombay, to Hindus as well as to Moslems.

OUTLINE OF MAHOMEDAN CRIMINAL LAW

Four Arabic words expressive of four kinds of punishment may be taken to disclose the basic principles of this law: *kisas* or retaliation; *diya* or blood-money; *hadd* or defined punishment (which cannot be reduced or increased); and *tazir* or discretionary punishment. The principle of retaliation applied to cases of wilful killing and to certain types of grave wounding or maiming and gave to the injured man or his *wali* or next of kin— in the case of a slave to his master—the right to inflict a like injury on the wrongdoer. According to Abu Hanifa the retaliatory killing should in every case be done with a sword—a rule which still, it is understood, governs capital sentences in Hyderabad, though by the beginning of the nineteenth century hanging was the method in general use in the Company's territories.[3] But the main features of *kisas* were that in some cases it was not available, e.g. where the person slain was a descendant of the slayer, and that it applied only when all the next of kin were entitled to demand it and did demand it. It was not the right of the public or of God but *hakk adami* or right of man, and when it was not exacted blood-money was payable. In cases of wilful murder the fine of blood was exigible only from the criminal himself. In other cases his *akela* (family or associates)

1 Stephen, *Nuncomar and Impey*, vol. 1, p. 40.
2 A full and clear account of the changing and tentative arrangements before 1790 is given in Beaufort's *Digest of the Criminal Law* (Calcutta), 1849, Bk 1, ch. 1. See preamble to Regulation IX of 1793.
3 Harington, *Analysis*, vol. 1, p. 284, Part II, Section 1.

were liable, but this was never applied in Bengal.[1] A conviction for murder could be founded on a confession, but for this purpose the confession must declare the act to have been wilful and whatever is stated in explanation has to be taken as part of the confession. Two male eye-witnesses of ascertained or apparent credit were necessary to establish a charge of murder in the absence of a confession, and as against a Mahomedan the witnesses were required to be of that religion. For less grave homicide not involving *kisas* or *hadd*, the testimony of one man and two women would be sufficient.

For intentional wounds and maiming a fine might be accepted in lieu of retaliation and this was the provision made by the law for unintentional injuries.[2]

Hadd, meaning boundary or limit, was applied to the fixed and immutable penalties prescribed by the law for certain offences—thus for *zina* (illicit intercourse), stoning or scourging; for falsely accusing a married woman of adultery, and for wine drinking, scourging; for theft, cutting off the hands; and for different types of robbery various punishments including mutilation or death or both. The savagery of the penalty was compensated by difficulty in getting a conviction. The execution of *hadd* was prevented by any doubt or legal defect; full legal evidence, e.g. two or (in the case of *zina*) four men of proved credit as witnesses, was required; a confession had to be made four times before the *kazi* and it could be retracted at any time; if the witnesses did not amount to the requisite number they might be held guilty of slander; if the case was proved they might have to begin the stoning. *Tazir*[3] as a kind of punishment found its way into Mahomedan law at a late stage for such transgressions as had no defined punishment. The kind and amount of the punishment were entirely within the judge's discretion. It might be imprisonment, exile, corporal punish-

---

1 Duncan, *Observations*, para. 79.
2 The *modus operandi* is given by the learned editor of Lane's translation of the *Thousand and One Nights*, 3 vols. 1883, see vol. I, p. 383, note 53 to ch. v. 'The fine for a member that is single (as the nose) is the whole price of blood, as for homicide...for a member of which there are two and not more (as a hand) half the price of blood; for one of which there are ten (a finger or toe) a tenth of the price of blood: but the fine of a man for maiming or injuring a woman is half of that for the same injury to a man; and that of a free person for injuring a slave varies according to the value of the slave. The fine for depriving a man of any of his five senses, or dangerously wounding him, or grievously disfiguring him for life, is the whole price of blood.'
3 Perhaps more correctly *ta'zir*.

ment, reprimand, boxing on the ear, or any other humiliating treatment—the offender might be exposed to the public gaze or led through the streets with face blackened or hair cut. In the *Arabian Nights* some of the interest is derived from the manner in which the unfettered judgment of those in authority was exercised in particular cases. It was especially open to the risks of bribery. In cases of *tazir* the conditions of a conviction were not so strict as for *hadd*, e.g. it might be inflicted on a retracted confession or on the evidence of a man and a woman or on 'strong presumption'. This part of the criminal law lent itself to control by the government of any particular place whose ordinances might lay down definite principles to regulate punishment in such cases. Even cases coming under *kisas* and *hadd*, if those punishments could not be inflicted owing to some exception, doubt or legal defect, could be dealt with by infliction of a lesser penalty by way of *tazir*. And there was the right of *siyāsat* (*seeasut, seesut*) or exemplary punishment inflicted by the sovereign for the protection of the public interest: in cases of a heinous and special nature the punishment might be equal to or even greater than that prescribed by the law of *kisas* or *hadd*.[1]

This doctrine of *siyāsat* played a great part under the Regulations. It is described by Jonathan Duncan as a

'corrective or supplementary doctrine which is well known and admitted in the practice of the courts in Bengal as being acknowledged to be a power vested in the Sultan Hakim, or ruler for the time being, whereby a criminal may for almost any atrocious act be lawfully or regularly put to death if the ruler aforesaid shall "*seasutun*" —or in the exercise of his discretionary coercive authority as entrusted to him for the public good—think fit to command it.'[2]

From the sanction which it gave to cruel punishments the Mahomedan law seems almost unspeakably severe. Yet the claim could be made for it officially[3] that

'As a system the Mahomedan criminal law is mild; for though some of the principles it sanctions be barbarous and cruel yet not only is the infliction of them rarely rendered compulsory on the magistrate, but the law seems to have been framed with more care to provide for the escape of criminals than to found conviction on sufficient evidence and to secure the adequate punishment of offenders.'

1 For a reference to it see Peacock C.J. judgment in *R.* v. *Khyroollah* (1866) 6 W.R. 21, 23 (Cr. R.). But it seems doubtful whether *futwa* of death by *siyāsat* could be pronounced on anyone not a murderer (cf. Beaufort's *Digest*, p. 155, para. 849).
2 *Observations*, para. 64.   3 *Parl. Papers*, 1831-2, vol. XII, p. 696.

While it is said that Mahomedan law prefers confessions to all other evidence, it must be noted that in cases which were considered as involving 'the right of God' the principle applied was that God is forbearing and requires no punishment of the transgressor. Both confessions and evidence were to be discouraged by the *kazi*. This doctrine was at its highest in cases of adultery where we also see the giving of evidence by witnesses made so burdensome and useless, that in the result the savage penalty of stoning prescribed as *hadd* could be incurred only by confession.

HOMICIDE

The Mahomedan law of homicide was if taken as a whole very complicated, technical and obscure. Justifiable homicide (*kuth-i-mobah*) included cases of retaliation, although no sentence had been passed by any *kazi*; and cases where the killing was done in preservation of property from theft or robbery; or in prevention of adultery or rape or other serious offences; or at the express desire of the person slain.

The two gravest of the five kinds of homicide recognized were wilful homicide (murder) and 'wilful-like' homicide. The school of Abu Hanifa, which had prevailed under the Moguls, did not class the voluntary act of killing as wilful homicide unless it was done with a deadly weapon—one from whose nature intention to kill could be inferred. This excluded many cases of intentional killing and included some cases where a deadly weapon had been used and death though not intended had been caused. 'Wilful-like' homicide covered cases of death voluntarily caused but with a weapon not likely to cause it. As this crime was not punished by retaliation of death but only by the fine of blood, expiation and exclusion from inheritance to the slain, the distinction between these two grades of homicide was of great importance. The question of intention, not being according to the prevailing view a question of fact to be answered upon the circumstances of each particular case, but a question of law to be answered according to the nature of the instrument or weapon used, great nicety of distinction was to be found in text writers of authority. What was the crime when death was voluntarily caused by a sharp instrument, by the iron edge or handle of a hoe, by a small needle or a packing needle, by fire, by biting, by throwing into an oven or cauldron, by drowning in water, by strangling, by means of a wild beast, by poison? To take the last case as an important illustration, the balance of opinion was that the design to kill is not inferable from the administration of poison because poison is occasionally given as a medicine, and it is possible that the person who gave it may not have known that the quantity was excessive.[1] The fine of blood (100 camels or 1000 dinars or (say) £250–£350) as penalty in many of such cases was not so much mild as absurd. So also in many cases coming under the third head of 'homicide', *kuth-i-khuta*—viz. killing by error, e.g. where the killer aiming at one person kills another.

In Harington's *Analysis* (1805–9)[2] we find a careful sketch of this law taken from the *Hidayah* and the *Fatawa Alamgiri*, and an account of the amendments introduced in his day by the Bengal Regulations.[3] The legislature of each of the three Presidencies in ways that differ more or less but have the same general intention proceeded with the work of amendment and adaptation of this law. Some might think, Harington reflects (vol. I, p. 341), that such a law was too bad for continuance. The French revolutionists for example would think so. Any other people than the British would have abolished it altogether and substituted ' a new code of laws founded on those of England or of some other country where the principles of legislation and good government are better known both in theory and practice than they could be to the people who, nearly twelve centuries ago, became subject to the arms, religion, and policy of Mohummud, or to those who have been since forced to acknowledge the arbitrary sway of his successors'. But he takes pride in the fact that the principles of Edmund Burke had been allowed to prevail; 'a disposition to preserve and an ability to improve, taken together, would be my standard of a statesman'.

The fact remained, however, that in this law there were rules and even principles which no civilized government could administer, true though it be that in their origin they had marked an advance from 'days of ignorance' in Arabia and elsewhere. As Sir Courtenay Ilbert bluntly puts it: 'It was impossible to enforce the law of retaliation for murder, of stoning for

1 Jonathan Duncan found it impossible to recommend for Malabar that poisoners should be executed (*Observations*, para. 47).
2 Vol. I, p. 215.
3 Cf. *Parl. Papers*, 1831–2, vol. XII, pp. 693 *et seq.*

sexual immorality or of mutilation for theft or to recognise the incapacity of unbelievers to give evidence in cases affecting Mahomedans.'[1]

THE BEGINNINGS IN 1772

The cloudy title of the Company to the *nizamat* made it slow to alter the criminal law. Hastings had begun inauspiciously by enacting in 1772 (art. 35) that dacoits (members of a robber gang) were to be executed in their village, the village fined, and the families of the dacoits made slaves of the State—a recourse to slavery which was unconvincingly defended in a letter written by the 'Committee of Circuit' (15 August 1772) on the ground (which was true enough) that in India slaves were treated as members of the family 'and often acquire a much happier state by their slavery than they could have hoped for by the enjoyment of their liberty'. Slavery by order of the British was not destined to last long: by 1833 it had become intolerable to opinion in England and the Charter Act of 1833 required the Company to abolish slavery: by an Act of 1843 the Indian Legislature forbade the Indian courts to recognize slavery as a status. As to mutilation, in Wilson's *Anglo-Muhammadan Law*[2] may be found a copy of a letter from Hastings to the Collector of Islamabad (11 July 1774) requiring him to permit certain sentences of mutilation to be carried out; and a letter of 1781 from the Collector to the officer commanding troops at Chittagong requiring him to assist in the carrying out of sentence of impalement upon four dacoits in different divisions of the province. Such were the beginnings.

HASTINGS'S PROPOSALS, 1773

By a letter of 10 July 1773, Hastings laid before his colleagues in the government a number of questions bearing upon the reform of the criminal law. He remarked upon the refusal of the courts acting in accordance with the Mahomedan law to pass sentence of death on dacoits unless murder had accompanied the robbery. He recalled that custom recognized the sovereign's right to interpose in special cases to strengthen the efficiency of the law (*siyāsat*); and proposed that a general order or commission should be obtained from the Nazim, authorizing that the penalties prescribed in 1772 should be inflicted on professed

1 *Government of India*, 1907 ed. p. 325.   2 6th ed. 1930, p. 26.

and notorious robbers, and that convicted felons or murderers not condemned to death and all persons sentenced to imprisonment for life should be sold as slaves or transported. 'The present reduced state of the Nazim and the little interest he has in the general welfare of the country' induced Hastings to think that the Company should exercise a right of adding to or commuting the sentences of the courts when this seemed necessary to supply deficiencies or correct irregularities. He objected to the distinction made by the courts, following Abu Hanifa, in cases of homicide, according to which the crime did not amount to murder if not committed with an instrument formed for shedding blood; with the result that though the intention of murder might be clearly proved, the penalty of death could not be imposed, and the murderer escaped with the 'fine of blood'. He objected too to the option granted by the law to the next of kin to claim or waive their right of retaliation, and to the rule that they should themselves take part in executing sentence of death. These proposals exhibit more concern for the efficiency of the law than for correcting its barbarities, but it is said that Hastings attempted to get rid of mutilation as a punishment.[1]

CORNWALLIS'S MINUTE, 1790

Nothing seems to have come of Hastings's recommendations until in a Minute of 1 December 1790, his successor, Lord Cornwallis, acknowledged that 'the general state of the administration of criminal justice throughout the provinces is exceedingly and notoriously defective'. He attributed this to two obvious causes—the gross defects in the Mahomedan law and the defects in the constitution of the courts. As to the former, he held that his government were competent to amend the law; both because it was the government of the country and also because the Regulating Act of 1773 had not in any way taken exception to the penalties prescribed by that government in 1772 for dacoity, or to the supervision of the criminal courts which had in 1772 been entrusted to the Company's servants. Accordingly, he proposed to make intent the criterion of murder, and not the nature of the instrument employed, thereby adopting the opinion of the two disciples Abu Yoosuf and Imam Mahomed, in preference to the opinion of their master. Also to take away

1 *Parl. Papers*, 1831–2, vol. XII, p. 696.

from next of kin their option to remit the penalty of death; and to abrogate amputation and mutilation as legal punishments, substituting fine and imprisonment in their place.

This Minute is perhaps sufficient of itself to show the truth of Lord Bryce's observation: 'It was inevitable that the English should take criminal justice into their own hands—the Romans had done the same in their provinces—and inevitable also that they should alter the penal law in conformity with their own ideas.'[1]

The proposals of Cornwallis were enacted in 1790 and the two years following, together with a provision that the religious tenets of a witness should not make him incompetent to give evidence. They found place in the Cornwallis Code of 1793.

II

SYSTEM OF 1793

On 1 May 1793 the Cornwallis Code was passed—a body of forty-eight enactments, mostly drafted by Sir George Barlow, which held the field for twenty years at least as 'the system of regulation and polity for the internal government of these provinces'.[2] Regulation IX of 1793 was in effect the criminal procedure code, but it included the necessary amendments of the Mahomedan law, restating the enactments of the last three years in that behalf. It may be read with certain further amendments made soon afterwards (Regulations IV and XIV of 1797, VIII of 1799, VIII of 1801). The civil judges of the district were to act as magistrates, dealing themselves with petty offences and committing other cases for trial to the courts of circuit. These were four in number and were composed of the judges of the provincial courts of appeal. The Nizamat Adalat or chief criminal court was, until 1801, composed of the Governor-General and members of council sitting at Calcutta: after 1801 it had three or more judges. It was assisted by a Chief Kazi and two *muftis*. While Europeans not being British subjects were amenable equally with Indians to the courts of circuit set up by the Regulation, European British subjects were treated as triable only by the Supreme Court at Calcutta—an arrangement modified by Act of Parliament in 1813 to provide for assaults

1 *Studies in History and Jurisprudence*, vol. I, p. 120.
2 Harington, *Analysis*, vol. I, p. 16.

and trespasses by such persons against Indians. The Act gave jurisdiction over these offences to certain local magistrates, subject to convictions being removable by certiorari into the Supreme Court; and Act IV of 1843 applied to them the ordinary system of appeal within the Company's courts. Speaking broadly, we may say that in one way or another to offences by European British subjects English principles of law had always been applied when the Penal Code came into force.

The Regulation, if we may so refer to Regulation IX of 1793 as it stood at the turn of the century after certain additions and amendments, discloses the general principles on which criminal justice was to proceed. The order of proceedings at a trial was to be charge, plea, evidence for the prosecution, defence, evidence for the defence, opinion or *futwa* of the law officer (*kazi* or *mufti*). If the Mahomedan law required the prosecutor to appear in person, he must do so; otherwise he might prosecute by an agent (*vakil*); though when his evidence was necessary, his attendance could be required. The evidence of witnesses was to be taken down in writing and read to or by the witness: leading questions were to be avoided: cross-examination by the parties or the judge was allowed. An admonition was to be given orally to each witness after he had been sworn, requiring him to speak truly what he personally knew as distinct from what he had heard from others. Confessions were 'always to be received with circumspection and tenderness'. The religious persuasions of witnesses were not to be considered a bar to conviction of a prisoner, but where the evidence of a witness would be deemed incompetent by Mahomedan law because he was not a Mahomedan, the law officer was to say what would have been his *futwa* had the witness been of that religion: thereupon the case was to be referred to the Nizamat Adalat, without sentence being passed by the trial court; and the Nizamat Adalat, if it thought fit, would act upon the evidence.

The basis of the Regulation was that Mahomedan law should determine the elements necessary to constitute the offence charged, the sufficiency of the evidence, and the punishment. The trial judge was ordinarily to pass sentence on the basis of the *futwa* and to grant his warrant for the carrying out of the sentence—that is if the *futwa* seemed to him to be consonant with natural justice as well as with the Mahomedan law; though sentences of death or life imprisonment were not to be carried out until the Nizamat Adalat had confirmed them. The law to be administered was a sacred law—the *sharia*, of which the *kazis* and *muftis* were authorized exponents. In the Mahomedan system a *mufti* was an exponent of the law for the assistance of the *kazi* or judge who applied the law in practice, but the *kazi* was often himself a qualified jurist (*akil-ul-ijtihad* or *mujtahid*) and in that case was not, according to high authority, obliged to follow the *mufti's* view if he differed from it (cf. Harington's *Analysis*, vol. I, pp. 225–33). However venal 'law officers' of the courts might be at times, it was difficult to contemplate that they should as a class be required to take part in inflicting death or imprisonment contrary to accepted doctrine —in effect, knowingly to deliver *futwas* contrary to the *sharia*. Lord Cornwallis, as his letter of 1 December 1790 shows, was quick to appreciate this. But he considered that Mahomedan law allowed government (the *hakim*) to give effect to a rational preference for the doctrine of the two disciples where they differed from Abu Hanifa, and that it was possible therefore to enact that intent and not the nature of the weapon should be the test of murder. So too he saw no reason why it should not be laid down that after conviction the law should take its course without reference to the will of the murdered man's heirs. Nor was there any reason why imprisonment as a milder form of punishment should not be substituted for that of mutilation. These reforms were accordingly enacted in 1790 and 1791 and restated in 1793.

BYE-PASSING THE *FUTWA*

But the need for reform in the law was more fundamental and the problem more complicated. A procedure was required whereby the *futwa* should be bye-passed or circumvented so as to permit of substantive reform: hence the device already noticed in connection with the evidence of witnesses who were not Mahomedans. The *futwa* could be taken in the usual course or it could be taken hypothetically, e.g. on the assumption that a witness had been a Mahomedan, on the assumption that the heir of the murdered man had prosecuted: thereupon the case could be referred to the Nizamat Adalat without sentence being passed by the trial court. This relieved the strain upon law officers of courts and placed responsibility upon members of Council as judges of the Nizamat Adalat.

HOMICIDE

This device in one or other of its forms was applied by Regulations of 1793, 1797, 1799 and 1801 to cases where the judge disagreed with the *futwa*; where the heir of a murdered man had either refused to prosecute or had pardoned or commuted the offence, or had failed to appear, or by reason of minority could not demand *kisas*; where *kisas* was not demandable by reason of relationship between slayer and slain, e.g. parent and child, master and slave; to cases of murder at the request of the person murdered; where the accused by Mahomedan law was not liable to *kisas* because it was not demandable against one of his accomplices. It was also applied to strengthen and make more reasonable the law against homicide which had become encumbered with a number of distinctions drawn not only by Abu Hanifa but also by the two disciples; also to deal with cases in which people had been killed for practising sorcery, and cases of throwing infants into the Ganges (Regulation IV of 1797, VI of 1802). Apart from wilful murder (*kutl-i-umd*) the law recognized as forms of illegal homicide (*jinayat*) certain other types of killing. These rendered the fine of blood payable by the criminal and his family or associates but did not entail the punishment of death. They included not only killing by negligence but also what was called *kutl-i-khuta* or erroneous homicide, which covered cases where the error was in the intention, e.g. firing at a man in mistake for an animal, also where the error was in the act, e.g. firing at an animal and hitting a man. It came to be held that if the accused deliberately intending to murder *A* killed *B*, he was liable only to pay the fine, and the same bad rule was applied in cases of wounding. To all such cases Regulation VIII of 1801 applied the device of taking the *futwa* upon the footing that the accused had committed the murder or the wounding intended and the matter was disposed of accordingly by the Nizamat Adalat or the trial court. If *diyat* or fine of blood became demandable in any case, the courts were to commute it to imprisonment. From Regulation XIV of 1797 we find that prisons were full of persons sentenced to pay to private individuals fines which they could never pay. The Nizamat Adalat was authorized to grant relief in such cases and criminal courts were forbidden to make orders for payment of damages to individuals or to impose any fines save to the use of government.

ROBBERY

Then as now the crime of gang robbery with violence was one of the terrors of life in many parts of the Lower Provinces. Of the matters coming under the general doctrine of *hadd* one was *sarika*[1] (*sirka*) or larceny in its two forms—*theft* or larceny by stealth and *robbery* or open larceny by force and violence. The basis of the offence of secret larceny or theft was that the property should have been in due custody (*hirz*), either *custody of place*, e.g. a house, tent, or *personal guard* as when the property though on a road is near to the owner and within his sight. The penalty for theft was amputation except when the value of the property stolen was below ten *dirhms* (between two and three rupees)—for the first offence amputation of the right hand, for the second of the left leg. *Tazir* or *siyāsat* might authorize further punishment extending to death; but, as in other cases of *hadd*, confessions and prosecutions were discouraged by the Mahomedan law and many exceptions had been introduced to render amputation for theft of rare occurrence. Thus it was not applied to thefts of small articles in common use, or where the property stolen belonged to a relative, or to the thief's master, or host, or where the thief had entered a house and taken the property but had been seized before removing it from the house. The owner had to attend and prosecute.

Robbery with violence (*kat 'ut-tarik*—that is, highway robbery), according to Abu Hanifa and other high authority, was not committed unless the act charged was done outside and at a distance from any city: according to some it must not take place between two cities, towns or villages and at a place less than three days and nights distance from a city. Abu Yoosuf took a wider view and held that the crime could be committed at any distance from a city or even within a city if done at night and on the highway. Other conditions insisted on were that the robbers must be strangers to the parties robbed; ten *dirhms* for each robber was the limit of value. For robbery the penalty was amputation of the right hand and left foot; and for murder in such cases, even if no robbery had taken place, death: not as a matter of *kisas* but as a matter of the right of God or public interest. For robbery with murder the penalty of death might or might not be preceded by amputation. All of the robbers were liable to death if one of the gang committed

1 Cf. Beaufort, *Digest*, Book vi, section iv, p. 618.

murder. But on the other hand all of them could take advantage of the fact that any one was a relation of the person robbed, or had a joint interest in the property taken—or any of the exceptions which prevented sentence of *hadd*.

For a crime so serious and so prevalent as dacoity it was necessary to have a much more strict and even justice, less barbarous and more effective. This was provided by Regulation LIII of 1803, which abolished the condition as to place—all places being put on the same footing whether or not they were on or near a highway or at a distance from any inhabited spot. It also abolished the network of distinctions as to one of the robbers being a minor or lunatic or relation of the person robbed or having an interest in the property, or his share of the plunder being less in value than ten *dirhms*. It abolished also the necessity of having evidence of a special kind and enabled convictions to be based upon confessions, evidence of credible witnesses, or strong circumstantial evidence. It detailed a procedure in which the law officer's *futwa*, the judge's sentence, and the reference to the Nizamat Adalat were assigned their respective parts, so that where robbery had been accompanied by murder all the participants should be sentenced to death, and where it had been accompanied by wounding, arson or other aggravations, to imprisonment and transportation for life, or even to the death penalty in heinous cases, on the well-settled principle of *siyāsat*. Seven years' imprisonment was provided for simple robbery; in exceptional cases fourteen. All these sentences might be mitigated by the trial court or the Nizamat Adalat, according to the nature of the case, in view of extenuating circumstances, or where, on consideration of the number of prisoners convicted of the same crime, the ends of justice permitted such a course.

Mere secret larceny or theft, whether from a person or a house, was left by section 5 of this Regulation to discretionary punishment (*tazir*), but if the entry into a house were followed by acts of violence, the persons taking part were liable to the same punishment as in the case of robbery with violence or dacoity. By this Regulation the liability to transportation was restricted to those who had been sentenced to imprisonment for life.

TAZIR

The same Regulation dealt comprehensively with the doctrine and practice of *tazir*, setting forth the three types or classes: (*a*) crimes not within *hadd* or *kisas*, (*b*) crimes within these categories but not so treated because of technical insufficiency of proof or because of special exception or scrupulous distinction (*shoobah*), (*c*) heinous crimes requiring exemplary punishment at the sovereign's discretion for the protection of the public (*siyāsat*). The *futwas* of the law officers were complained of on the ground that, especially in the second class of cases, the punishment was too often awarded according to the degree of proof—being either awarded on insufficient proof of guilt or, in heinous cases, being inadequate to the crime proved. It was provided accordingly that when a prisoner was found liable to discretionary punishment (*tazir, ukuba, siyāsat*) the *futwa* should declare this generally with the grounds therefor, leaving the punishment to be assessed by the Judge or in some cases by the Nizamat Adalat. Where a Regulation had prescribed the penalty there was no difficulty. When the Judge did not consider the case proved he was not to sentence the prisoner at all, whatever might be the *futwa*. If the case was one within the second of the three classes above-mentioned, a second *futwa* was to be taken specifying the punishment of *hadd* or *kisas* to which the prisoner would have been liable, but for the exception or technical insufficiency of evidence; and the Judge was to pass sentence accordingly, commuting any punishment as required by the Regulations. For offences for which no stated penalty had been prescribed by Regulation or provided by the Mahomedan law, the maximum punishment was to be thirty-nine stripes and imprisonment with hard labour for seven years.

PUBLIC EXPOSURE AND MARKING

Among the matters left by the Mahomedan law to discretionary punishment were the offences of perjury and forgery and their derivatives. *Tusheer* or exposure in a public place with circumstances of ignominy was the proper penalty for perjury according to Abu Hanifa, but the disciples prescribed whipping and imprisonment. Regulations XVII of 1797 and VIII of 1803 prescribed for the Lower and Upper Provinces respectively that the *futwa* should state the penalty according to both opinions;

and that the judge should sentence the accused on conviction according to one or other of these opinions as he should see fit, or in bad cases to suffer punishment according to both opinions. The former of these Regulations authorized judges when awarding *tusheer* to add a direction that words expressive of the crime should be marked on the forehead of the prisoner by a process which had been applied by section 11 of Regulation IV of 1797 to convicts sentenced to imprisonment for life. 'This inscription is to be made by the process termed *godena* (*godna*), by which the Hindoo women ornament their faces and which leaves a blue mark that cannot be effaced without tearing off the skin.' In 1807 these provisions were rescinded and the law stiffened by Regulation II of that year which gave simple working definitions of perjury, subornation of perjury and forgery; and directed that if the judge thought the prisoner a proper object of corporal and ignominious punishment he should sentence him to public exposure (*tusheer*), to be marked by *godena*, to thirty stripes and to imprisonment with hard labour for not less than four or more than seven years. If in any case this sentence was thought by the judge to be too severe, he could refer the case to the Nizamat Adalat. By section 12 of Regulation XVII of 1817, marking by *godena* was abolished in such cases, though it was retained for convicts sentenced to imprisonment for life. By 1837 public degradation took the form of being made to ride upon an ass. Macaulay compares it with the English pillory but proposed in his Penal Code to abolish this sort of punishment altogether. By Act II of 1849 both marking by *godena* and *tusheer* or public exposure were abolished as punishment throughout the whole of British India.

OVER-RULING OR DISPENSING WITH THE *FUTWA*

By 1810 the amendments made by Regulation to the Mahomedan law and to the procedure by *futwa* had produced considerable complication. Regulation I of 1810 gave power to the executive to dispense with 'law officers' altogether at any particular criminal trial, and provided that in such case no sentence should be passed by the court of circuit, but that the case should be referred to the Nizamat Adalat, any witness whose competency might be in doubt having been examined. Apart from such cases, the *futwa* or declaration of the law was an essential step, though the judge as we have seen could refer the case to the Nizamat Adalat if he disagreed with the *futwa*: thereupon the law officers of the Nizamat Adalat gave a further *futwa* and that court passed final sentence. By Regulation XVII of 1817 power was given to two or more judges of that court to convict and pass sentence, although its own law officers were in favour of acquittal; and in effect to override any objection by a law officer to receiving evidence because the witness was a police officer or other officer of government, or on any other grounds which the trial judge thought unreasonable though valid by Mahomedan law. The penalties for homicide, robbery, perjury and forgery, and for offences against the coinage were re-declared or made more stringent by this Regulation. In this and in earlier Regulations it was provided not only that civil and other courts should commit for trial persons whom they considered to have given false evidence before them, but that, without the order of such court, accusations of perjury against witnesses should not be brought to trial. These are still features of the law of India.

ADULTERY

The crimes which Mahomedan law included under the head of *zina* came under the doctrine of *hadd* and carried penalties of stoning or scourging, according as they amounted to adultery or only to fornication. In cases of adultery, rape or incest, Regulation XVII of 1817 complains that the Mahomedan law of evidence rendered a legal conviction almost impossible and that the law officers of the Nizamat Adalat had declared presumptive evidence to be insufficient. That these opinions represented truly the standpoint of the *sharia* is clear enough. The twenty-fourth *sura* of the Koran and the incident there mentioned of the wrongful accusations made against Ayesha explain a good deal of the strictness of the law in this regard, but the penalty of stoning to death accounts for it even more plainly. Here especially effect was given to the general doctrine applicable to all cases of *hakk Allah* or right of God that it was even more meritorious to conceal offences than to prove them. 'God loves those of his servants that cover their sins' is a traditional saying.[1] The need for four competent male witnesses was

---

1 Cf. *Encyclopaedia of Islam*, sub voce Adhab. Harington's *Analysis*, vol. 1, p. 291.

rigorously insisted on, and if less than four in number, the witnesses were liable to the punishment for slander. Their probity was moreover to be established by inquiry. Accordingly, it was enacted by Regulation XVII of 1817 that this class of offence could be made out by presumptive evidence, i.e. credible testimony and circumstantial evidence; and that a suitable penalty could be imposed not exceeding thirty-nine stripes or imprisonment with hard labour for seven years. Married women were not to be prosecuted on such charges save by their husbands. From Jonathan Duncan's report on Malabar we learn that in 1792 the punishments for adultery were in practice enforced only against women.[1] But when the husband complained against his wife the adulterer was liable to be prosecuted also.[2] Cases of rape were to be referred to the Nizamat Adalat if a conviction was obtained.

So much pains had been taken to enable the Nizamat Adalat to convict, notwithstanding that the *futwa* did not find against the prisoner, that Regulation IV of 1822 comes almost as comic relief, containing as it does the discovery that the Regulations had nowhere provided that the Nizamat Adalat could acquit a prisoner notwithstanding his conviction by the *futwa* of its law officers. This Regulation also provided that that court need not give effect to any plea that a murderer was only liable to *diyat* or fine of blood because the person murdered had been detected in the act of fornication with the wife or relation of the murderer: a plea which had been upheld by *futwa* in the Nizamat Adalat.

END OF THE SYSTEM AS A GENERAL LAW, 1832

Regulation VI of 1832 marks the end of the Mahomedan criminal law as a general law applicable to all persons. It recited that it was desirable to enable European functionaries who preside in civil and criminal courts to avail themselves of the assistance of respectable natives in the decision of suits or trials. It set out three ways in which civil courts could do this— by referring the suit or one or more points arising in a suit to them as a panchayet, by having them as assessors, or employing them more nearly as a jury. The decision in all cases was,

1 See his report entitled *Observations on the Administration of Justice*, section XLIV. This is the tract referred to in Bombay Regulation V of 1799.
2 Beaufort's *Digest*, p. 580, para. 3021.

however, to be the court's own decision. While civil courts could follow one or other of these courses only when specially empowered to do so, the commissioners of circuit or judges of sessions were all at liberty to follow them and in that case to dispense with the *futwa*: but if the crime was not one which the judge was empowered by Regulation to punish, the case was to be referred to the Nizamat Adalat.

This Regulation recited that it was offensive to the feelings of many persons who do not profess the Mahomedan faith to be liable to trial and punishment under the provisions of the Mahomedan criminal code, and that the Regulations now rendered it unnecessary to maintain that form of trial towards such persons. It referred to the power of a single judge of the Nizamat Adalat to overrule *futwas* as showing that in such cases there was not always any need to require a *futwa*. It enacted that non-Muslims, when brought to trial for an offence cognisable under the general regulations, might claim to be exempted from trial under the Mahomedan criminal code and that in other cases the judge of Nizamat Adalat was to exercise a discretion in requiring or not requiring a *futwa*.

This was the governing Regulation in Beaufort's and Campbell's time. The latter points out[1] that miscellaneous offences, not specially provided for by the Regulations, ought properly to be punished only as being crimes by the Mahomedan law and that this Regulation, while giving exemption to non-Muslims from the operation of that law, did not explain by what law a Hindu or European claiming this exemption was to be tried. He adds in a note:

'An odd case occurred a few years ago at Benares of a half-caste who was convicted and sentenced to imprisonment for adultery, but was pardoned by Government on the ground of *his being a Christian*— a fact which certainly does not seem a mitigation of the offence.'

Beaufort's summary of the practice is to the effect that under this Regulation 'the court now never calls for a *futwa* except when in a case tried in a sessions court before a law officer the sessions judge recommends a sentence of death or in any special case where a reference is thought necessary'.[2] But Campbell's description of the working of this 'jury' system is by no means flattering.[3]

1 *Modern India*, pp. 465–6. 2 *Digest*, p. 181, para. 990, note (*a*).
3 *Modern India*, p. 473.

'No one is compelled to serve on the jury; it is alien to the feelings
and customs of the country, people cannot be induced voluntarily
to sit upon it, and for all practical purposes it is an entire failure.
The Punchayet or jury of arbitrators, chosen by two parties to decide
between them in civil cases, is a native institution, but to be summoned by Government to decide on the guilt or innocence of a
person in whom they take no interest is a hardship and unprofitable
responsibility much disliked by all natives. In fact, the judge generally
puts into the box some of the pleaders and such people about the
court, in order to comply with the law, intimates to them very
broadly his opinion, they always agree with him and there is no
more trouble. For having taken their opinion he may decide as he
chooses.'

III

AGRA OR BENARES AND THE CEDED DISTRICTS

The above account of the course of the criminal law in Bengal
may be taken as applicable to Benares and what were called
the Ceded Provinces[1]—the main part of the territory which in
1834 became the province of Agra. But there was occasion
for some special legislation also. It was necessary to treat as
murder the practice among Rajkoomars of starving female
infants to death (Regulation III of 1804), and to take steps
against the practice of sitting *dhurna* (Regulation XXI of 1795,
III of 1804; cf. VII of 1820 and section 508 of the Indian Penal
Code), whereby Brahmins intimidated people by inducing them
to believe that they had been made objects of divine displeasure.
Regulation XXI of 1795 dealt also with other practices whereby
Brahmins, if they were served with a writ or other process, were
wont to threaten to kill women or children. It contained a
noticeable provision that on the question whether the offence
of *dhurna* had been committed a Hindu pandit was to give a
bebusta (opinion) to the court of circuit in lieu of the *futwa* of the
Mahomedan law officer. This procedure was ended by Regulation VII of 1820, which restored the *futwa* declaring that
dhurna was obnoxious to the Mahomedan law as oppression
(*zulm*). By section 23 of Regulation XVI of 1795 Brahmins were
not in the 'province of Benares' to be punishable with death:
transportation was substituted for the capital sentence[2] until
Regulation XVII of 1817, section 15 abolished the privilege.

1 Districts around Benares had been ceded by the ruler of Oudh in 1775 and the
'Ceded Territories' by his successor in 1801.
2 This would seem to have been the rule in Benares since 1790.

These matters have an interest as showing special points of contact with the religion and usages of the Hindu population to whom the Mahomedan law was applied. In the holy city of Benares and its surrounding districts the intensity of Hindu feeling and the vitality of Hindu practice were plainly at their highest.

IV

MADRAS

Legislation in Madras pursued a similar course. Regulations VII and VIII of 1802 constituted four courts of circuit and a superior criminal court (*Foujdarry Adalat*), the latter to sit in the Presidency town. It regulated them so as to secure a general compliance with the Mahomedan law subject to certain express amendments. It followed closely Bengal Regulation IX of 1793 and the Cornwallis Code. When the Mahomedan law required the presence of the prosecutor he was to attend. An admonition was to be read out to witnesses instead of requiring them to take an oath; and their evidence was to be recorded. Persons of any religion were competent witnesses, and the law officers were to say what their *futwa* would have been had the witnesses been Mahomedans. Provision was made for referring all sentences of death or imprisonment for life, and all cases in which the judge disagreed with the *futwa*, to the Foujdarry Adalat; for requiring the *futwa* to be given on the assumption that retaliation (*kisas*) had been demanded; for proceeding on the doctrine of the two disciples which regarded intention as the test of wilful murder; for substituting transportation for imprisonment, and imprisonment for mutilation, or for blood-money, and so forth. The Foujdarry Adalat was to pass sentence of death in cases in which the *futwa* had declared the accused not liable to *kisas*, on the ground of relationship to the slain; or when the murder had been done at the request of the party slain, or when an accomplice was not liable to *kisas*. When the prescribed punishment was too severe the court could suspend its sentence and submit the case to the Governor in Council for mitigation of penalty, and it could offer pardon to a person willing to give evidence for the prosecution if the Governor in Council approved. In 1803 Regulation XV repeated Bengal Regulation LIII of the same year, which dealt with the doctrine of *tazir* and with robbery with violence. Perjury and forgery were also weak spots in the criminal law and Regulation VI of 1811 provided for public exposure, marking on the forehead, thirty stripes and imprisonment as deterrents. By Regulation I of 1808 the Foujdarry Adalat was allowed to convict without a *futwa* in certain cases. By Regulation I of 1825 it was given discretion to remit any sentence which seemed too severe although by Mahomedan law it was prescribed, and to take into account evidence inadmissible by Mahomedan law. By Act I of 1840 it was relieved from the obligation to take a *futwa* from its law officers at all, but the absence of a *futwa* was not to dispense with the Mahomedan law in any case to which it was still applicable. This reform was applied to the Foujdarry Adalat only and not to any lower court. To dispense with the *futwa* was a serious step and the approval of the Indian Law Commission was first obtained.[1]

---

1 'It has so far been dispensed with in Bengal, except in cases of murder; and the Law Commission imagine that the greater part of the existing criminal law being to be found in the Madras Code of Regulations, and the rest with little or no exception in recorded precedents or in books which are readily accessible, the Madras judges would be competent to administer it without the aid of those officers....It would, they conceive, render Persian records of trials unnecessary in that court, and be attended with considerable saving of time in the administration of criminal justice in the most important class of cases' (Letter 30 May 1837; *Parl. Papers*, 1842, vol. xxx).

CHAPTER XI

HINDU CRIMINAL LAW: BOMBAY

THE LAW OF CRIME A PERSONAL LAW

THE administration of criminal justice proceeded in Bombay upon lines different from those laid down for Bengal and Madras—naturally enough, since large territories made part of the Bombay province had not been at the time of annexation under Muslim rule. In a letter of 1822 Elphinstone describes the Bombay system:

'We do not as in Bengal profess to adopt the Mohammedan code. We profess to apply that code to Mohammedan persons, the Hindoo code to Hindoos, who form by far the greatest part of the subjects. The Mohammedan law is almost as much a dead letter in practice with us as it is in Bengal, and the Hindoo law generally gives the Raja on all occasions the choice of all possible punishments....The consequence is that the judge has to make a new law for each case.'[1]

Provision having been made by Regulation I of 1799 for forming a code of Regulations, Regulation V of that year set up a system of criminal law. The 36th section shows that to Christians and Parsees the English law was to be applied; while in the case of Hindus and Mahomedans the 'native expositors' were to be asked what punishment the law of the prisoner assigned to the offence which the judges of the Court of Sessions found on the facts to have been committed. The Regulation contained many of the amendments to the Mahomedan law which we have already noticed in Bengal and Madras, including provision for a reference to the Governor in Council in cases of death sentence or imprisonment for life, or when the judges disapproved of the exposition of the law by the Kazi. In particular it referred to 'the tract entitled *Observations* now constituting part of the criminal code for the province of Malabar' as a guide both in Mahomedan and Hindu cases. Regulation III of 1802 repeated the same provisions for Surat and Regulation II of 1805 applied them to Gujerat. Regulation III of 1802 made further modifications of the Mahomedan law as to retaliation, culpable homicide and perjury in the same manner as had been found necessary elsewhere. Section 15 of

1 *Life of Elphinstone*, by Sir T. E. Colebrooke, 1882, vol. II, p. 125.

that Regulation provided for the more severe punishment of Hindus convicted of perjury—making them and Parsees liable to *godena* or marking on the forehead. The grant of pardon to an approver was made possible with the consent of the Governor in Council by order of the chief criminal court in Bombay instituted under Regulation IX of 1812.

In 1819 the territory subject to the Government of Bombay became much enlarged by annexation of the Maratha districts of the Deccan which had been under Baji Rao II, and Elphinstone, who had carried out this policy and had made an elaborate report on the conditions in the new territories, became Governor of Bombay. In 1827, at the end of his period of office, there were passed at his instigation and under his influence and supervision a series of Regulations which came to be known as the Elphinstone Code, and which put the law of the enlarged province of Bombay upon a new footing. To appreciate the criminal law enforced for the period before that Code it is necessary to have some idea of the main features of the Hindu criminal law, how far it had been enforced before the British administration, and to what extent it had been retained.

THE HINDU LAW OF CRIME

According to the *dharma-sastras*, a substantial amount of criminal law comes under the heading of *vyavahara*, which cannot in these texts be translated simply as 'civil justice' but is more nearly equivalent to the wider phrase 'judicial matters'. *Vyavahara* means law in the modern sense, business intercourse legally interpreted, legal procedure. There is no formal distinction between civil and criminal law till the term *vyavahara* is divided by later writers into 'cases of property' and 'cases of hurt'.[1] Manu's[2] eighteen titles of the law, 'topics which give rise to law suits' (*vyavaharasthitau*), turn out to be taken with little change from the Arthasastra of Kautilya.[3] They include (11) assault, (12) defamation, (13) theft, (14) robbery and violence (*sahasa*), (15) adultery. These same headings occur in much the same order in Yajnavalkya's second chapter[4] (*Vyavaharadhyaya*). They occur again in the *Vyavahara Mayukha*[5] of Nilkantha, which begins with a wide definition of *vyavahara* or, as Mandlik trans-

---

1 *Cambridge History of India*, vol. 1, p. 281, Professor Washburn Hopkins of Yale.
2 Manu, viii, v, 4–7.   3 Jayaswal's *Manu and Yajnavalkya*, p. 116.
4 Mandlik, pp. 232–43.   5 *Ibid.* pp. 137–53.

lates it, 'judicial proceeding'. The *Mayukha*, as showing what these eighteen divisions are, quotes the opening words of Yajnavalkya's second chapter: 'If one aggrieved by others in a way contrary to the Smritis and the established usage complain to the king, that subject is one of the titles of *vyavahara* or a judicial proceeding.' In his Tagore Lectures for 1917 Mr Jayaswal devotes two lectures to the criminal law as it appears in *Manu and Yajnavalkya* (lectures VIII and IX).[1] He considers that the latter made a workable code of criminal law by returning to the older and milder law which had been in force before the 'ferocious puritanism and blood-thirsty religious zeal of the Manavan Code', and thus promoted the peace, progress and culture of the Gupta period. His view is that the legal genius of the race then reached its pinnacle of glory but that 'in criminal law it found nothing to add: it accepted Yajnavalkya as final'. Until we have put on one side the extravagances of the Manavan Code, which are attributable to its ferocious objection to the Sudra Buddhist and to his claims to be listened to as a religious teacher, we do not, in Mr Jayaswal's opinion, get back to the ancient system of the Arthasastra[2] of Kautilya, which was later to be taken by Yajnavalkya as the basis of his teaching upon crimes. The commentator nearest, in Mr Jayaswal's opinion, to the sense of the ancient law is Medhatithi.

THE *VYAVAHARA MAYUKHA* OF NILKANTHA (A.D. 1650)

By reason of its late date and its authority in the Mahratta country we may notice the *Mayukha's* chapters on assault, theft, violence (*sahasa*) and adultery. These contain citations from

---

1 Manu's date is generally taken as between 200 B.C. and A.D. 200. Yajnavalkya is fourth century A.D. Narada fifth century A.D. Brihaspati A.D. 600 or 700. Mayukha seventeenth century. Jayaswal puts Kautilya's date as 300 B.C., Manu as 150 B.C. and Yajnavalkya as A.D. 150.

2 *Arthasastra* (science of polity). As for the Arthasastra of Kautilya we have mention of it in such later works of the Jaina Agama as the *Anuyogadvara* and other sutras. As the Jatakas and other Pali canonical texts clearly attest, the science of royal polity was developing under the name of *Rajadhamma* or principles of royal polity. The Samanas and Brahmanas including the Sakyaputtiyas contributed much to the development of this important branch of learning. In one of the oldest Pali fragments we are given a list of topics that determined the scope of a work on royal polity. The list comprises the topics concerning the kings, the thieves, robbers, bandits and plunderers, the Mahamattas or ministers and high officials, the army, dangers, wars, foodstuffs, drinks, clothes, beds, articles of luxury, friends and relations, conveyances, villages, towns, cities and countries, men, women, warriors, etc. (*India as Described in Early Texts of Buddhism and Jainism*, by Bimala Churn Law, D.Litt., Luzac and Co., London, 1941, p. 257.)

Manu, Yajnavalkya, Brihaspati, Narada and others, and in general maintain the principle that the heinousness of the crime is related to the superior or inferior position of the person injured as compared with the wrongdoer. On 'assault' it quotes Manu and Yajnavalkya for the rule that the limb with which a Sudra assaults a Brahmin shall be cut off, but it quotes other and milder texts as well. On the whole abuse and assault are dealt with by imposing fines. For theft in most cases fines are to be imposed. Theft is divided into open and secret theft and includes cheating. In this chapter the texts cited authorize in particular circumstances banishment, beating, the cutting off of fingers, of a hand, of a foot; and hanging. The last mentioned is, for example, Brihaspati's prescription for highwaymen. We get here as in Yajnavalkya the rule that the village or locality of the theft is to be held responsible if the thief is not caught, unless he can be shown to have escaped into another district. Kidnapping women and stealing cattle are dealt with by special ferocity—burning, mutilating and drowning. The offence of *sahasa* (violence) is said by Brihaspati to include four crimes— manslaughter, robbery, assault on another man's wife, and assault (*parushya*) in the sense which covers abusive language. The punishment of death for murderers is authorized except in the case of a Brahmin who is to suffer public exposure and be banished. A Brahmin may, however, be killed in self-defence. For rape of a married woman capital punishment is also authorized and there are various scales of fine for adultery according to the circumstances, but when the woman is of higher caste mutilation is also provided.

JONATHAN DUNCAN AND MOUNTSTUART ELPHINSTONE

If we find it difficult, from the number of counsellors mentioned in such a treatise, to gather any precise rules of criminal law, the difficulties of the first British administrators, as the eighteenth century gave way to the nineteenth, were even greater, as they faced their task in Malabar and in what is now the Bombay province. The leading figures are two—Jonathan Duncan and Mountstuart Elphinstone. The tract entitled *Observations*, referred to in Regulation V of 1799, is the work of a very successful and distinguished administrator, Jonathan Duncan, who had been sent at the head of a Commission from Bengal and Bombay 'to

inspect into the state and condition of the Province of Malabar'
after the cession of that country by Tippoo in 1792. The inspection
took place in 1792–3 and the *Observations* are dated 6 July 1793.[1]
Duncan as Resident at Benares from 1788 had been familiar
with the administration of the Mahomedan criminal law under
the Governor-General and Council of Bengal. On the recommendation of Cornwallis he was to become Governor of Bombay
in 1795—an office which he held for sixteen years until his death
in 1811. Both in Benares and afterwards in Kathiawar he
exerted himself to put down the practice of infanticide. But in
1793 for his information as to the Hindu criminal law he was
dependent on that 'Code of Gentoo Laws' which had been
written at Warren Hastings' behest by certain pandits of
Bengal. It had been written in Sanskrit and translated by one
of its authors into Persian. In 1775 it was translated from the
Persian into English by Nathaniel Brassey Halhed, a young man
who when at Oxford had been led to study Arabic by Sir William
Jones and had as a 'writer' in India attracted Hastings' attention. This was published in London in 1776: further editions
appeared in 1777 and 1781 as well as a French translation at
Paris in 1778. Like Charles Hamilton's translation of the *Hedaya*
—another work for which Hastings' enterprise must have credit
—it suffers from the Persian translation being but a loose and
inaccurate version of the original. We need not here take account
of its deficiencies as a manual of civil law—e.g. it contains very
little about Contracts—which were pointed out in a kindly way
by Sir William Jones in his celebrated letter of 19 March 1788
to Lord Cornwallis outlining his scheme for digesting the native
laws. Among the 'subjects rather curious than useful' we find
a good deal about criminal law in the Gentoo Code, whereas
the code which Jones projected was to be concerned only with
Contracts and Succession: there is almost nothing bearing upon
criminal law in Jagannatha's *Digest* which Henry Colebrooke
translated and published in 1798. Whether Elphinstone in 1819,
when he wrote his *Report on the Territories conquered from the
Paishwa*,[2] had better means of information as to the criminal law
to be found in the Hindu texts, I do not know. But both of these
distinguished administrators were careful to examine into the
law actually enforced by way of criminal justice before the

---

1 They are in the third volume of *Reports and Regulations, Malabar*, published at
Bombay.　　　　　　　　　　　　　　　　2 Published 1821, Calcutta.

British occupation—the one in Malabar (which was under Bombay till it was annexed to the Madras Presidency in 1801), the other in the Maratha territories in the Deccan. Elphinstone had acquired an intimate knowledge of the Maratha country as his *Report* shows: much more profound than Duncan can be supposed to have obtained as head of a visiting Commission to Malabar, dependent to a large extent on reports from the various Rajas who had held sway under Tippoo and before his time.

THE GENTOO CODE (A.D. 1776)

The Hindu criminal law as presented in the 'Gentoo Code' is full of impracticable and absurd directions which cannot represent any systematic practice. Over a very large part of India— a part which included Bengal—the Hindu law had for centuries ceased to have any reality so far as crime was concerned, the Mahomedan law being the public law of the land. The Gentoo Code in 1775 represented the notions of a long dead past so far as regards criminal law. It is not easy to see how Hindu society with its multiplicity of independent chiefs each exercising arbitrary power, though influenced more or less by respect for the Brahmin and his learning, could very well give rise to a coherent system deserving to be called a Hindu law of crime. What is put forward by the text-writers as a legal rule is often no more than the fanciful suggestion of a Brahmin writer legislating *in vacuo*. A long *catena* of absurdities could be quoted from the Gentoo Code—in many cases the absurdity consists in a perverted notion of 'making the punishment fit the crime'; in others in the minute distinctions upon which the tariff of fines is built; in others in the savagery with which crimes are punished when committed against Brahmins or persons of higher caste than the wrongdoer. Thus in Chapter xv which treats of defamation all possible slanders are imagined and a fine attached to each; and in Chapter xvi all the possible types and methods of assault are specified and a fine provided in each case. So too we get provisions:

If a man strikes a Bramin with his hand, the Magistrate shall cut off that man's hand (p. 233). If a Magistrate has committed a crime and any person upon discovery of that crime should beat and ill-use the Magistrate, in that case whatever be the crime of murdering one hundred Bramins such crime shall be accounted to that person; and the Magistrate shall thrust an iron spit through him and roast

him at the fire (pp. 233–4). If a Sooder sits upon the carpet of a
Bramin in that case the Magistrate having thrust a hot iron into his
buttock and branded him shall banish him the kingdom or else he
shall cut off his buttock (p. 234). If a man sells silver or any other
article made to counterfeit gold, the Magistrate shall break his hand,
nose and teeth and fine him one thousand pieces of cowries; if he
is constantly guilty of such practices the Magistrate shall cut him
into pieces with a razor (p. 245). If a Bice (Vaisya) commit adultery
with a woman of the Bramin caste who has no master, with her
consent, the Magistrate shall confine him one year in prison and
fine him one thousand pieces of cowries; if the woman has a master
the Magistrate shall bind him upon a hot iron plate, wind the grass
beena round his body and burn him, or burn him with the grass *kose*
(p. 272).

In an affair concerning a horse, if any person gives false evidence
his guilt is as great as the guilt of murdering one hundred persons.
In an affair concerning gold, if any person gives false evidence whatever guilt would be incurred in murdering all the men who have
been born or who shall be born in the world shall be imputed to
him (p. 128). If a Sooder gets by heart the Beids of the Shaster the
Magistrate shall put him to death (p. 296).

WAS HINDU LAW APPLIED IN PRACTICE?

Such provisions or most of them are extravagances even from
the standpoint of the Indian Raja at the beginning of the nineteenth century, who was not in general fanatically inclined
towards Brahminism. They render very blunt the edge of the
warning with which they are accompanied: 'If a magistrate
doth not inflict punishment according to the Shaster his subjects
and his kingdom and his possessions and the children of his
relations become miserable and contemptible' (p. 297); but they
have their importance when we come to ask to what extent this
law was applied in fact. Elphinstone says of the Maratha
country that:

'even in common criminal trials no law seems ever to be referred to
except in cases connected with religion where shastrees were sometimes consulted. The only rule seems to have been the custom of the
country and the Magistrates notice [notion] of expediency. The
Hindoo law was quite disused, probably owing to its absurdity; and
although every man is tolerably acquainted with its rules in civil
cases, I do not believe anyone but the very learned has the least
notion of its criminal enactments.'[1]

In Malabar some thirty years earlier Duncan and his Commission had been told by one of the Rajas (Cartinaad) that

1 *Report*, p. 53.

'in this country the custom of settling matters by a person who knows the laws never was introduced...nor is the manner of punishment taken from any written books...it is true that in differences between Brahmins they consult their books and report to the Raja who, with the approbation of the Brahmins, passes sentence'. And another Raja had reported: 'I have enquired of the Brahmins if there are any books which treat of these things but they tell me there are none now in the possession of the people of this country. I have nevertheless desired them to procure them.' And another report concluded with an intimation that other districts had different customs.

Finding, however, that the punishments applied to the various species of crime did not differ widely but had 'a general similitude from one end of the province of Malabar to the other' and were similar to what was laid down in the 'Gentoo Code', Duncan concluded that they were derived from the Hindu law as their common source, though he found 'the Bengal Code', as he calls it, more full and accurate in the classification of offences and 'breathing rather a greater spirit of mildness', e.g. in not prescribing the death penalty for killing a cow or robbing the storehouse of the Magistrate.

'However the details that have been furnished on these subjects by the several Rajahs of the province of Malabar may have passed to their knowledge through tradition more than by any written record, yet the principles thereof are generally the same as the existing Hindoo laws in other parts of India' (section xxxiv).

THE CRIMINAL PROVISIONS OF THE GENTOO CODE

It is one thing to find that such punishments as were inflicted for certain offences resembled those which the Gentoo Code authorized; it is another thing altogether to find that whatever that Code authorized was being in fact carried out. Much of it can only have been a dead letter. If, however, we take as broad a view as possible of the provisions of the Gentoo Code about the commonest types of crime, we find—subject to exceptions for the cases of Brahmins and women—as follows: The penalty for murder is death. Theft is divided into two classes—open and concealed according to the taking. Where the crime consists in fraud, e.g. deceit practised in selling goods, it is called open theft. Housebreaking is an example of concealed theft. Open theft is punishable in general by fine: concealed theft is visited with the loss of a hand or foot, but grave cases like housebreaking and highway robbery are also visited with death. Adultery by a man of inferior caste with a woman of a superior caste who has a master is punishable with death. The woman who commits adultery with a man of lower caste is to be subjected to public exposure naked upon an ass; in some cases cast out of the city, in others eaten by dogs or burnt. Assault is punished with fines graduated in the most meticulous manner; so also is defamation or false abuse. The penalties denounced for giving false evidence are of a rhetorical character, so much so that one suspects that no penalty was in practice inflicted.

PUNISHMENTS IN MALABAR: DUNCAN'S PROPOSALS

The evidence before Duncan's Commission satisfied him that in Malabar capital punishment was inflicted for (1) a sudra slaying a Brahmin or a cow, or (2) wounding either so as to draw blood, (3) a man of low caste lying with a Brahmin's wife, (4) robbing a temple, (5) robbing the Raja's treasury, (6) housebreaking, highway robbery, or great robbery, (7) repeated thefts, (8) wilful homicide. Slavery was the punishment imposed on higher caste women for sexual offences with lower caste men. Expulsion from caste was inflicted on Brahmins for robbery, eating with inferior castes, lying with low-caste women. Whipping, fine and confiscation of goods were punishments suitable to cases of small thefts and robberies, but mutilation was regarded as the ordinary punishment for theft and robbery.

On a review of these matters and of the Mahomedan law with which he was much more familiar, Duncan proposed that in Malabar treason or rebellion should entail forfeiture of lands; and that accomplices of chief rebels should be dealt with as for highway robbery, or in minor cases by imprisonment and fine: that wilful murder should be punished by hanging and less heinous cases by fine and imprisonment; that Brahmins and Hindu women should not be put to death though Mahomedan women should suffer death for murder, according to their own law; that in no case should fines be exacted from relations; that for wounding or maiming the *lex talionis* might be enforced; for robbery loss of life might be imposed but mutilation was to be abolished and imprisonment substituted for it; for false evidence whipping, branding and imprisonment might be inflicted on

Hindus as well as on Mahomedans, since it seemed by the Gentoo Code to be a crime held in the utmost abhorrence by Hindu lawgivers. Cheating and forgery were to be dealt with by imprisonment and whipping and by requiring full restitution to be made. In cases of loss of caste, adultery, eating forbidden food, the judge was not to refuse to take cognisance but to employ as arbitrators principal persons of the religion concerned, confirming their award or mitigating it. He had noticed in dealing with the Mahomedan criminal law as to adultery that this law was now only applicable to the woman (section XLIV). He has praise for the details of the provisions against committing nuisance which are to be found in Chapter XII of the Gentoo Code.

PUNISHMENTS IN THE MARATHA COUNTRY BEFORE 1819

The customary punishments which Elphinstone found to be enforced in the Maratha country of the Deccan in 1819 are thus described by him:[1]

'Murder unless attended by peculiar atrocity appears never to have been capital, and was usually punished by fine. Highway robbery was generally punished with death because it was generally committed by low people, for a greater distinction was made in the punishment on account of the caste of the criminal than the nature of the crime. A man of tolerable caste was seldom put to death except for offences against the State. In such cases birth seems to have been no protection...yet it is well observed by Mr Chaplin that treason and rebellion were thought less of than with us. This originated in a want of steadiness, not of severity, in the Government. When it suited a temporary convenience an accommodation was made with a rebel, who was immediately restored not only to safety but to favour....Punishments, though public, were always executed with little ceremony or form. Brahmin prisoners who could not be executed were poisoned or made away with by deleterious food... women were never put to death: long confinement and the cutting off the nose, ears and breast were the severest punishments inflicted on them. Mutilation was very common and the person who had his hand, foot, ears or nose cut off was turned loose as soon as the sentence was executed and left to his fate. Imprisonment in hill forts and dungeons was common, and the prisoners, unless they were people of consideration, were always neglected and sometimes allowed to starve. Prisoners for theft were often whipped, at intervals, to make them discover where the stolen property was hidden....Flogging with a martingale was very common in trifling offences such as petty thefts. But the commonest of all punishments was fine and con-

1 *Report*, pp. 53–5.

fiscation of goods to which the Mamlatdar was so much prompted by his avarice that it was often difficult to say whether it was inflicted as the regular punishment or merely made use of as a pretence for gaining wealth....No other punishment, it may be averred, was ever inflicted on a man who could afford to pay a fine; and on the whole the criminal system of the Marrathas was in the last state of disorder and corruption.'

THE ELPHINSTONE CODE 1827

His experience of this large tract of country, which came under the Bombay Presidency at the time when he became Governor, impressed Elphinstone with the need for a better and more uniform system of law, civil and criminal, throughout the now extensive province. Like some of his friends he was a great admirer of Bentham; and in 1827 the Elphinstone Code took shape as a formal and ordered set of Regulations (about thirty in number) drafted upon a uniform system—an improvement in certain details upon the Cornwallis Code of 1793. Of Sir George William Anderson (1791–1857), who became one of Macaulay's colleagues on the first Indian Law Commission, it is said by a biographer:[1]

'He was employed by Mr Elphinstone in passing the first systematic code of laws attempted in British India known as the Bombay Code of 1827 which was a great advance upon anything previously attempted in India, and served to prove, by thirty years' experience of its working, that there was no difficulty in applying a general code, founded upon European principles, to the mixed populations of India.'

CRIMINAL CODE OF 1827

By Regulation XIV of 1827, a logical and self-contained penal code was included in it. Fitzjames Stephen described this Regulation as—

'a body of substantial criminal law which remained in force until it was superseded by the Criminal Code,[2] and which had very considerable merits, though it would probably not have supported the test of strict professional criticism to which indeed it was not intended to be subjected.'[3]

The preamble recited that it had been the practice of the British Government of Bombay to apply to its subjects respec-

1 Sir Alexander Arbuthnot in *D.N.B.*
2 That is, the Indian Penal Code.
3 *Sessional Proceedings of the National Association for the Promotion of Social Service for* 1872–3, p. 8, cited in Cotton's *Elphinstone*, p. 181.

tively their peculiar laws, modified and amended as necessity required by Regulations passed and published; the courts of justice ascertaining the native law in each case as it occurred by a reference to the law officer of the religion of the offender. The Regulation claimed to be an expression of the 'general result of the practice of the courts' which would 'secure the more steady observance of the principle of administering to individuals the law of their religion', while it would also 'provide a code easy of access for those individuals of the community to whom, as not being subject to any specific national or religious code of criminal law, the English law has with considerable inconvenience been hitherto applied'.

In fact this Code by section 7 provided that in addition to the crimes specified therein, offences declared by the religious law of the person charged which constituted a breach of morality, or the peace, or good order of society, should be liable to such punishment as that law provided if it was one of the forms of punishment recognized by the Code, and if not should be visited with an equivalent and appropriate punishment of a recognized kind. To this extent the Code was not completely self-contained. Indeed, it was a sketchy rather than a thorough performance of which the first Indian Law Commission expressed but a poor opinion. It attempted to deal with everything in forty-one sections, and the roughness of its classification tended to confound minor offences with graver ones.

In their letter to Lord Auckland of 14 October 1837, which was prefixed to their draft of the Penal Code, they say:

'The penal law of the Bombay Presidency has over the penal law of the other Presidencies no superiority except that of being digested. In framing it the principles according to which crimes ought to be classified and punishments apportioned, have been less regarded than in the legislation of Bengal and Madras.

...We have said enough to show that it is owing, not at all to the law, but solely to the discretion and humanity of the judges, that great cruelty and injustice is not daily perpetrated in the criminal courts of the Bombay Presidency.'

All the same, it may be noted, Macaulay like everyone else had the highest respect for Elphinstone—'a great and accomplished man as any that I have ever known', he said in 1856.[1]

1 Trevelyan's *Life of Macaulay*, vol. II, p. 404.

CHAPTER XII

INDIAN PENAL CODE

BEFORE 1833, in each of the three Presidencies—Bengal, Madras and Bombay—the Governor-General or Governor and the Council over which he presided were not only the chief executive authority but also exercised legislative powers under authority from Acts of Parliament. Their enactments were called 'Regulations'. Though their legislative competence was far from absolute—for most purposes European British subjects and the Presidency towns were beyond their scope—the whole system of revenue and judicature which the Company enforced throughout each Presidency had been set up, amended and expanded by 'Regulations' framed and passed by these Councils. Each of the three statute books contained voluminous and complex provisions touching sometimes with a light but more generally a heavy hand most of the features of Indian life. These enactments dated back in the case of Bengal to the Cornwallis Code of 1793, and in the case of Madras to the year 1802 when legislation on the Bengal model was begun for Madras. In Bombay the legislation of the early years of the century had been revised and restated in the Elphinstone Code of 1827.

The results arrived at by 1833 had many defects in point of substance and few merits in point of form. William Morley[1] defends the Regulations, saying that they were 'formed, modified and abrogated, according to the peculiar circumstances of time and place, with an ability and moderation which reflects equal honour on the lawgivers themselves and the country which gave them birth'. He praises the method of 'gradually building up the law in proportion as the facts arise which it is to regulate', and considers that under a complication of difficulties they worked well in practice. He admits that the Regulations seem at first sight to be 'an incongruous and indigested mass' and that the study of them is both intricate and difficult, saying that 'on this account some hasty and thoughtless persons have been induced to pass an indiscriminate censure upon a system which they, possibly, wanted time or industry to acquire, or capacity

---

1 Morley, *Administration of Justice in British India*, 1858, p. 158; *Digest*, vol. I, p. clv.

to understand'. No doubt, as the history of philosophy has been said to be 'philosophy itself taking its time', so the Regulations may be treated as showing the forces of order and of enlightenment taking their time. The tentative amendments, the partial and imperfect solutions, the makeshift devices which constitute a gradual process of improvement were in the circumstances of the time and of the country a true method of progress and in general the only method which would work. But the results of such a process are almost necessarily defective, calling loudly for analytical scrutiny and for simplification. The general opinion entertained of the Regulations among historians is not quite so favourable as Morley's. Thus:

'At this time each of the three Presidencies enjoyed equal legislative powers; though the Governor-General possessed a right of veto over the legislation of the subordinate governments, it had in fact been little exercised. Thus had come into existence three series of regulations, as these enactments were called, frequently ill-drawn, for they had been drafted by inexperienced persons with little skilled advice; frequently conflicting, in some cases as a result of varying conditions but in others merely by accident; and in all cases enforceable only in the Company's courts because they had never been submitted to and registered by the King's courts.'[1]

Criminal law was no exception to the general rule. In Bengal and Madras the Mahomedan criminal law had been continued as the law of the land applicable to Hindus as well as Mahomedans. In Bombay the endeavour had been to apply Hindu criminal law to Hindus, and the Mahomedan law to Mahomedans only. The Regulations contained many notable provisions which represent the attempt made in each Presidency to adapt the Mahomedan and other law to the conditions of India and to make it consonant in some degree with British rule. The defects of the law in each Presidency were emphasized by the lack of uniformity in the laws of the Presidencies even more than when the same defects reappeared in each; and side by side with the penal law, thus variously adapted to the country districts of the provinces, the law of England remained in the three Presidency towns the basis of the criminal jurisdiction of the Supreme Courts, untouched by any Regulations.

With the Indian Law Commission, the time had come when the criminal law of the Regulations had to be considered as a

---

1 *Cambridge History of the British Empire*, vol. v, p. 5. For Fitzjames Stephen's view see Hunter's *Life of the Earl of Mayo*, 1876, vol. II, pp. 183–6.

whole, and in 1836–7 the impression made upon Macaulay and his colleagues was most unfavourable. In the covering letter of 14 October 1837, to Lord Auckland, great play is made by the Commissioners of the discrepant laws of the different parts of India. It is noticed, for example, as regards forgery and perjury that in Bengal serious forgeries were punishable with double the term of imprisonment for perjury; in Bombay perjury was punishable with double the imprisonment provided for the most aggravated forgeries; while in Madras the two offences were exactly on the same footing. That in Bombay the escape of a convict was punishable with double the imprisonment assigned for it in either of the other Presidencies, while coining was punishable with little more than half what the other Presidencies assigned. That in Bengal the seller of stamps without a licence was liable to a moderate fine and in Madras to a short imprisonment, while the purchaser was not punished at all; yet in Bombay both were liable to imprisonment for five years and a flogging. We may add here the terse summing up of Whitley Stokes: 'The Anglo-Indian Regulations, made by these different legislatures, contained widely different provisions, many of which were amazingly unwise'.[1] Lord Bryce[2] speaks of their work as done 'in a very haphazard fashion'. 'The criminal law became a patchwork of enactments so confused that it was the first subject which invited codification.'

Sir George Campbell indeed thought in 1852 that 'the Commission was unfortunate in its first subject. The criminal law, though imperfect, was more suitable than most parts of our system, and it was the system of civil and criminal procedure which it was most urgently necessary to regulate.'[3] But this was rather captious criticism—all the more so that, while the proposal to codify first the penal law had been Macaulay's own, Government in 1837 was pressing for its completion.[4] Campbell admitted that 'a systematisation of the criminal laws would be a great good, necessary in the second degree'. Indeed, on his own showing,[5] 'our criminal law is very much a patchwork

1 *Anglo-Indian Codes*, vol. 1, p. 2.
2 *Studies in History and Jurisprudence*, vol. 1, p. 120.
3 *Modern India*, 1852, p. 521. Bethune is said to have been of the same opinion. *Parl. Papers*, 1852–3, vol. XXXI, p. 253.
4 According to Sir E. Ryan the urgency was that Europeans who were permitted since 1833 to settle in the mofussil could not be made amenable to the mofussil courts so long as these administered Mahomedan criminal law (*Parl. Papers*, 1853–8, vol. XXXI, p. 238).   5 *Modern India*, 1852, p. 465.

made up of pieces, engrafted at all times and seasons on a ground nearly covered and obliterated.... The general result is that all the worst and most common crimes are satisfactorily provided for by special enactments; but that there is a very great want of definition, accuracy and uniformity as to the miscellaneous offences...we have the main points of a tolerable system: but it wants remodelling, classification and codification.'

Again, no review of the position of the criminal law in the thirties can omit to take account of the fact that far-reaching reform on specific points was becoming or had become irresistible. Thus only in 1825 had women been exempted from flogging as a punishment (Regulation XII, section 3), but Regulation II of 1834, section 2, abolished this punishment altogether in the Bengal Presidency; *sati* had been made illegal by Bengal Regulation XVII of 1829; slavery as we see from the Charter Act (1833) had become intolerable to English opinion; exceptionally drastic legislation was required to put down *thuggee* (*thagi*) (Acts XXX of 1836, XVIII of 1837, XVIII of 1839 and others); public exposure as a punishment was no longer approved (Act II of 1849); and the forfeiture of property on account of change of religion was abolished by Act XXI of 1850, extending to the whole of British India the provision made by section 9 of Bengal Regulation VII of 1832, though many people thought that on this point the native laws should not be touched.[1]

The Charter Act of 1833 introduced a single legislature for the whole of British India with jurisdiction to legislate for all persons and for the Presidency towns as well as for the mofussil. The Company's monopoly of Indian trade had been ended by the Act of 1813, but now the Company was to close down its trading activities altogether, and an influx of Europeans and others was to be expected since they were no longer to be 'interlopers'. Parliament, while recognizing that a complete uniformity of law was impossible, set up a Commission to give India a common law—that is to provide a general law applicable *prima facie* to everyone in British India, though particular classes might have to be exempted from its rules as to particular matters. The purpose was 'that such laws as may be applicable in common to all classes of the inhabitants of the said territories, due regard being had to the rights, feelings and peculiar usages of

[1] Morley's *Digest*, vol. I, p. clxxxi.

the people, should be enacted' (section 53). Macaulay's speech upon the second reading (10 July 1833) is justly celebrated and his work in India as the first legal member of Council (1834–8) had effects both lasting and extensive. Without injustice to any of his colleagues on the Indian Law Commission the draft of the Penal Code may be attributed to him. Three of them at least were distinguished men—Mr Charles Hay Cameron, a barrister from England who went to India to join the Commission in 1835, is described by Leslie Stephen as 'a disciple and ultimately the last disciple of Jeremy Bentham'. He became in 1843 Legal Member of Council after Mr Andrew Amos. John Macpherson Macleod (he became a K.C.S.I. (1866) and a Privy Councillor (1871)) was an experienced civil servant from Madras who had been secretary to that Government in more than one department. George William Anderson, of the Bombay service, had taken part in the framing of the Elphinstone Code of 1827 and had distinguished himself as a judge of the Company's chief court of appeal. He became a member of the Bombay Council in 1838, and after his retirement became Governor of Ceylon in 1849 and a K.C.B. Cameron and Macleod were members of the Law Commission which was appointed under the Act of 1853 and sat in England. Macleod was included in the later Commissions which were appointed in 1861–7 and which by 1870 had produced seven reports containing drafts of codifying Acts. Macaulay speaks highly of all three of his colleagues, but in 1836 illness had deprived him of their assistance.

In a letter written by Macaulay on 15 June 1837, we learn: 'the Penal Code of India is finished and is in the press. The illness of two of my colleagues threw the work almost entirely on me.'[1] In the following January he refers to it as 'a sort of work which must wait long for justice, as I well knew when I laboured at it'.[2] But in truth everything had to wait—the many projects for the restatement and reform of the civil law as well as the new penal code. When twenty years had passed and the time came for a new Charter Act in 1853, nothing had reached the statute book. This was not because the Law Members who succeeded Macaulay—Amos, Cameron, Bethune and Peacock— were wanting in ability or were lukewarm about law reform, though doubtless the loss of Macaulay was a great loss in drive

1 Trevelyan's *Life of Macaulay*, vol. I, p. 417.   2 *Ibid.* vol. II, p. 43.

and in influence. Fitzjames Stephen attributes it to the many preoccupations of Government in those difficult times—the Afghan disasters and triumphs, the war in Central India, the wars with the Sikhs and Lord Dalhousie's annexations, which he says threw law reform into the background and produced a state of mind not very favourable to it. As the movement is generally acknowledged to have its origin in certain correspondence between Metcalfe and the Bengal judges in 1829, we should perhaps be careful to note that strong opposition was offered to Macaulay's draft by many of the Indian judges. Hence for one reason or another 'his successors made remarks on it for twenty years' as Stephen says. The Government of India got rather tired of it and on 26 April 1845, a secretary wrote on their behalf to the Law Commission asking them to revise their draft with a view to its adoption with amendments 'or to its final disposal otherwise'. In 1846 and again in 1847 Mr C. H. Cameron and Mr D. Eliott reported at length the results of a detailed revision.[1] Ten years more carry us to 1857, with Bethune and Peacock as Law Members in the meanwhile. Bethune revised and altered the Code so much as to make it a new code in principle, according to Sir E. Ryan's evidence given in 1853,[2] and his altered version was sent back to India in 1852, the year in which Peacock became Law Member. We may accept Stephen's narrative[3] as we are little likely to get a juster judgment:

'Then came the Mutiny which in its essence was the breakdown of an old system; the renunciation of an attempt to effect an impossible compromise between the Asiatic and the European view of things, legal, military and administrative. The effect of the Mutiny on the statute book was unmistakable. The Code of Civil Procedure was enacted in 1859. The Penal Code was enacted in 1860 and came into operation on January 1, 1862. The credit of passing the Penal Code into law, and of giving to every part of it the improvements which practical skill and technical knowledge could bestow, is due to Sir Barnes Peacock, who held Macaulay's place during the most anxious years through which the Indian Empire has passed.'[4]

That it has established itself as an eminently successful code of law both in India and elsewhere may now be affirmed without fear of contradiction. It is working as law in so many parts of

1 *Parl. Papers*, 1847–8, vol. xxviii.
2 *Ibid.* 1852–3, vol. xxxi, p. 238.
3 Trevelyan's *Macaulay*, vol. i, pp. 417–18.   4 1852–9.

the world that it may be regarded as having passed the highest objective test. Whether we say with Stephen that it has been 'triumphantly successful' or with Bryce that it is 'universally approved'; whether or not we remember Trevelyan's *mot* about 'the gratitude of Indian civilians, the younger of whom carry it about in their saddle-bags and the older in their heads', its merits are acknowledged so ungrudgingly that one would hardly have supposed that a body of rules could have commanded so much admiration for being comprehensible and concise. The praise of its form is due in part to the reasons which make specially acceptable in India a system which guards the liberty of the subject by showing in an exhaustive series of plain statements what acts and omissions are by the law made punishable. The basis of the Code lies in the second section: 'Every person shall be liable to punishment under this Code and not otherwise for every act or omission contrary to the provisions thereof.' In stating the elements of each offence and the punishment provided for it, the Code uses the most ordinary English terms to distinguish the different offences, thus giving point and precision to the English language and making for accuracy of thought in practical affairs. Whether much of the clarity of the Code is due to the employment of illustrations—a device suggested by Bentham—may be doubted. The literary or historical prototypes of a few of these are noticed by Trevelyan[1] but add little or nothing to their worth. In the letter to Lord Auckland which accompanied the original draft (14 October 1837) the Commissioners say clearly: 'The definitions and enacting clauses contain the whole law. The illustrations make nothing law which would not be law without them', and again that 'our illustrations are never intended to supply any omission in the written law'. But the Commission which sat in England and drafted the Indian Succession Act of 1865 laid greater stress on illustrations, saying in their report of 23 January 1863 that 'the illustrations are not merely examples of the law in operation but are the law itself showing by examples what it is', and contending that as much law has been made by judicial decisions so law may without impropriety be said to be made by the illustrations. The device was employed in the seventies, when Fitzjames Stephen and Hobhouse were Law Members, in the Evidence Act, the Contract Act and the Specific Relief Act.

1 *Life of Macaulay*, vol. 1, p. 415.

But, as is noticed by Sir Francis Oldfield, it plays no considerable part in any subsequent codification of importance.[1]

In point of form the merits of the Code remove it to a distance which for practical purposes is as far from the complexity of the English common law as from the 'distinctions' of Abu Hanifa or the two disciples. But beyond all controversy the substance is taken from the English law. 'The draft and the revision' in Stephen's view 'are both eminently creditable to their authors; and the result of their successive efforts has been to reproduce in a concise and even beautiful form the spirit of the law of England; the most technical, the most clumsy, and the most bewildering of all systems of criminal law...his draft gives the substance of the criminal law of England, down to its minute working details, in a compass which by comparison with the original may be regarded as almost absurdly small.'[2] Sir Henry Maine[3] puts the same praise the other way round, when he speaks of 'that admirable Penal Code which was not the least achievement of Lord Macaulay's genius, and which is undoubtedly destined to serve some day as a model for the criminal law of England'. Lord Bryce, too, is rightly emphatic that the deviations from English rules which may be found in it do not affect the general proposition that it is substantially English,[4] and Whitley Stokes[5] says: 'As in the case of the other Codes... its basis is the law of England, stript of technicality and local peculiarities, shortened, simplified, made intelligible and precise....' In this respect Bryce also puts the Penal Code on the same footing as the various civil codes which followed it in India.

But in this matter of planting English law in India the Penal Code, having been drafted by 1837, stands in a somewhat different case from the civil codes—more correctly from the various chapters of the Civil Code—which were later to be projected for India. By 1861 the task of law reform in India had been shifted to England, the Charter Act of 1853 having set up a new Commission to sit in London. It consisted of distinguished English judges and others, and in 1855 it arrived at certain governing principles which modified considerably the enthusiastic Benthamism which had inspired Macaulay and

1 *Cambridge History of India*, vol. VI, ch. XXI, p. 388.
2 Trevelyan, *Macaulay*, vol. I, p. 417.
3 *Village Communities in the East and West*, 1871, p. 115.
4 *Studies*, vol. I, p. 126.
5 *Anglo-Indian Codes*, vol. I, p. 71.

others in the thirties. They are to be found in its report dated 13 December 1855, and may be summarized by saying that in the codes to be drafted for India (a) the law of England should be the basis, (b) that it should be greatly simplified, (c) that not all subjects should be codified, (d) that particular classes should sometimes be excepted from the codified provisions as regards particular matters, (e) that save for such special exceptions the rules of the code should be the law of the land applicable to everyone, (f) that religious laws like the Mahomedan and Hindu law should not be codified. On 2 December 1861—the year after the Penal Code had been enacted—these recommendations were formally accepted by the Secretary of State, who issued a commission to Sir John Romilly, Sir William Earle, Sir Edward Ryan, Sir James Shaw Willes and others to carry out on this footing the project for a Civil Code. Matters stood in that position when Maine in 1862 became Law Member and the Succession Act of 1865 was carried through the Legislative Council almost in the exact terms of the Commission's draft.

But the Penal Code had in effect been drafted in the 'thirties and its English character is accounted for more by the abilities and standpoint of Macaulay—at all times a redoubtable champion of modern culture and institutions in preference to those of oriental origin. His speech on the second reading of the Act of 1833, while it contains the admission that complete uniformity of law was not practicable, discloses only a poor measure of respect for the native laws which Warren Hastings and others had refused to abrogate or supersede. The draft Code of 1837 may be thought to fall into line with Macaulay's victory in Council (7 March 1835) upon the education question over H. T. Prinsep and H. H. Wilson when Lord William Bentinck decided that 'The great object of the British Government ought to be the promotion of European literature and science among the natives of India'.

In a penal code devised for British India in 1837 it would be difficult to contest the wisdom of taking the English law as a basis provided that it was simplified and adapted with systematic care to Indian needs. Since the time of Cornwallis it had been *chose jugée* that the criminal jurisdiction could not be exercised without regard to British notions of justice, whether in substance or in method, and the Regulations had in fact introduced much law upon that footing—apart altogether from the fact that the

Presidency towns had worked with English law since 1726. What profit was to be expected from going to other systems for a model? It is hardly intelligent to attribute the admitted success of the Code to the negative fact that in it the English law has parted with its English dress or been disengaged from the accidents of its history. Its merits must lie in the last resort upon the fairness and soundness of its principles—the acumen which sees the right test of criminality, the restraint which avoids imposing unnecessary restrictions upon individuals.

This, however, is not at all the standpoint of Macaulay and his colleagues in their covering letter to Lord Auckland of 14 October 1837. The criminal law of the Hindus, of the Mahomedans, of the Regulations, and, with greater emphasis than ever, the criminal law of England are roundly condemned both as foreign and as defective—the English law, it seems, had just been pronounced by Commissioners appointed to inquire into it to be 'so defective that it can be reformed only by being entirely taken to pieces and reconstructed'.[1] Hence Lord Auckland is informed not only that 'it appears to us that none of the systems of penal law established in British India has any claim to our attention except what it may derive from its own internal excellence' but also that 'no existing system has furnished us even with a groundwork'.

'Under these circumstances we have not thought it desirable to take as the groundwork of the Code any of the systems of law now in force in any part of India. We have indeed to the best of our ability compared the Code with all those systems and we have taken suggestions from all; but we have not adopted a single provision merely because it formed a part of any of those systems.... We have derived much valuable assistance from the French Code[2] and from decisions of the French Courts of Justice on questions touching the construction of that Code. We have derived assistance still more valuable from the Code of Louisiana[3] prepared by the late Mr Livingston. We are the more desirous to acknowledge our obligation to that eminent jurist because we have found ourselves under the necessity of combating his opinions on some important questions.'

The French Code was doubtless of great help as a model and upon many questions of form: on specific points it afforded some valuable suggestions which were utilized for India, e.g. the period of twenty days' pain or disablement as a test whether

1 Letter to Lord John Russell, 19 January 1837.
2 1810.   3 1821.

hurt (harm) was 'grievous'; the distinction between a more and a less heinous kind of 'uttering' false coin. I cannot find that in the end the Louisiana Code contributed a great deal, but Mr Livingston's opinions seem to have called forth all Macaulay's power of combat and analysis, particularly upon the subject of offences against the human body. The English criminal law of 1837 and of the twenty years or so before that was savagely unjust in the penalties which it prescribed for some offences of a common type—produced as they were, or at least rendered inevitable—by the social conditions of the time. The use made of capital punishment was in some respects absurdly indiscriminate. These features were apt to obscure such merits as the law might have in its precise definition of offences and in the common sense of the distinctions which judges had developed in charging juries. Macaulay had from his earliest youth regarded it perhaps too exclusively as something to be reformed. In a letter written at the age of eighteen to his father, whose name is still held in high esteem as a reformer, he refers to Sir Samuel Romilly's death in terms coloured no doubt by his father's philanthropic zeal: 'How long may a penal code, at once too sanguinary and too lenient, half written in blood like Draco's and half undefined and loose as the common law of a tribe of savages, be the curse and disgrace of the country?'[1] As he reviewed his draft in 1837 he might well feel that he had travelled very far from this and that a simple and humane code must be fundamentally different.

In the long notes appended to the draft (lettered A to R)—'eighteen notes each in itself an essay'—every chapter of the Code is explained and defended. We see here if anywhere Macaulay's assumptions and lines of reasoning and his 'very intense labour'.[2] In some measure they explain his curious unawareness of the English law as the basis of his thinking—the mine which he was working. That no law 'has any claim to our attention except what it may derive from its own internal excellence' and that 'no single provision had been adopted merely because it formed a part of any system then in force in India' and even that the law of England 'needed to be taken to pieces and reconstructed'—these considerations taken together had not successfully expelled the law of England with a fork. But the notes upon each chapter do firmly impress upon the

1 9 November 1818. Trevelyan, vol. I, p. 89.   2 *Ibid.* vol. I, p. 465.

reader that, greater even than the modification of English rules which were directed to meet specialities of Indian conditions, were those which are due to an opinion that the various rules of law in force in England were capable of improvement and simplification. Right reason and not local colour accounts for most of the departures. It is impossible to simplify without amending; and if on each topic one set oneself to note all the variations, one might easily end by losing sight of the ground-work that had been left untouched. Thus theft (section 378) differs from larceny in England in a number of respects, e.g. intention to deprive the owner of his property is not a necessary element. But who would fail to recognize the English legal notion behind the English word, though 'asportation' is not mentioned, when he reads 'whoever intending to take dis-honestly any movable property...moves that property in order to such taking'. Again, in the offence of defamation (section 499) no difference is made between spoken and written words: in Macaulay's draft it was proposed that truth should be a complete defence but this suggestion was not in the end adopted. With or without such amendments—small differences may be the most confusing—who would fail to see that section 499 is a revision of the English law? A good deal has been said in the courts about the utility or inutility of English decisions in inter-preting the Code. As in the case of the law of evidence, of contract and in other matters, the two laws were sufficiently alike and unlike to make English decisions both treacherous and difficult to ignore until the Indian courts had covered the ground by decisions of their own.

We are, however, concerned to notice how problems special to India have been solved. It is clear from the Commission's notes to their draft that the special conditions have been as carefully considered with a view to avoid making conduct punishable where no sufficient advantage was likely to accrue from applying the criminal law, as from the standpoint of making special provision against crimes produced by Indian con-ditions. Whitley Stokes[1]—who had a unique knowledge of the Indian statute-book and may be regarded as the last of the great codifiers among Law Members—claims for the Penal Code:

'Besides repressing the crimes common to all countries, it has abated if not extirpated the crimes peculiar to India, such as *thuggee*,

1 *Anglo-Indian Codes*, vol. I, p. 71.

professional sodomy, dedicating girls to a life of temple harlotry, human sacrifices, exposing infants, burning widows, burying lepers alive, gang robbery, torturing peasants and witnesses, sitting *dharna*.'

That a good police administration should find it impossible to put down such practices by reason of defects in the Penal Code would indeed be a misfortune—a sad commentary on the Code as on the country. But we do find in detail that great attention has been paid in the Code to India's special problems, which arise not merely out of the religions and usages of the people but out of the distances, the contours, the climate of the country and the racial distinctions among those who in different ages have poured into it from the north. Thus, to take a very obvious point, it was essential to the very chance of peace in India that rules should be elaborated to punish mischief done to religious places or insults offered to objects of veneration. Yet how great is the care needed to provide for such matters may perhaps be seen from the exception added to the section which prohibits the sale of obscene books or pictures (section 292)—an exception required to permit such things when kept or used for religious purposes. Again one may ask how does a uniform Penal Code treat such a crime as bigamy in a country inhabited by Hindus and Mahomedans? The section (494) is very simple: 'Whoever having a husband or wife living marries in any case in which such marriage is void by reason of its taking place during the life of such husband or wife'—in fact, the personal law prevails. The acceptance of a bribe by a public servant (section 161) and the giving of the bribe, which is an abetment (section 116), are dealt with in view of the fact that in India the giver is so often a person struggling against oppression by the taker. Adultery as a form of *zina* at the Mahomedan law had at one time been visited with the savage penalty of stoning to death, prescribed as *hadd* or punishment which could not be altered. This resulted in convictions being unobtainable except indeed upon confession. Macaulay's draft did not make adultery a crime, but section 497 of the Code in its final form made it an offence punishable (with five years' imprisonment and fine) on the part of the man, though not on the part of the woman.[1] The woman's husband must prosecute. The Code contains no provision against incest,

---

[1] On this point the law made a *volte-face*. In 1793 Jonathan Duncan in his *Observations* on Malabar pointed out that the Mahomedan law against adultery had come to be applied only against women.

nor till recently was there legislation against child marriage; but in view of child marriage it was provided that if a wife was under ten years of age intercourse by her husband amounted to the offence of rape (section 375). The age has now been raised to thirteen.

As regards the right of self-defence, Macaulay was desirous to encourage and not to restrict it, as might have been necessary with 'a bold and high spirited people accustomed to take law into their own hands and go beyond the limits of moderation'. Criminal intimidation was an offence under the Code before it had been made a statutory offence in England. Special provision of severe penalties was made for cases where bodily hurt is inflicted by way of torture. 'The execrable cruelties which are committed by robbers in this country for the purpose of extorting property or information relating to property render it absolutely necessary here.'

The offence which is and always will be of supreme interest to inhabitants of those parts of India where people live in houses at some distance from one another was dealt with frequently by the Regulations under the name of dacoity. In the Code (section 391) this is retained and specially defined as meaning (in effect) robbery committed or attempted by five or more persons. The maximum punishment is transportation for life.

The nature and importance of this offence are not easily grasped without some acquaintance with Indian conditions. Sir George Campbell says that it

'seems indeed almost peculiar to India, being open plunder by armed bands, and yet not open resistance to Government, the bands collecting at night and disappearing in the day time in a way which can only be effected in very peculiar circumstances'.[1]

'The crime of dacoitee or gang robbery is distinguished from ordinary robbery by the numbers engaged forming a gang; and from burglary[2] by the use of *open and intentional violence*. There may be many persons concerned in a burglary or theft, and being disturbed they may murder or wound; but dacoits do not *attempt* concealment, they disguise their faces but make an open attack with lights, etc., and for the time defy the inhabitants of the neighbourhood. Herein the crime as practised in India is well defined and distinguished from anything else.'[3]

The old rule—as much Mahomedan as English—is retained

---

1 *Modern India*, p. 502.
2 In the Code the word 'burglary' gives place to 'house-breaking by night'.
3 *Modern India*, p. 469.

that if any one person commits murder in committing dacoity, every one of the dacoits may be punished with death (section 396).

Membership of a gang of persons associated for the purpose of habitually committing dacoity is an offence of itself (section 400) and may be punished with transportation for life—a principle introduced by Act XXIV of 1843 on the analogy of the enactments directed against *thuggee* (cf. Act XXX of 1836). By section 310 of the Code a *thug* is defined as a person habitually associated with others to commit robbery or child-stealing by means of or accompanied with murder. This offence is punishable with transportation for life.

The definitions (section 300) which determine whether culpable homicide amounts or does not amount to murder were considered by Whitley Stokes to be 'the weakest part of the Code',[1] but they are cumbrous rather than difficult or objectionable; they do not seem to vary substantially from the English law save in rejecting the rule that a person is guilty of culpable homicide if he accidentally causes death while engaged in an unlawful act. This is one of the few points of substance upon which Macaulay would seem to have agreed with Livingston. Until 1870 (Act XXVII) causing death by a rash and negligent act not amounting to culpable homicide was not made penal under the Code: such acts would have been punished in England as manslaughter.

The fabrication, giving or corruptly using of false evidence is severely dealt with in its different forms and gradations: Macaulay with difficulty restrained himself from including false *pleading* in the category of perjury. Forgery or the making of a false document is dealt with according as it is simple forgery (punishable with two years' imprisonment) or forgery of a public register or a valuable security or a will, which entails much longer imprisonment. These offences, fatally easy to commit, had always given trouble in India, partly because the Mahomedan law did not take them seriously enough, being inclined to treat them as sufficiently punished by *tusheer* or public exposure with ignominy,[2] and partly (as Nuncomar's case had shown) because the English law had become indiscriminate in its severity.

General features of Macaulay's draft speak clearly of his

---

1 *Anglo-Indian Codes*, vol. I, p. 41.
2 Cf. Bengal Regulations XVII of 1797, VIII of 1803, II of 1807.

broad-mindedness and humanity. Thus the offences punishable with death though in form six were really only two—treason and murder;[1] and where sentence of death was competent it was not in general compulsory, it being open to the court to inflict transportation save where the murderer is a life convict already.[2] Transportation was to be limited to cases of life sentence as had been the practice, but the Code as passed permits, in two exceptional cases, of transportation for seven years and upwards. It was open to the court to award all or part of a fine to the sufferer as compensation. Between 1837 and 1860 slavery had been considered by the Law Commission after Macaulay had left India and Act V of 1843 had been passed to abolish it; but in Macaulay's draft of 1837 no difference was made where an offence was committed by a master against his slave. Acts not generally objectionable might be forbidden by local authorities for special reason if they became dangerous to the public tranquillity or health. Public exposure as a punishment was rejected. Nor was flogging included as a recognized punishment in Macaulay's draft; for young offenders and for petty offences it had recently been abolished and he did not wish to reintroduce it; for other cases he objected to it as a 'cruel punishment'. It was, however, introduced by the Whipping Act (VI of 1864) which as amended by Act IV of 1909 and Act XVII of 1914 allows of this punishment being inflicted for certain offences by juveniles and for cases of theft, house trespass, rape and certain other cases.

An old friend in a new house is the offence of 'sitting *dharna*', which in Benares and elsewhere had been made penal by Regulations.[3] It consisted of sitting fasting at the door of a house or tent to compel payment of a debt; originally this was done by a Brahman either on his own behalf or that of another; if the suitor were to die the consequences would fall upon the debtor. In section 508 it appears in the first illustration as a case of trying to cause a person to do something by inducing him to believe that otherwise he would be a victim of divine displeasure. Macaulay observes in Note J that such practices were rightly punishable. No doubt he was well warranted in this

---

1 Gour's *Penal Law*, vol. i, p. 215.   2 Section 303.
3 Bengal Regulations XXI of 1795, III of 1804, VII of 1820. It is spelt *dhurna* in the Code. Cf. Manu, viii, 48–50; Yajnavalkya, ii, 40; Jayaswal's *Tagore Lectures*, 1917, Calcutta, 1930, pp. 136, 182.

opinion, but it is not without point to observe that in the Hindu system at one time this practice played a part which was by no means wholly anti-social. In Elphinstone's report[1] upon the Maratha territory of the Deccan (1819), which has been considered to be 'the most valuable evidence we possess as to the working of the primitive Hindu system unaffected by Muhammadan law',[2] we find a system of dunning under the name *takaza* employed under the Marathas for inducing or compelling assent to the calling of a panchayet to deal with a grievance— a result 'which might not have been gained from the indolence of the magistrate'.

'When a matter had once come to trial it was always expected that Government should enforce the decision; but with the irregularity so characteristic of the Marrattas, the plaintiff was often permitted to enforce them himself, and this was effected by means of the system called Tukkazza, which, though it strictly means only Dunning, is here employed for everything from simple importunity up to placing a guard over a man, preventing his eating, tying him neck and heels, or making him stand on one leg with a heavy stone on his head under a vertical sun. . .' (p. 87).

'If a man have a demand from his inferior or his equal, he places him under restraint, prevents his leaving his house or eating and even compels him to sit in the sun until he comes to some accommodation. If the debtor were a superior, the creditors had first recourse to supplications and appeals to the honour and sense of shame of the other party: he laid himself on his threshold, threw himself on his road, clamoured before his door, or he employed others to do all this for him: he would even sit down and fast before the debtor's door, during which time the other was compelled to fast also, or he would appeal to the Gods and invoke their curses upon the person by whom he was injured' (p. 93).

In the chapter on 'Debts and Interest' in Arthur Steele's *Summary of the Law and Customs of Hindoo Castes within the Dekhun Provinces*[3] we have again a careful account of this custom or system of 'private redress'.

'*Tukazu.* The custom of Tukazu under the late Government was of various kinds. If the parties were Sahookars (money-dealers), or the debtor a man of fortune, it was usual for the creditor to demand payment verbally or bring the debtor to his own house. Then to send a Gomashta (agent) to his house to demand payment; then to seat a man near his house, and should the debtor not request his creditor to take him off by a Munna chithee (written submission to

---

1 *Report on the Territories conquered from the Paishwa*, published at Calcutta, 1821, p. 87.
2 J. S. Cotton's *Elphinstone*, pp. 148–9.
3 1827 ed. p. 264. New ed. London, 1868, p. 267.

arbitration) he would be obliged to comply with the man's demand for daily subsistence (4 annas etc.), the owner fasting the whole time from morning till evening and accusing the debtor as the cause thereof. (This variety only of Tukazu exists at present—*sidenote*.) Should the debtor still persist in not coming to some agreement, the dun would forbid any water to be brought inside the house, and subsequently plant several hired men of the debtor's caste at his door, who would forbid the cooking of food within the house from morning to evening and receive their hire from the debtor. This practice continued daily till the parties came to some settlement of the debt. In Tukazu the creditor cannot exercise violence towards his debtor, nor dun his wife or family, nor take away property without his permission. Among Tylung Brahmins and Gosaeens, it was not usual to place any hired person at the debtor's door, but the creditor remained himself on the spot, fasting, abusing him, and demanding payment, or he stood with a stone placed on his head, or his Sendee (lock of hair unshaven) plaited and fastened to a peg at the debtor's door; he even threatened to hang himself, or confine the debtor in a room. The sin of these self-inflicted acts is considered to rest with the debtor who is the cause of them; nevertheless men in power would repel such attempts to obtain payment by violence.'

In Note J the original draftsmen bracket together the practices known as *dharna* and *traga*. It would not appear that these names stand for different types of conduct;[1] but we may observe about the latter that when in 1858 John Stuart Mill came as almost his last act of service to the Company to write a defence of their régime,[2] he chose this as one of the features to be noticed (like piracy, infanticide, slavery, *sati*, witchcraft, etc.) in connection with 'Judicature and Legislation', as matters upon which the Company had not been unsuccessful. His paragraph on 'Tragga' is as follows:

'The insecurity of rights and the imperfection of the tribunals, under the native Governments, had introduced on the part of those who were, or believed themselves to be injured a singular mode of extorting redress. They hired a person of one of the religious classes to threaten that unless the demand, whatever it might be, was complied with, he would kill or wound himself or someone else; thereby, it was supposed, entailing the guilt of murder or of wounding on the person whose alleged injustice was the original cause of the act. If the threat proved ineffectual, the honour of the threatener was engaged to carry it into practical effect; and many suicides or murders were committed from this cause. This barbarous practice, known by the name of Tragga, has been almost entirely suppressed, partly by penal laws, and partly by affording more legitimate means of enforcing just claims.'

1 Both are given and explained in Wilson's *Glossary*.
2 *Memorandum of the Improvements in the Administration of India during the last Thirty Years* (1858).

In Sir Hari Singh Gour's well-known and thorough commentary[1] on the Penal Code he observes that 'it is a standing complaint against the Code that it is Draconian in its severity as regards punishments'. An example of such criticism may be of interest; it is taken from the *Madras Law Journal* for 1929.[2]

'The Penal Code is one of the much praised Acts of Indian Legislature and in spite of its many defects has served its purpose fairly well. Its sentences can hardly be said to be other than monstrous. No civilised country to-day imposes such heavy sentences as does the Penal Code. Heavy sentences have long gone out of fashion in England and the odour of sanctity and perfection attaching to the Penal Code should not deter indigenous legislatures to thoroughly revise the sentences and bring them into conformity with modern civilised standards.'

If the criticism is to be put in this way, it should be noticed that in Note A to the draft of 1837 the Commissioners pointed out that if Indian prisons were better managed the length of sentences might be decreased. 'We entertain a confident hope that it will shortly be found practicable greatly to reduce the terms of imprisonment which we propose.' In Mill's pamphlet of 1858 we get a short statement of the events which had intervened:

'In the course of the last few years the system of prison discipline in India has undergone a complete and most salutary revolution. The origin of this reform may be dated from the report of a committee appointed in Calcutta in 1838, composed chiefly of the principal members[3] and secretary of the Indian Law Commission.

'Up to this time those inmates of jails who were under sentence of labour, were employed almost exclusively (in fetters) on the roads: which rendered prison discipline almost impossible, as the prisoners could nearly always, by the connivance of their guards, command intercourse with friends and relations; and the engineer officers, in their anxiety to obtain efficient work, fed them highly, and treated them in other respects with an indulgence entirely inconsistent with the purposes of punishment. At the same time, the mortality from exposure and unhealthy localities was great. The committee showed that the State were absolute losers by employing convict labour on the roads; that it would be a positive saving to keep them in idleness in the jails, as the cost of extra superintendence and guards considerably exceeded the expense at which the work they did could be executed by hired labour. Since this time outdoor convict labour has been abandoned, and the prisoners are employed within the jails in various manufactures; and this employment which commenced in 1843 has every year become more profitable....

1 *Penal Law of British India*, 5th ed. 1936, vol. I, p. 213.
2 57 *Madras Law Journal*, p. 60.   3 Macaulay had left India.

'Prisoners sentenced for long terms of years are now removed to large central jails; and the change has been attended with great improvement in general management and discipline....'

It was right therefore that the sentences proposed in 1837 should be reconsidered when in the fifties the draft Code was revised before enactment. The policy of prescribing minimum sentences was abandoned and these were dropped from the draft. Since the definition of the offence was in a number of cases altered the maximum punishments provided in the draft and in the Code respectively are not always strictly comparable, but the result of a comparison seems to be that in most cases the maximum originally provided was retained; and that where it was altered the increases are as noticeable, though I do not say as numerous, as the reductions.[1] However, the Code when it prescribes punishments prescribes maximum amounts and no court is in

---

1 Illustrations are given hereunder: plain figures are used to denote the sections of the Code and figures in brackets to denote the clauses in the draft of 1837.

Unaltered

  161 (138), public servant taking bribe, 3 years.
  193 (190), false evidence, 7 years.
  298 (282), words wounding religious feelings, 1 year.
  323 (318), hurt, 1 year.
  359 (355), kidnapping, 7 years.
  379 (364), theft, 3 years.
  384 (369), extortion, 3 years.
  406 (387), criminal breach of trust, 3 years.
  417 (394), cheating, 1 year.
  453 (431), housebreaking, 2 years.
  456 (435), housebreaking by night, 3 years.
  465 (443), forgery (simple), 2 years.

Reduced

  Concealing design to wage war (110), 14 years; 123, 10 years.
  Depredation on foreign territories (115), 14 years; 126, 7 years.
  Defiling place of worship (275), 7 years; 295, 2 years.
  Disturbing religious worship (276), 3 years; 296, 1 year.
  Grievous hurt (319), 10 years; 325, 7 years.
  Robbery (377), 14 years; 392, 10 years.

Increased

  Waging war against Native State (114), banishment or 3 years; 125, transportation for life or 7 years.
  Abetting mutiny (116), 7 years; 131, 10 years.
  Abetting mutiny if mutiny occurs (117), transportation for life; 132, death.
  Abetting desertion (120), 1 year; 135, 2 years.
  Taking bribe to influence public servant (139), 6 months; 162, 3 years.
  Public servant illegally engaged in trade (147), 3 months; 168, 1 year.
  Threat to public servant (184), 1 year; 189, 2 years.
  Counterfeiting King's coin (233), 7 years; 232, 10 years.
  Delivering counterfeit coin (240), 3 years; 239, 5 years.
  Do. in the case of King's coin (241), 7 years; 240, 10 years.
  Rape (360), 14 years; 376, transportation for life.

general[1] obliged to pass any higher sentence than it thinks sufficient. The very different degrees of heinousness among offences of the same class are—at least as regards some crimes— proverbial: indeed, an over-minute classification of crimes would only bring complexity and difficulty without corresponding advantage. The sentence of transportation though nominally retained is in process of being abandoned in effect. Whether a more lenient administration of the law as regards certain crimes would be a successful reform is a question which cannot be answered off-hand in the negative, but it may be doubted whether there is much to be gained by restricting the punishments which the Code permits as maxima. The matter might well be reviewed in all its aspects by a competent committee in the Indian Legislative Assembly or elsewhere.

[1] For three offences the imprisonment must be rigorous (sections 194, 226 and 449). Sections 397 and 398 prescribe a minimum of seven years for robbery and dacoity if deadly weapons are employed.

LIST OF CASES CITED

INDEX

For EU product safety concerns, contact us at Calle de José Abascal, 56–1°,
28003 Madrid, Spain or eugpsr@cambridge.org.

www.ingramcontent.com/pod-product-compliance
Ingram Content Group UK Ltd.
Pitfield, Milton Keynes, MK11 3LW, UK
UKHW010336140625
459647UK00010B/636